Advance Praise for

The Destiny of Our Stars

McNeill-Moretti discusses processing the loss of her husband in this inspirational memoir. The author reflects on how the events of her life prepared her to handle widowhood and aided in her long journey to a state of healthy acceptance. McNeill-Moretti's confessional prose blends introspection with a kind of spiritual poetry: "I'm grateful I found the way back to my life, albeit I know I will never be the same person I once was," she writes. There are funny moments as well to balance out the sad in this raw, unique, and distinctive memoir of loss and change.

—Kirkus Reviews

The Destiny of Our Stars is an excellent read about the step-by-step journey of the grieving process. It reminds us that time does not heal all wounds, but requires a steady grip on the shock, numbness, and emotional highs and lows it deals one. The author, Greta McNeill-Moretti, fluidly takes the reader through not just the ups and downs of her grief of losing her husband, and love of her life, but also her life's journey that brought her there. She keeps the well-written narrative interesting, intriguing, and at times hysterical. Reading this book will make you realize that grief does not follow a predictable path, but is a process of adjustment.

—Thomas E. Mullin, Advance Reader

Greta McNeill-Moretti's *The Destiny of Our Stars* is a heartfelt memoir about love, loss, and renewal. At its core, it's the story of a woman navigating widowhood after losing her soulmate, Lawrence, to brain cancer. The book moves from raw grief to spiritual awakening, with reflections on fate, synchronicity, and the mysterious ways the universe brings meaning to suffering. It's not just a chronicle of mourning; it's a roadmap through the darkest corners of heartbreak toward the quiet light of acceptance and hope.

Her words are simple, but they cut deep. She uses humor in surprising places, and it works. It keeps the story grounded and human. Sometimes her honesty stings, but that's what makes it beautiful. It's a book that feels lived, not written from a distance. It's impossible not to root for her as she rebuilds her world, piece by piece. She writes about compassion, family, and friendship in ways that make you think about your own life. She doesn't let you skim through her pain. She makes you sit with it, the way grief makes you sit still until you learn to move again.

I'd recommend *The Destiny of Our Stars* to anyone who has lost someone they love or who simply wants to understand what real resilience looks like. It's for people who appreciate writing that's emotional but never self-pitying, and who don't mind tears mixed with laughter. This book is raw, deeply personal, and surprisingly comforting. It reminds you that even when life shatters, the pieces can still reflect light.

—Thomas Anderson, Editor in Chief, Literary Titan

The DESTINY *of* OUR STARS

GRETA MCNEILL-MORETTI

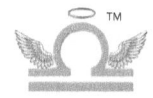

THE DESTINY OF OUR STARS
Greta McNeill-Moretti

COPYRIGHT © 2025 by Greta McNeill-Moretti

This book is a memoir and is designed to provide information in regard to the subject matter covered. While the publisher and author have used their best efforts in preparing this book, they make no representations or warranties with respect to the accuracy or completeness of the contents of this book and specifically disclaim any implied warranties of merchantability or fitness for a particular purpose. No warranty may be created or extended by sales representatives or written sales materials. It is sold with the understanding that neither the author nor the publisher is engaged in rendering legal, investment, accounting or other professional services. This book should not be used in place of professional mental health counseling. If you are feeling unwell, you should consult with a professional when appropriate. The advice and strategies contained herein may not be suitable for your situation. All persons and stories mentioned in this memoir have been recollected to the best of the author's memory throughout her life, whether they are living or deceased. Neither the publisher nor the author shall be liable for any loss of profit or any other commercial damages, including but not limited to special, incidental, consequential, personal, or other damages.

Book Cover Design and Interior Formatting by
Glen Edelstein, Hudson Valley Book Design

ISBN: 979-8-9995413-0-7 Trade Paperback
ISBN: 979-8-9995413-1-4 Hardcover
ISBN: 979-8-9995413-2-1 Audiobook
ISBN: 979-8-9995413-3-8 eBook

Library of Congress Control Number: 2025915522

THE DESTINY OF OUR STARS

PLEASE DONATE

United Hospice
Joe Raso Hospice Residence
415 Buena Vista Rd, New City, NY 10956

"Ensuring comfort when time matters most
providing compassion and support
putting the patient first, as they realize their end of life journey."

They were the angels on Earth
who offered emotional and spiritual support
to my beloved Larry and our entire family.

With their round-the-clock, amazing medical care
in their beautiful and peaceful setting
they brought dedication, beauty, and tranquility
to softly ease the end of a remarkable life.

Lawrence P. Moretti

DEDICATION

MAY THIS BOOK SERVE AS a living tribute to my devoted husband, Lawrence Peter Moretti, who was my profound inspiration, my light, my heart, my unsung hero who braved the storm. He was a beautiful and gentle soul who taught me how to live my life humbly with respect, humanity, and grace. This remarkable man was the greatest gift ever given to me, the love of my life, and my true soulmate. He was the one who lifted my spirit and brightened my days, who gave me strength to find the courage to reach for the stars and realize my dreams. I celebrate his life so beautifully lived, and remain endlessly grateful for his unwavering support, compassion, and love. Until we meet again my beloved, I am eternally yours. Thank you for loving me, and for your special words whispered to me constantly throughout our life together:

I loved you before I met you
I love you now
I will always love you

CONTENTS

Dedication · vii

A Message to My Readers · xi

Introduction · 1

Chapter 1   *The Lover's Goodbye* · 5

Chapter 2   *Expecting the Unexpected*
             (A Bell's Not a Bell 'Till You Ring It) · · · · · · · · · · · 19

Chapter 3   *The "C" Word* · 37

Chapter 4   *Ajna Chakra*
             (My Paradox of Illusion) · 51

Chapter 5   *Insights Gained, Possibilities Explored* · · · · · · · · · · · 59

Chapter 6   *Allow Me to Introduce Myself* · · · · · · · · · · · · · · · · 67

Chapter 7   *The One* · 87

Chapter 8   *A Tapestry of Cultures* · 95

Chapter 9   *Bloodlines From Love, Blended With Loyalty* · · · · · 109

Chapter 10   *The Shape of Loss* · 125

Chapter 11   *Finding Hope Through Gifted Signs* · · · · · · · · · · · · 143

Chapter 12   *The Reawakening* · 167

Chapter 13   *Wistful Nostalgia* · 175

Chapter 14   *Reflections on Synchronicity* · · · · · · · · · · · · · · · · · · 185

Chapter 15   *Finding Your New Life Path* · · · · · · · · · · · · · · · · · · 205

Heartfelt Poem · 220

Acknowledgments · 247

Works Cited · 251

A MESSAGE TO MY READERS

Life has a funny way of happening without notice. One minute every-thing's fine, and then it pulls the rug right out from under your feet. I guess the only constant is change, and most significant events in life often occur without a grand announcement. A catastrophic turning point took me on quite an adventure, but it certainly wasn't a fun and carefully planned package tour; it was more like an impromptu odyssey that I didn't see coming. To put it bluntly, it was more of a seismic crack in my life where everything shifted, and the ground gave way beneath me. The bottom literally fell out of my world, and nothing has been the same since.

You see, I found the love of my life, my soulmate, at 17, married him five years later, and was blessed with two wonderful sons, beautiful homes, several cherished dogs, and let's not leave out one bird and a few fish. Everything felt in place. Then, a watershed moment upended our happiness. Our serenity was shattered one portentous day when cancer metastasized its way into our happy world, bringing unforeseen challenges and anguish. My husband, Lawrence, was diagnosed with Glioblastoma, brain cancer. I guess it's a testament to destiny's diver-gent design, how our path was suddenly and irrevocably altered by fate. The fight for life truly began, and our primal instinct to survive surged to the forefront. We faced this devastating illness together for a little over two years until he succumbed to the disease.

After I lost him, my heartache was complicated. Numbness and rage became the dual landscapes of my grief. Some days, I felt deper-sonalized and moved through life mechanically as if I were living in an emotional vacuum. Other days, I was consumed with rage; the real-ization of a beautiful life, brutally snatched away, unjustly stolen. At my lowest ebb, I believed there was nothing left to live for. It was at that moment that I was gifted an awe-inspiring experience offering a paradigm shift in understanding; a divine intervention that illuminated a path to acceptance and genuine peace. It was a revelation to discover that the love I had for him, which seemed to be the source of my pain, actually became my power, my greatest strength.

In the days that followed, one of the most important decisions I made was recommitting to writing; I found it to be an essential step in my healing. Yes, for many years life interceded, but I believe my dreams of writing were merely deferred, never forgotten. Ultimately, it culminated in this moment, bringing me to you today. I had no idea that one day I would write this book, my memoir, and how an extraordinary event would awaken my entire outlook and help lead me back to my authentic self again. I'm just an ordinary girl from New York, and my story is one of a pivot. "Better bend than break" aptly summarizes my experiences and resonates deeply with my narrative. It showcases how flexibility, not rigidity, ensures survival.

Navigating this period of formidable obstacles, then finally finding my way out of the other side of tragedy, has taught me that if we greet the world with an open heart, life sends us breadcrumbs of meaning; coincidences, clues, synchronicities to light our way through the darkest tempests. Grief can be a long passage, but everyone carries the inner fortitude to reach the other side, and the human heart can mend and rebuild itself after everything it has suffered. Painful endings are not final; they are catalysts for transformation and renewal. I learned the hard way how breakages and repairs are a part of life, and I found the beauty in the scars and imperfections.

The healing journey begins with a conscious choice to embrace hope over despair, because when you cultivate positivity, joy, and growth, it provides a path to a purposeful existence. It empowers you to step into your full potential, to live a life of clarity and contribution, flourishing in the light, rather than being consumed by the shadows.

This is my story

INTRODUCTION

"WIDOWED" IS A LEGAL TERM that describes a person who has lost their spouse through death and has not remarried; hence, widow refers to a woman, and widower refers to a man. But, to me, the word *widowed* is all-inclusive, whether married or not. For those of us who endure the heartbreak of widowhood, grief becomes a visceral reminder, a poignant reflection of the emptiness, the pain, and a testament to the love we still carry for them, and will forever. Every single one of us feels nuances of love. It's the human heart's compassionate inner-life force, our connection, and the glue that holds humanity together. Love transcends all borders, cultures, and creeds, regardless of background or circumstance. We're not isolated entities, but part of a much larger web of life that is interconnected, and when we experience the deep, profound loss of a soulmate, it severs a strong and meaningful connection to our human social ecology. It is a major life change that creates turmoil in our emotional well-being, causing pain and imbalance. But, as time passes, it will be the memories that will remain, our solace; they are integral to our personal narratives, for they will never disappear. They will linger in our hearts, then transform, shape us, and eventually remind us of what mattered most. And through loss, we, the widowed, become forever united.

First and foremost, I would like to extend to you my deepest and most sincere condolences for your loss. Mere words, whether spoken or written by me here, can't take away the devastation you're feeling. Please know that I walk in your shoes, and that you're not alone. I know from my own personal experience that there is no language that can adequately capture the heartache of losing a soulmate. It disrupts the very fabric of our being and alters our life. It's as if a guiding star has fallen, faded away, and when that light waned, the very vibrancy and color of our world diminished with it.

But, within these pages, I can offer you my gentle hand to hold, and invite you to share in my story, as I pass along a little wisdom to help guide you towards healing. I will do it with an honest, open heart, and provide a sense of comfort as you embrace a future which now lies ahead for you. Here, you will learn about resilience, and how strength propels us all to move forward. So, if you allow me to be your refuge from pain, I promise that I'll softly replace your distress with peace. Let me be a guiding light on your path to unleashing your dreams which will lead you towards a renewed purpose for your life. Let's spark your passions, that inner fire, as you embrace a more optimistic tomorrow. There are endless possibilities, as we search in our quest for renewed happiness. Yes, joy and fulfillment can be brought back into our lives, even after we have stood in the rain, drenched in the defeat of our sorrows. After the darkest of storms, we can find inspiration and hope from the beautiful rainbows which appear suddenly, briefly, and we can look forward to the promise of a new day that will bring a fresh start, where we embrace the unknown as we rise from the ashes and begin anew.

My life took a very different path when a powerful synchronicity fell into it. I experienced a life-altering event, which led to a momentous transformation, and unlocked a new chapter to begin. Despite the passage of one year after my beloved's death, I still couldn't heal. I kept reliving the trauma, and felt trapped by a mental barrier built by my despair. That was until two days occurred, when this sign happened, challenging me and giving me the enlightenment I desperately needed. It guided me towards a place of revelation, where I found healing, and peace. It was the start of significant change. It taught me how to release the past and make a conscious decision to accept what I could not change, reclaim my life, and to keep my heart open to what destiny has aligned for me. Reality has taught me about truth; my dreams pushed me in the direction in which I was meant to travel; and fate guided me here to you.

But, have you ever wondered if your life has only one predetermined partner? Think about it for a moment. Could it be true that our lives, which are in constant motion, shift alignment as we navigate through this realm that is being steered by something much greater than us, or, purposely guided towards a path, one in which we didn't choose? Suppose there really is something larger, a phenomenon which exists beyond our knowledge that knows *all* as it changes our entity's course through our existence here. Destiny. How was it that you found the soulmate you loved at that exact time when you did, in that exact place where you were? Was it your fate? Could a miracle such as this happen more than once in a person's life? Personally, the way I felt about a man the night we met, was as if I loved him from a previous lifetime; it was soul recognition. Farfetched, perhaps, yet I cannot even dismiss the concept of déjà vu, for I strongly believe in both. I have had no choice, as I've been given far too many signs in my life to believe otherwise.

Come with me into the heart of my emotional loss; together, we'll uncover the courage to continue your life and find unexpected moments of laughter. You see, it's not always about the journey, my friends; it's about the ride. The destination is overrated, as the true treasure isn't the arrival. Cherish the process, the joy, and the memories made along the way as you embark on your next chapter in life. And buckle up, because you are in for the adventure of my lifetime.

CHAPTER 1

THE LOVER'S GOODBYE

WIDOW IS A WORD THAT I never thought would be used to describe me. You see, forever was something that I was promised; how long he would love me, how long he would protect me, and how long he would stay by my side. That was until one day when the universe decided to punch a hole into our world and tear out my heart, my soul, my very reason for living. Exactly one year after I lost him, I received a sign, a message of sorts, which brought with it comfort, peace, and a reason to carry on and never give up. Synchronicity is a gift, and this one was surely the greatest and most willful that was ever presented to me. It helped me to finally start the heartbreaking process of acceptance, of coming to terms with my loss, and at the same time, pointed me in a direction where I would find renewed passion for my life.

I know what it's like to lose someone you love dearly, and how it leaves significant scars, for grief most certainly is the price we pay for love. Seldom is this type of transition, this type of loss, ever peaceful for us, the ones who remain. We all have different relationships with our loved ones, and we all grieve in different ways when they're taken from us. Grief is universal, personal, and as individual as a fingerprint; every person experiences its nuances differently. It's also ambiguous, confusing, like being suspended within a moment, caught between what was, and all the memories that were still to be made, what could have been. If you're someone who has lost a great love in your life, someone who was your soulmate, then truth be told, there is rarely a comparison when it comes to this type of devastating loss, as all words fall short when trying to describe it.

The famous actor Jim Carrey once said: "Grief is not just an emotion; it's an unraveling, a space where something once lived, but is now gone. It carves through you, leaving a hollow ache where love once resided."

When I first began to mourn for my beloved, it was an ineffable grief that felt like an open wound, and I knew that this was going to be an unresolved trauma that would surely leave an indelible mark. Only time helped the raw edges of my sorrow begin to soften, yet its imprint remains with me always; the memories that we made, and recollections from what now seems to be another lifetime away, one that was once ours. I don't think that any of us ever move on completely; instead, we move with it. We move with multiple, distinctive layers of pain, like our own unique tapestry woven with discomfort. But, the one connection we all share, that's hardly ever spoken about, is the silence; it's deafening. And it's not because we have nothing to say. And it's not because we don't care. It is because this is how we drift through the solitude, as we try to adapt, and persevere. Our hearts are now so heavy that we cannot put our pain into words.

For those of us who lived through this storm, we're tired of having held everything together, and we can't express our emotions out loud anymore because some of us fought battles that were out of our reach, even though we crept on our bellies as close to the enemy as we could. For those of us who grappled with disbelief after being shell shocked from unexpected and sudden demises, well, the very loudest of cries, trying to reason with "why" are simply never heard. After the silence, it is that final parting that lingers, with all of our questions and concluding moments left unresolved. Yes, some of our chapters run their course, but some end abruptly. Either way, it doesn't really matter, as this type of grief ebbs and flows and feels like life's profound betrayal. The irreplaceable attachment that both you and your soulmate once shared makes this particular type of loss feel as if there is no more hope. You're absolutely empty, and it's hard to find even the slightest semblance of the comfort they say you need when your heart feels crushed and your belief system has been shattered into a million pieces.

This powerful experience, the soulmate union, is epic. It's an intense, unique connection that transcends beyond typical romantic relationships. You were so deeply attached to your partner that it feels like a part of you has died too, especially your identity. The numbness and uncertainty leaves you feeling afraid, alone, and lost in the dark. It's overwhelming, and leaves you questioning how you will ever find happiness or meaning in life without them ever again. You begin to examine your own purpose, question why you exist, and wonder how or if you'll be able to cope.

In addition to everything else, we grievers also carry the trauma of how our loved ones died. The emotional distress related to the circumstances of the death, be it sudden or a long and arduous illness, greatly impacts and affects a person's ability to function in everyday life, and leads to an ongoing psychological impact beyond just the loss itself. Many of us then struggle with the idea of our own mortality. How do we stay left behind after they have been taken from us? The reality is, we are not meant to fully understand the reasoning behind why our beloveds have gone, and it's so hard to try to learn how to release the need for those answers. We're told we must attempt to find peace, which is nearly impossible when so many shadows are chasing us.

But, how do you prevail when you feel guilty for still being alive? It's as if you are betraying their memory by experiencing any kind of positive emotion without them. It's called "survivor's guilt," and is very common. In general terms, it's the type of guilt associated with surviving, while the person you deeply loved has died, or suffered significantly. But, survivor's guilt is not one size fits all.

It can be tied to one, specific event like an accident, where you feel responsible for the death of someone else. They call this "**event-based**." Or, it can be a feeling of underserved survival, because you have what someone else no longer does. It is not linked to one, specific event; it's much broader. They call this "**existential guilt**." Or, it can be regarding actions/inactions during a distinct event. They call this "**survivor's guilt with specific incident**."

There are so many variations of survivor's guilt, and an enormous amount of research pertaining to this subject, but basically you feel like you shouldn't be allowed any joy while the person you deeply loved is no longer present. However, it's important to know that this is a normal part of grief, and that it's okay to allow yourself to feel both sadness and happiness simultaneously.

Grief is very complex. *Common guilt symptoms are . . .*

* ... *guilty for not trying harder to save them; self blaming; illusions of control.*
* ... *guilty for past disagreements; why didn't you give them more love, support, patience?*
* ... *guilty for worrying about your own future, because your loved one no longer has one.*
* ... *guilty about moving on too quickly, not honoring their memory longer.*
* ... *guilty for feeling happy; shouldn't you feel worthless, undeserving?*
* ... *guilty for being angry with them for leaving.*

There are a million "*guilties,*" too many to count.

Allowing yourself to experience joy again is not a sign of betraying your soulmate or being disloyal to them; but, rather a sign of healing and moving forward. Think about what your beloved would want for you. Mine wanted me to get on with my life and do the things I had not been able to do while caring for him. We must honor their memory by continuing to live.

But, as we grieve we must also examine the state of what is left of our spirit, which is an amazingly strong life force in itself. It's an invisible spark of life that animates all living creatures. Soul and spirit are not interchangeable terms. A soul is the essence of a person's individual identity, and is closely tied to their physical body and experiences in the world. It is considered to be the part of us that lives on after death. Our spirit is often described as our breath of life, the more divine aspect, and is typically seen as the part of a person that connects with something much greater, and the spiritual realm. In summary, while the terms "soul" and "spirit" can sometimes be used broadly to refer to a person's inner self, there is a distinction between them, with the soul representing the individual's conscious being, and the spirit representing their connection to God.

When we enter into a loving, intimate relationship, giving all to another being, we share our experiences, our beliefs, and our intellects as we allow ourselves to tear down our walls, and be vulnerable as we open up and give everything we have with our heart, soul, body, mind, and spirit. Soulmate is a deep and insightful connection on so many levels. With effortless communication, there is a sense of mutual growth and inspiration, where you can always be your most authentic self without the fear of judgment. You feel as if you've known each other forever, and have complete acceptance of each other's flaws.

When we look at the difference between a soulmate and a compatible partner in life, it's vast. Yet, they share similar traits; interests, standards of living, goals, faith, the ability to address challenges, and financial intentions. Compatible mates share a partnership that is steady, and comfortable. There can be contentment, and there can be love, but not on the deepest level. When the death of one partner occurs, there is grieving that can present itself in a variety of ways, but they navigate this experience a bit differently as they adjust to their new life, and then move forward. Perhaps the surviving partner/spouse initially scrambles to tie up loose ends, but when all is said and done, when the dust settles, and everything has been neatly tied into a bow, whether complicated or not, their life goes on as expected, and they honor the memories of their loved ones.

In contrast, soulmates have an almost mystical connection on a soul level. There is an immediate recognition, an intense emotional bond, as they experience the most extreme level of love a human being is capable of. Some have even described it as agape, a godly love. In psychology, Eros, the God of love (also known as Cupid in Roman mythology, the son of Venus) is known for his ability to shoot arrows that strike mere mortals to awaken them with an intense, fiery feeling in their heart. He is often associated with sexual and erotic love, emphasizing immense physical attraction, affection, and embodies the concept of the chemistry of passion and desire.

The soulmate relationship changes everything, and is unconditional. They acknowledge the entirety of the other, genuinely embrace everything about the other, bury their souls in each other, and sacrifice everything to save the other. They are masters of selflessness and give each other unwavering support, all that they are without hesitation, never give up, and never accept anything less. Their love for each other is the most important thing, even above money, no matter how their finances stack up, material possessions always take a back seat. Instead, their priority is each other's arms, each other's touch, where they know they will always be loved, protected, warm, and safe. They depend upon each other for emotional support, rather than surrounding structural support. They grieve longer, for their hearts truly break when they lose their mate, and it's an unending struggle trying to find ways to cope, and to survive.

Additionally, they not only honor the memories of their loved one, but the past becomes a bittersweet treasure-trove filled with immense regret, sorrow, lost love, and an unending, deep ache of loss. It becomes a vicious cycle as you find yourself constantly reliving moments with them, pining for the connection you had, and desperately wishing you could experience those times again. There is tremendous denial on the long path of processing the unflinching reality of letting go of this great kindred spirit you had in your life.

I know that some days the challenge to move forward seems insurmountable. They were your protector, the hero who defended you, and brought out the best version of you. They understood your perspectives, and shared all of your dreams, and heard all of your unspoken thoughts and felt your pain as their own. Your soulmate was the one with whom you shared your most intimate hours, who awakened that spirit inside of you, and who animated your heart to come alive. When your soulmate dies, your happily-ever-after departs from your life, and that finality forces you into a silent space of introspection as you wrestle with the logic behind the rationale of events, searching for the reasons why. Sometimes you feel it becomes impossible to find ways to ease the intensity of your despair.

I vividly remember a dark and somber day at the beginning of August 2023. I ran errands; first dropping into my local post office, then to a nearby food mart to pick up cookies, and last, leaving my beloved's best gray suit at the dry cleaners. One could surmise this was a normal day in a quotidian life filled with daily tasks, except that this day was far from normal and entailed atypical, deliberate, and specific activities. The post office helped expedite a down payment for cremation expenses. The cookies were traveling with me to a hospice residence where my beloved lay in bed slowly dying; they were his favorite. The suit I dropped off was for his funeral. The reality of it hit me as I drove halfway up the parkway, and I quickly pulled my car over to the shoulder. I released the guttural cries of a woman preparing for the end of a life, the life of a man she had loved more than anything in her entire existence. Sick to my stomach, I quickly swung open the car door and vomited.

As I entered his room with cookies, a smile, and my usual huge bear hug, he hadn't a clue. It was just another day in my life of painful denial, as I stood watching my beloved, the man I always kept within my safe keeping, slip through my fingers. My existence, as I once knew it, had deteriorated into a checklist of to do's so everything would go seamlessly and perfectly at the end. I shined his shoes, chose his shirt, tie, and jewelry, along with a small, matching lavender-colored pocket square, so that when the time came, and well wishers visited to pay their last respects, he'd be remembered as they knew him.

Immediately after I lost him, I experienced a decline into depression that I was not even aware of. I kept busy going about my daily life, and constantly blamed myself for things that were completely out of my control. I was so angry. Six months slipped by, and there was a tipping point which pushed me over the edge. A crisis unfolded, and my mental health completely deteriorated, and it culminated in a nervous breakdown. I took to my bed for approximately three months. At the same time, I also had this fear, that if I did anything really stupid, it would have been an aberration to God, and that I'd end up burning in hell for all eternity. Catholic guilt. Maybe at that specific point in time, that's what saved me. Well, that, and I believed that killing myself was something I was incapable of, as I didn't think I had the courage. I thought I was what someone might refer to as the Webster's Dictionary definition of "chicken shit." At that time, if you were to look it up, my picture would have been staring right back at you. No, I didn't have the audacity then to take my own life. I'm not sure if suicide has anything to do with braveness; it's more a feeling of being out of options, which I thought at that time I still had plenty of. But, tired of tying myself into a pretzel looking for even one, I stopped contemplating the idea of snuffing my life out, and instead I searched for the deepest trench I could crawl into and wished and hoped that the world would just leave me alone and go away. But, life's not as easy as that. It catches up to you. After this abnormally long period of limbo, I eventually sought therapy to help me cut through the thick fog, and to distinguish right from wrong. Therapy sessions started nine months after the passing of my beloved. With intense hours under a professional's care, I thought I found my way back into a "somewhat" rational mindset. I was mistaken.

I struggled in therapy. One day, the breach got too wide, and I couldn't find any more footholds to scale without a trapdoor opening beneath me, or core strength to climb that rope out. That's when chicken shit got seriously, and game changingly overruled; I raised my white flag, and threw in my towel of defeat. Sane people would have picked up the phone to their therapist; instead, following yet another sleepless night, heavy drinking commenced with the dawn. On an empty stomach, I started with red wine, leading into vodka, then searching around the house for medications that were used to heavily sedate my husband when he had his seizures. There weren't any. Left drunk, I went back to my bed and called a friend. My one option left. I purposely didn't choose to contact my children; I refrained from sharing my tortured despondency with them, as they were in no position to bear any additional burden. Parents are supposed to be stable, strong role models, who set examples, not behave irrationally or become overwhelmed, disconnected, and falling apart. Instead, I sent out an S.O.S, and this friend dropped everything; he came running.

He knew something wasn't right, and I was actually embarrassed that I had scraped the bottom of that moral barrel, as this wasn't the hill I actually wanted to die on. He came into my bedroom, climbed into my bed and sat there for hours talking to me.

He let me drink, and he let my cry. Yes, the pain of my beloved's loss was immense, but not an excuse to end my own life. I was so lost. My friend talked me off of that ledge, recognized when I was coming close to the point of no longer crying wolf, threw me a lifeline, and gave me the motivation I needed to find all the reasons why I deserved to carry on. He persuaded me to continue with therapy. At that point I decided to try to straighten out, stop feeling sorry for myself, and concentrated my hardest once again to move forward, to somehow find my path to wellness. But, in all honesty I was still struggling. A short time later, on the anniversary of my beloved's passing, in a moment of pure chance, synchronicity saw a wandering lost soul, and stepped in to save my life.

Depression, for me, was not logical; it was desperate and irrational. The type of depression I had was referred to as "complicated grief," where the intense sadness associated with my loss became overwhelming and interfered with my daily life; it consumed me. I had zero interest in everything around me. I completely withdrew from society, had difficulty making decisions, severe sleep disturbances, I felt worthless, and at the end, I developed a fearless attitude towards death, culminating in thoughts of self-harm. My feelings became debilitating and significantly impacted my daily functioning. Depression can trick a person into thinking that their thoughts are the truth, but there is help out there, so please, reach for it. Pick up the phone to someone, a professional, a family member, a good friend, anyone, and **FIGHT** your way back. I did.

When I was in counseling, my therapist asked me a question: "Would you do it all over again if you knew the outcome, the heartbreak, if you were told ahead of time that you'd be the last one standing?" That was a tough one, and I thought about it hard, and then I replied simply, "Yes." Essentially, it's choosing to live fully, even with the knowledge of a tragic ending. I now believe we are the lucky ones, the chosen few who have experienced firsthand that rare and truest of love stories. We are the ones where the universe deliberately intervened one day and steered us in a direction where we found our center point for whom we were destined. A few of you didn't even know it at the time. You may have thought you met your soulmate by chance, but I believe you were wrong. It was fate, something I strongly believe in. I've been given too many signs in my life to believe otherwise. You may not understand it now, and the amount of time it will take varies from one person to the next, but we are truly capable of carrying on with our lives while concomitantly holding onto the beautiful memories we had with our soulmates.

I talk about my beloved all the time so I can keep him close to me; I even talk to him when I'm alone, and of course, my tears still fall. You see, my greatest fear is forgetting his laughter, his voice, so I won't ever allow that to happen. I understand how death is a state of no longer being, and so very far away. It is that place of which there is no return, and for most of us, the hardest fact of life to accept, especially when we can't find the closure we crave. For some, there will never be closure. But, healing, peace, and acceptance come from within us, but only over time. Most people find themselves wondering how our soulmate's impact on us resonates beyond our physical proximity; life beyond the veil. There are still nights when I feel him with me, in between pauses of my thoughts, as if he's watching, waiting. Science has told us that we are all made up of energy, so in essence, while we're still alive, the basic building blocks of physical matter are energy fields. Ultimately, we are composed of atoms, and the majority of our physical mass is a manifestation of that energy. It's those rapidly-moving particles that are the fundamental aspect of physical reality. When we leave our bodies through death, our energy remains.

Yes, the lover's goodbye is painful, yet can also be transformative if we use it as a catalyst for personal growth. As we shed the old, and begin to embrace the new, all of it can lead to a profound inner strength, and the emergence of self-discovery. This is the time to forgive yourself for all that you meant to do, but couldn't; for all those days you doubted your own self-worth, and for all those instances you replayed, over and over in your mind, the things that you could not change. Now is the opportune moment to show yourself grace with compassion, and know that your value was not undermined by the fact that they left, as it wasn't their choice to leave. They say that over time we learn to accept what was out of our hands and finally find peace from what we could not control. There is a quiet victory in finding the courage to unearth your resilience to heal, and to learn how to nurture your strength, and this is where time becomes our friend.

It is at this point that we are all given a choice. We can allow grief to remain a stronghold within our hearts, where we rebel out of despair and defeat, and permit bitterness to develop and gain its foothold. In essence, you enable grief to evolve into a state of erosion which can take away from the value of your life. On the other hand, what if you chose to rebound? That would entail making a concerted effort to turn away from focusing on just the negative. That's when our spirit recognizes this so that you can move ahead. When you take responsibility for yourself, and start to embrace and cultivate a positive mindset as you rebuild your life, you start to see the bigger picture, and you begin to feel hopeful again.

Over time, I've had no choice but to accept the word *widow*, which is a noun, not an adjective, but ironically now describes me. I think, however, we're all basically simple beings wishing to go through life hoping that we'll just be happy, that we don't ever hurt anyone, and that we'll fall in love, and for some, maybe even start a family. I thought I was following this rule of thumb, but one night I very unexpectedly fell out of charted waters, and slipped into something extraordinary. I fell instantly, absolutely, deeply, entirely in love with a man who was destined for me, another soul I already knew and recognized from another lifetime the moment I saw him. I know, it sounds crazy, but for those of you who've experienced this kind of connection, you know exactly what I'm talking about, and it's rare. Losing this type of great love in your life is mind-bendingly crippling. There were days that I wished there was a magic pill I could swallow that would wipe out all of the love and memories, and just make them vanish forever, for they debilitated me.

Sadly, it's not just humans who insightfully feel the depths of loss.

There have even been instances of this in the animal kingdom, a strong case in point being elephants. They are extremely intelligent, socially complex, and emotionally capable creatures. They have been observed mourning their dead, even in the wild. There are also at least two instances, both in captivity, where elephants have died from grief after the death of their mate.

Tarsiers are 100% carnivorous primates, and are known for becoming distressed, or even dying if they are separated from their mate, or if their mate dies. This behavior is the result of extremely strong social bonds. Most times, they depend upon on their mate for survival and emotional support.

It's also been evidenced that dolphins and even some whales actually carry their dead mates or their dead calves around in their mouths, mourning them, exhibiting very long periods of distress. They are extremely social mammals, and just like us, they have what is called von Economo neurons, a special type of neuron named after an Austrian neurologist, Constantin von Economo. It's found in the brains of humans and other animals and mammals, and regulates social and emotional cognition. It displays empathy.

Gorillas are known for mourning their dead and remain close by the body for very long periods of time as well. Younger primates have been observed sleeping in the same nesting area next to their older, deceased family members. Some vocalize distressing sounds. Gorilla mothers exhibit behaviors, like carrying their deceased babies for multiple days. This is looked upon as grieving. They stay near their dead, staring at them, touching them, smelling them, some even grooming them after death. We humans don't own love or grief. These heartfelt emotions are widespread in animals as well.

Honestly, losing my beloved was the hardest and toughest reality that I ever had to face. It may have been the end of our love story, but I now believe that it's not the end of finding a new purpose for my life that could bring me joy. Our new lives will bring the dawning of significantly new avenues to explore. Often, richer, brand-new, multifaceted friendships are possible and achievable. There could also be new employment or volunteering opportunities, going back to school and learning new skills, moving to a new home, or even perhaps one day, finding another intimate love. Your new life might allow you to express yourself through art, writing, music, or any activity that allows you to tap into your creativity. Life is about experiences, gaining knowledge and insights, accepting change, and stepping out of one's comfort zone. In discovering new things that make you happy, you'll feel a sense of accomplishment as they reward you and propel you forward so that you can enjoy the life that you are so deserving of. I believe we should try our best to dwell on the beauty in our lives, not on the pitfalls, try to discover what is left for us, and live out the remainder of our days as fully as possible. But, it's the unsteadiness of venturing back out into the world, that initial step, which is the most frightening. When do you hit the gas pedal, and when do you pump the brakes?

It is arduous, and downright grueling at times, as we try to move ahead, because we still face a tremendous amount of obstacles. Our paths will be filled with challenges, such as watching life go on all around us, which can sometimes feel unbearable. Whether we acknowledge it or not, watching other people paired up, healthy, happy, and enjoying their lives when ours have been completely destroyed and pulled inside out is difficult to handle. But, in order to try to enrich our lives as we move forward, how do we sideline these emotions? Is there a way to move past the grief and in some way recover while we are striving to start over?

There is no all true, perfect, or exact cure to this disconnection we feel, because for most of us that simply doesn't exist on this side of widowhood. To reconnect with your individual identity, and the sense of self which existed before you committed to your relationship with your soulmate, is essentially about rediscovering your own interests and passions. These are goals that might have been put on hold while building the life you had with your beloved. In trying to heal, it's similar to figuring out who you want to be when you grow up. As we acknowledge the way loss can so totally break us, we realize we have no choice but to rebuild from the bottom up.

As you experiment with different approaches as to what makes you happy through trial and error, you begin to see a glimmer of a life that might be worth living. In this process of rediscovery, it's a daily exercise of your mind as you devote your focus to shifting towards the "me" dynamic, and renewing that spirit inside of you, strengthening your values, and envisioning how you can use the tools from your relationship in order to move forward. So, we ask ourselves: What can we do to bring a lifelong positive effect on our capacity to find happiness? What makes us feel alive? We start by looking within, and go back to that time before "me" became "we."

CHAPTER 2

EXPECTING THE UNEXPECTED

(A Bell's Not a Bell 'Till You Ring It)

THEY SAY THERE ARE FIVE stages of grief:

Denial: This can't be happening to me, to us!
Anger: Why did this happen? Is there someone I can blame?
Bargaining: Make this go away and I swear to God I will . . .
Depression: I can't bear this; I'm too sad to do anything, I give up.
Acceptance: I acknowledge what has happened, I cannot change it, and I must move forward.

Note that these stages are not meant to be packaged up neatly, as nothing is typical. Grieving is as individual and as abstract as we are, and it is not a linear process. Loss and grief are not the same for everyone. Here's a more detailed explanation:

Shock, disbelief: It's unbelievably hard to accept death. We question whether the loss really happened. Not believing or accepting that it really occurred is a normal reaction. When it first happens, in some cases, you talk yourself into thinking it was all a mistake and that your loved one is actually still here. "It can't possibility be my beloved, it's someone else, everyone has it all confused, as this cannot be happening to me, to us."

Anger: This often comes into play, and is extremely common. Maybe you're angry with the person who died for not being around anymore. Maybe you blame the caregivers for not doing enough. Maybe you even blame God. You begin to find small injustices and magnify them, making them significant, when in actuality they're not. Letting go of the anger is part of the process that only time can heal. It's a crucial step in healing that only we can reason with and control it to fade so the wounds can finally mend.

Profound sadness: This can often lead to feeling alone or isolated. We believe that no one can possibly understand the depth of our grief, and that in itself drives us even deeper into our sorrow. It feels like a part of you is missing; that piece which is irreplaceable. It leads to a sense of emptiness and despair that can be incredibly difficult to maneuver alone.

Guilt: Regretting what you said or did, or didn't do and should have done. You question everything and try to analyze every sinking feeling about the death. You blame yourself for poor decisions or things that were completely out of your control, convincing yourself that you could have changed the outcome. As previously stated, there are a million guilties . . .

Fear: Anxiety is triggered on so many levels. It's a buildup of grief as you face life without your soulmate. You feel vulnerable and uncertain about your future alone, as well as an acute awareness of your own mortality.

Pain: Grief is not just emotional; it presents physically too. Expect triggers from simple, ordinary things that can turn out to be long-term challenges. Examples are: Places, scents, familiar songs, sounds, events, i.e., birthdays, holidays, anniversaries. The list goes on, but when you become aware of them, you give yourself a better edge at keeping them at bay. Plan ahead and use strategies to support yourself compassionately, treat yourself kindly, and without judgment. There is a psychological impact as the intense sense of loss and longing associated with losing a soulmate can lead to decreased motivation, social withdrawal, and overall feelings of emptiness, further contributing to physical changes. The brain processes emotional pain similarly to physical pain, activating similar neural pathways which can manifest as physical symptoms and lead to significant effects in your body. There are individual variations, degrees, and severities of physical symptoms which can be different for everyone's unique personality, coping mechanisms, and the nature of their relationship with their soulmate.

I can personally attest that losing your soulmate sets off a whirlwind of crazy and intense emotions and physical changes, especially during that first year, and for some even into the next few years to come. For instance, personality changes, such as being more irritable, less patient, or no longer having the tolerance for other people's "small" problems may surface. You experience an intolerable yearning for them with a sense of incompleteness, obsessiveness, or sometimes even delusional thoughts. You'll find difficulty communicating with other people, sometimes needing to redefine the roles of family and friends who, unexpectedly, are no longer there when you need them. You may become more isolated, either by choice or circumstance, and begin to feel like an outcast.

Not only are you feeling alone, you feel downright invisible at times. At first, I found that some people could not face me; they literally avoided me. They couldn't find the words, so they thought it was best not to say anything and avoided me altogether. Look, I get it; it's hard for some people, but I am still alive and I sure could have used a friend, more so then than ever.

Then there were the people who, if I brought up my beloved, would just stop talking, or change the subject, as though he had never existed. They would start stumbling over their words, trying to find ways of talking about something totally unrelated. The fact of the matter was, I was onto them, and it hurt me when they avoided the subject and wouldn't acknowledge that he was part of who I am.

You may experience a sense of feeling as if you're adrift in your own life, as the depth of the relationship you shared with your beloved is so deeply and suddenly absent. What if there are children? Now you're not only dealing with your own grief, but you find yourself also navigating theirs when they look towards you for guidance and support.

Then, there comes the dilemma of the material possessions left behind. This decluttering, also known as "grief cleaning," is the process of letting go of the things which are tied to a deceased loved one. The clothes where their scent still lingers, or jewelry carrying enormous sentimental ties that you gave to each other, and in our case, supplies donated to help with disability needs. Everything was everywhere. My beloved was gone, as I sat surrounded by everything he wore, right down to the clippers I used when I cut his nails, and the intimate cologne he preferred, Lagerfeld. The stair lift, the wheelchair, the walker, the cane, the special seat he sat on when I helped to shower him, even the bed guard, all lay idle, now waiting for the next person to support. It was all too overwhelming; I knew I couldn't take my time as I revisited all the rooms where parts of his existence still remained. So many gloomy corners, nooks where he once sat, his chair was like a ghost, areas that became so empty without him. I knew it all had to change before I lost my mind, and I had to make quick decisions. His possessions were literally destroying me. So, I gave back. I loaded up my car and drove to the nursing home that took great care of him when he needed it, and I donated it all so others could benefit. I then went into his closet and folded all of his clothes, and had our two sons sift through it all and take whatever they wanted. The rest went to our very close and dear family and friends, the remainder to charity. It was how he wanted it. I kept his favorite shirt so that I could sleep in it, but to this very day I have not been able to. I couldn't bear seeing his possessions anymore; it was heartbreaking, dismal, paralyzing, and blocked me from finding any semblance of healing.

Do what is right for you, and take your time. In my case, my emotions impacted my decision and I had no alternative but to let go of everything quickly. Everyone is different. I found it to be a highly triggering process; it seemed like everything had a memory tied to it; even the most absurd, nonsensical items, i.e. a stack of business cards he kept from people I wasn't even acquainted with. They all meant something to him; not to me. There was also a small American flag pin I found in the back of his drawer that lit up which he wore on his jacket collar one Fourth of July many years ago. If I allowed it all to consume me, these negligible things would have left me in a puddle on the floor for the rest of my days.

It can be such an emotional project, but it can also present the opportunity to not only honor memories, but create space for new beginnings. I recommend that you begin in short bursts, rather than trying to tackle everything at once, like I did. Yes, there are items now that I wish I could get back. Break it down into manageable time slots, and get help from friends and family if you think it would make it easier. If you're still not ready to part with something, store it. It's a temporary solution that will give you much needed time to process your emotions and to make decisions at a later date.

About those delusional thoughts: In my particular case, approximately four months after I lost my beloved, I found myself displaying extremely out-of-character behavior. I joined online dating sites on a whim, then canceled the same subscriptions the very next day, as I certainly was not in my right state-of-mind at all. At that time, another man in my life would have been way beyond superfluous; just about as useless as a submarine needing screen doors. It was the loneliness; it was unbearable. I even made contact with an old boyfriend from way back in the day, someone who had tried to contact me several times during my marriage, with whom I never engaged. I felt as if I were grasping for any attachment that might help to alleviate the emptiness that was left inside of me. He was extremely happy to hear from me, of course. He was also married, but flirted with me anyway. In a strange way, I was hoping that something might materialize from it, but as I was revisiting this past relationship, I realized how totally inappropriate it was for me. In hindsight, it was also disrespectful to my soulmate, for if he knew how I was behaving it would have broken his heart. He had always felt that I deserved the best and would have been surprised at how I had lowered my standards. I came to my senses and realized it wasn't a healthy choice for me to make in initiating contact with him in the first place, and I decided to cut off all communication after only a few conversations.

When you're so desperately lonely and not thinking straight, your mind tricks you into believing that finding a romantic level of relation with another human being will take away all of your sadness, but in reality all it does is make you feel worse because you weren't ready at all; you hadn't taken the time needed to heal. I took a step back, forgave myself for acting like a fool, and moved forward knowing I'm still living and learning. You must forgive yourself, especially at this confusing time in your life, as we were made to learn from our mistakes. Hindsight offers clarity and you must be gentle on yourself, even when you make poor decisions.

You can seek support from a healthcare professional, perhaps 1:1 with a grief therapist, or even attend grief support groups. This is a crucial and challenging time. Like I said before, there's no shame in reaching out and admitting how you feel, as you'll need tools to help steer you forward, tools that you can use for the rest of your life. Suffering from this type of loss is something one cannot do alone, I can personally attest to that, and I am not ashamed to say so.

Some people don't wish to waste their time on professionals, as they feel they cannot possibly understand what they're going through, because they may never have experienced it themselves. I disagree with this way of thinking. However, I also understand how these types of people prefer the company of others who are in the same boat. I keep an open mind. Personally, I went this route in addition to professional therapy. My husband succumbed to brain cancer, so I contacted The Glioblastoma Support Network and the National Brain Tumor Society which are resources for the widowed and others who have lost a loved one to this horrible disease. Here I found other people who understood. They were sympathetic listeners, these new acquaintances with whom I've established connections, since we all shared the same battles and traumas.

These resources can also include online support groups and educational materials. So you see, there's something out there for you. We just have to own up to the fact that we're lonely, hurting, and willing to share our sorrows as we make that first step in being transparent and asking for help. There's no one size fits all; square pegs can't always fit into round holes. I'm just advising that you try to look for the best match for you. There are also self-care practices, such as engaging in healthy lifestyle habits like regular exercise, a balanced diet, sufficient sleep, and partaking in social interactions which can aid in managing the physical and emotional impacts of grief as well. I know, easier said than done, so I'm going to try my best to help and break it down for you:

Sleep patterns are disrupted and are number one on my list of ailments. Either you sleep too much or can't sleep at all. You can experience difficulty in falling asleep, waking frequently, or feeling exhausted, even after sleeping eight hours (if you're that lucky), due to constant rumination about your loss. I preferred not to take the medications that my doctor was willing to prescribe, as I was afraid of becoming that crazy lady that the local police find singing and dancing down the street, naked, at 3:30 a.m., so I rely solely on over-the-counter remedies like taking magnesium at night, then melatonin. On really bad nights, I take just a tiny nip of a strong nighttime cold/flu remedy (not nearly the amount advised), or something my friend turned me on to, an antihistamine medication specifically formulated for children. I have also picked up a generic formulation specifically made to help you sleep, but won't make you feel groggy in the morning. Sometimes it works, but other times it doesn't. These are some of the crutches that work for me, but I use them infrequently, as they can help at first, but over time your body becomes dependent upon them and you'll find that they don't work quite as well, or you may need a larger dose in order to achieve the same effect. Therefore, I caution you to use these judiciously. There are many more remedies you can try out there, you just need to find what works for you and not feel guilty when you utilize them. You need to help yourself. No one else can.

At night, I find myself either writing or watching comedy shows on TV. It helps as everything kicks in and finally makes my eyes heavy. I do take everything with caution, as I also must take my regularly prescribed daily medications. Although not many at all, they are enough to give me pause when I supplement with something to try and sleep. So, if you do take daily medications, ask your doctor first what the contraindications might be if you combine them with a nighttime sleep aid. Think before you pop, that's my motto. Believe it or not, most nights I find myself dozing off to shows that are ridiculously funny, like Seinfeld, or an animated show called Family Guy, or my other, favorite cartoon, called South Park. I used to watch that one years ago with my two sons; a silly, stupid series which I still find crazy-funny. I think it's quick-witted, realistic, and very well-written. I remember watching an episode one night where two teachers, a man and a woman, were in charge of teaching the boys and the girls about sex education separately. Neither one of them knew what they were doing, as both were still virgins themselves, and way beyond past the age for marriage. I guess the topic got them pretty excited and they ended up sneaking away and awkwardly getting it on, almost killing each other in the process! It was absolutely hilarious, to the point that I peed myself. So, when I'm watching TV, I'd rather laugh myself to sleep than cry. For me, a change of underwear is well worth it.

There can be hormonal fluctuations when one experiences grief as deep as this, as the body releases stress hormones, such as cortisol, which can disrupt various bodily functions, like sleep, appetite, and your immune response. It may not be a bad idea to ask your physician if you should have your pituitary and thyroid glands checked in the process just to be sure everything's A-ok.

Your immune system can falter, so if you suspect that your immune system is somewhat off kilter, or weakened due to stress, you can try to boost it by eating a balanced diet rich in fruits and vegetables. Also, try your best to get enough sleep (I know, it's hard), exercise regularly, manage your stress levels, practice good hygiene, such as washing your hands often and avoiding other people whom you suspect are sick, and above all, stay hydrated by drinking lots of water. Take your current weight and divide it by two, then the remaining number is how many ounces of water you should try to be drinking daily. Consider supplements like vitamin C and zinc, but only after consulting your doctor. If you suspect a serious issue, turn to a healthcare professional to rule out any underlying medical conditions you may not have been aware of. My best advice is to have a complete physical in order to get a clear snapshot of where you stand, without sugarcoating anything that would embarrass you. This is the time for blunt honesty, and to face head on, how this loss has affected you in more ways than one.

Your appetite may also suffer, which can lead to weight loss or gain. I overate as a coping mechanism. When my beloved was sick, I gained an enormous amount of weight, which was extremely stressful on my 5' 5" frame. I remember trying on a dress for his funeral, staring at myself in the mirror wondering who the bloated, blood sausage staring back at me was. I would overeat from all the stress, and yes, I also began to drink. Maybe some of you have also abused some kind of substance. Vodka was my *go-to* every night after a long day of caring for my husband. It dulled my pain just enough to drift to sleep, but like the old saying goes, I was up when I should've been down, so my sleep patterns were highly disrupted, as I became my own worst enemy. It was the last thing I should have done, allowing my own health to suffer, but that's what we do when our beloveds are sick; we put ourselves on the back burner and scramble our brains until we're cooked. Many times I questioned whether I was drinking to ease the pain or to punish myself for not doing more to help him. I can now say that I did all that I could and that I was physically and emotionally wiped out.

Eventually, all the harm I did to myself caught up with me. After he died, I tried to follow his advice to take good care of myself. I immediately had a complete physical, and slowly, began the journey back to me. Albeit, I was left staring at high blood pressure and was also now pre-diabetic. It all scared the hell out of me. Medication has helped me, and I also toned the drinking way down. I made a firm commitment to drink myself sober again (now I drink a lot of water) and it's certainly not an everyday occurrence anymore, but I do engage in an occasional fine glass of wine from time to time. I'm not a nun. In fact, far from it, which you're about to find out! Soon, the extra weight slipped off, as I was never meant to carry that on my frame anyway. Simply by eating sensibly and healthily, with a normal daily caloric intake for a female my height and age, *everything in moderation* worked for me. I try to move more too, which helps. I admit I do hate to exercise, but the old fashioned method still applies: Stop shoving food and substances down your throat to appease your feelings, eat less, eat healthy, and move your ass. I started moving mine and over time walking helped to bring it back up to where it's supposed to be, and might I add, it's quite a nice one. *Just sayin'* . . .

Your skin also reacts and changes, even though you're probably trying to follow your usual routine. You need to address those changes as they occur. Grief can significantly change your skin by causing it to appear dry and dull. You can become more prone to wrinkles due to the stress hormone cortisol, which breaks down collagen and actually accelerates the aging process when produced in excess during periods of intense grief. It can also manifest as visible signs like increased acne breakouts, redness and rosacea (which is a condition that causes pimples and broken blood vessels), or an uneven skin tone due to a disrupted skin barrier function due to your body's "fight-or-flight" response.

Your hair can fall out, which actually happened to me. Look, we're sharing here, and I've never been one to hold back; just ask my family or any one of my friends. When I would brush my hair in the morning, I started noticing clumps of it caught in the bristles, and some in the sink. Then, I'd shower and additional tufts would be left in my hands. I remember one day getting ready to meet up with a friend. It was approximately 14 months after my husband died. I styled my hair as usual, but this time I used that sneaky little *back of head* mirror which I pulled out from the wall, and I angled it so I could view my reflection in the huge vanity mirror behind me. It revealed I was missing half of my head of hair, and I had huge bald spots! I thought I was doing everything right since embarking on my new healthy lifestyle which included supplements i.e., multivitamins, biotin, collagen, etc., so I couldn't figure out what I was doing wrong. The only thing I overlooked was the fact that when grief first hit me, it got way beyond dark and grim.

I still have my moments of weeping, although not nearly as stormy. For all of us, grief takes its toll, whether we are left with physical deficits or emotional scars. In most cases, it's both. But, answer me this: Why is it that the hair on my head is falling out, yet the battle with those three, stubborn chin hairs haven't been informed that we lost this war? I should be so lucky, so thank God for tweezers. In my case, testing revealed nothing specific, so I had no choice but to accept my hair loss. But, I always think quickly on my feet, so I became well acquainted with hair pieces and partial wigs, aka toppers. There really are many choices out there, very realistic, and if you can't do it by yourself, I can assure you there are wonderful hairdressers who can cut and style them to suit you perfectly. Whether you're a man or a woman, they can also tutor you so that you feel adept at doing it on your own. Don't be embarrassed to ask for help; hairdressers see it all the time, that's what they're there for. I get lots of compliments on my *hair* and my reply is usually always the same, "Thank you, I'll let *her* know you liked it." That's when they realize it's not all mine. Everything rolls off my back nowadays, I've always been an open book. So what if a strong wind blows it off your head one day when you're out in public? Laugh, pick it up, shake it out and plop it back onto your noggin (make sure it's bubble gum free), and this time, may I suggest that you use stronger clips? Like I said, just laugh at yourself. Folks, it's just hair, and while I wouldn't mind one bit if mine decided to grow back, I have no problem wearing wigs. At this point, there's no room for embarrassment. I think we've been through enough.

You can have changes in digestive issues such as stomach upset, nausea, diarrhea, or constipation due to stress hormones impacting your digestive system. My best advice is to eat healthy, don't forget to drink plenty of water, exercise your body and your mind, and just be kind to yourself. Our emotions absolutely impact our physical health, and these changes are usually reflected in your colon. Daily probiotics are live microorganisms that provide health benefits when consumed in adequate amounts. It's as easy as taking one capsule per day. Or, they are also typically found in fermented foods such as sauerkraut, kimchi, natto, tempeh, pickles, and yogurt. Look for yogurt labeled as *live and active cultures* or *probiotic*. These yogurts contain live bacteria that can benefit gut health. Greek yogurt often contains a higher concentration of probiotics than regular yogurt, is thicker, and has more protein. Other foods such as miso, olives, dark chocolate (which contains prebiotics that feed probiotics), kvass (a fermented beverage containing antioxidant properties), and cottage cheese are also good for your digestive system. However, not all dairy products and fermented foods contain probiotics. Look for labels that indicate *live and active cultures*. Heat can kill probiotics, so it's best to consume these foods raw or with minimal cooking. If you ever get stuck, and all else fails, I hear

29

that glycerin suppositories are God's gift to humanity. Natural, fast, job done. I guess this too shall pass? Pun intended. But, maybe someone ought to get back to me on *that* one . . .

You may even experience cardiovascular complications stemming from the intense emotional and physical stress of grief and loss associated with losing your soulmate. In extreme cases, the stress of losing your beloved can trigger symptoms resembling a heart attack, known as "broken heart syndrome." The medical term for this is called Takotsubo cardiomyopathy. I cover that later here, as it happened to a very dear and close friend of mine, and in her particular case could not have been prevented no matter how many people at that time tried to intervene, as she would not accept help. It mimics the symptoms of a heart attack: Chest pain, which feels like a squeezing or tightness in the chest; shortness of breath, which may occur suddenly or worsen with exertion; dizziness or lightheadedness, which makes you feel faint or even have a loss of consciousness; irregular heartbeat, where you feel a racing, skipped, or fluttering heartbeat; fatigue or weakness; profuse sweating. If you experience any of these symptoms, I recommend that you call 911, or go to the nearest emergency room immediately. Only a doctor can determine the cause of your symptoms and provide appropriate care.

You can experience physical tension in the head, neck, and shoulders as a result of all the emotional strain. Try booking regular appointments for a good deep-tissue massage. Treat yourself, you deserve it! And for all of you ladies out there, it wouldn't hurt to ask for Gaston, that tall, strapping French masseur, aka massage therapist, whose six-pack is made of steel, and fingers that know precisely how to knead. Il est beau. Opt for him in lieu of Gertrude, that short, stout, big-boned gorilla who you know is going to hurt you. I think my hormones are running amok again, which brings me to the next ailment.

Widow's fire refers to the intense desire for sexual intimacy that some people experience following the death of their partner. Essentially it's a form of grief related to the loss of a sexual connection with their mate. This feeling can last for months or even years, depending on the individual and their grieving process, with many experiencing it within the first few months after their loss.

Yes, this also happened to me. I'm a hot mess, aren't I? Heck, I admit it's not entirely over yet, and these feelings first emerged only a few months after my beloved died. Hence, the online dating sites. It came out of left field, out of nowhere. What was happening to me? Physically, I felt like I was jumping out of my skin. I was irritable for no reason, antsy, plain and simple: Horny as hell! Of course, there are things one can do to satisfy a physical need quickly, *or not*, like crossing the great divide and finding some southern comfort, aka, self-please, and then get a good night's sleep. But, then I realized what I missed the most was the intimacy I shared with my husband, as nothing ever interfered with that until he got sick and even then we worked around it. That's what I loved the most in our relationship. We always had this need to physically touch each other every day, all the time, even if it was just as simple as holding hands, him giving me a little slap on my butt when I walked by, or grabbing each other for a quick hug. It didn't matter, as long as we had a physical connection we knew our world was going to be ok. That's what really bothered me. What I was truly lacking was all of those tender moments with him, snuggling up together, me laying in the crook of his arm, smooching, just talking each other to sleep, and saying, "I love you."

Still, having sex sure would be great, and I do miss it. A LOT. Listen, at this point I would prefer the company of a real man as opposed to a BOB (battery-operated boyfriend), but I'm also no prude, I've been down that road too, both alone and with my lover, and I have no complaints. No, I have still not met anyone, but in all fairness, I truly haven't made a concerted effort to look, either. But, one day that will change. However, I don't think there's any strap-on erotic stimulator, sex-shaped toy, or Buzz Lightyear Humpty Who Ha that would ring the bells in my head, but hey, never say never, to each their own, as I am not one to judge, so whatever floats your boat! That's my philosophy. Just don't get yourself into a jam and end up in the ER, and certainly don't tell the nurses you accidentally fell onto that flashlight 'cause the dang thing got stuck up your ass. They're not going to believe you. Or, when you thought a showerhead would do the trick, but you got a little carried away and now that hose you're dragging out of your butthole resembles a tail! The plumbing got stuck and now there's no backing out. Just kidding, but do take good care of yourself, and be safe. These crazy sex hormone rushes are normal. Try not to be lascivious towards someone who is physically, actively running away from you, take the hint. Above all, remember that sex is fun! Just don't hurt yourself in the process.

My good friend Fran, who has a drawer filled with fun sex toys, called me the other day to inform me that a discreet, brown-papered package was on its way to my house. "Greta, you're so naïve, such a nerd. I'm popping a little gift into the mail for you right now; not The Rabbit, but I guarantee this nifty little gadget is gonna blow your socks off!" I am someone who has good rhythm, but coordination is not my strong point. I'm that dimwit who trips going upstairs, and still gets confused over righty-tighty, lefty-loosey. I can see it now: Halfway through pleasuring myself, springs pop, slippery pieces go flying everywhere, and now I'm sporting a brand new shiner, as my excited dog Harry starts playing floor hockey with his new pulsating Bananarama meat substitute on the floor. Talk about a mood buster. Well, Fran's discreet brown Amazon box arrived the very next day, so I decided to dip my toe back into pleasurable waters that night. I put my new Ladies Home Companion to the test, and without any slip-ups, the multiple levels of vibration gave me a full-blown party of one. My toes curled as if the universe threw a confetti parade in my hoo-ha; what a sweet surprise in my little slice of heaven! A huge brav"O" to you Fran! A dear friend who recognized when I needed more than just a little helping hand. Ring a ding ding!

Widow's fog refers to a mental state of confusion and difficulty concentrating that can occur after losing a spouse, often described as a "brain fog," where basic tasks seem challenging. For most people, this fog tends to last between six months to a year, but can sometimes extend longer, depending upon individual circumstances and coping mechanisms. Be kind to yourself, it's not your fault. I've been through it, and I can promise you that the professionals all say that it will get easier if you give yourself time. Things will become clearer, it won't last forever. Or, at least I hope not, for I still find myself going into rooms wondering what the hell I went in there for, or, when I find my iPhone in the freezer, the oven, or the mailbox. When it's totally lost, I just call my cell from the house phone. I'm always thankful the ringing isn't coming from my dog's stomach. Actually, I'm starting to get used to being this way. Perhaps it's just a part of aging. So for now, I'll consider myself lucky, that on good days, I still remember to put my underwear on in the morning.

Broken Heart Syndrome is a topic that I wish to revisit, as this was how I lost a very dear friend many years ago. Her name was Annette. She was so full of life; educated, intelligent, and funny. She was born and raised in an Italian section of Brooklyn, New York. She met her soulmate when she went to work for him managing his engineering firm in New York City. This firm was also the first to hire my husband immediately after his graduation from Manhattan University in the Bronx. The owner, Dr. Tonis Raamot was from a little country called Estonia, a country in Northern Europe which borders the Baltic Sea and the Gulf of Finland. Tonis, or Toni as we would all call him, was born and raised there. He was a very tall and gentle giant, generous to a fault, a kind man who always offered everyone his smile. He held a PhD in Civil Engineering and was brilliant, but it was his off-cuff sense of humor which everyone found so endearing, as he was unconsciously funny, but never knew it. He was divorced, with older children, and fell in love with Annette the moment he saw her, and hired her on the spot. Street-smart, Italian Annette from Brooklyn and brilliant Toni from Estonia were an unlikely pair to the outside world looking in, but as fate would have it, the greatest match for each other. It wasn't long before they married and lived a storybook romantic life.

They were married for ten beautiful and happy years, until Toni became ill unexpectedly and died very quickly from a staph infection in his early sixties. My husband and I were devastated, as Toni and my husband were very close. Toni respected my husband and grew to love him like he was his own son. But, it was Annette who took it the hardest. From time to time we would look in on her, or have occasional dinners at her house with her immediate family always present, as they didn't ever want to leave her alone. Oh, there were many doctor visits, medications, therapies, interventions, and grief programs that she attended, but nothing helped.

Still, she was somehow able to make me laugh once when she compared an Irish church, basement grief therapy circle to an Italian one. She told me that all who attended the Irish church sessions kept most of their feelings to themselves, each politely waiting for their turn to speak, spoke quietly when the group leader called upon them, and were well-mannered and courteous, not to mention, not one wet eye in the house. All were stoic and thoughtful.

Whereas, at the Italian church sessions, everyone was in mourning, and no one held back. There was wailing, crying, and screaming to the point where one person actually passed out. There were tears, tissue boxes, and emotions flying everywhere. She said the circle leader was a priest and was almost trampled because everyone pulled out pictures of their dearly departed loved ones asking this poor guy to bless their photos. Everyone wore black and everyone had a story and they weren't leaving until it was told. Italians are extremely emotional, family-oriented and loving people, and they don't hide their feelings. One never needs to guess what they're thinking. Personally, I applaud their transparency; the statistics on their dying from stress conditions resulting from difficulty expressing emotion must be the lowest in recorded history.

Everyone around her watched her grieve for her beloved Toni, as she became emotionally and physically sicker from her never-ending grief. Months and months of misery and suffering passed. The last conversation we had on the phone was her calling me from Toni's car, which she still could not part with. As she sat in the driver's seat in her garage sobbing, she explained to me how she had just found a few of Toni's hairs still caught in the visor. Toni was so tall that his head nearly touched the ceiling in most cars, which would explain why he could only buy a very large Cadillac, as he couldn't fit in most other models. She was beyond inconsolable on that particular day. In hindsight, I never quite understood the gravity of what she went through until I witnessed it with my own eyes when I saw her in person, or my own ears when I heard her tortured voice on the other end of the phone that day. She had lost her soulmate, the greatest love of her life, and for a little over three years she grieved for him until her poor little body gave out. Annette was diagnosed with broken heart syndrome, stress cardiomyopathy, Takotsubo syndrome, which over time weakened her heart muscle and led to her death. She is buried alongside her beloved Toni in the Green-Wood Cemetery in Brooklyn, New York and their gravestone reads "No Greater Love." Perhaps there never was, or at the very least, not for them.

When I think back, I remember all those sweet actions Toni would do for her, the romantic words he would whisper in her ear and how she would giggle, the little post-it notes he would stick on the side of the saucer which held the tea he had just made for her, writing how he missed her, even though Annette was literally sitting in the next room watching TV. The never-ending forehead kisses he gently placed, and how they always held hands; too many gestures of love to mention. With all of my heart, I miss them both, those two beautiful and sincere people who did everything for everyone, both taken out of this life too soon. I wish them Godspeed, and I keep the faith and believe in my heart that they are together again, for that is what soulmates do. They find each other.

CHAPTER 3

THE "C" WORD

CANCER KNOWS NO AGE, COLOR, gender or creed. It comes for you when it's least expected and touches upon people from every walk of life. It's not choosey. It was the last thing I ever thought would happen, but one day it came for us.

Our journey began in July 2021 with a diagnosis, followed by two years of my beloved battling brain cancer, which was deemed terminal from the get-go. It came with no warning and created a tremendous struggle to live through. After he died, I was so worn out, it was as if there was no life left within me. I tried to let him go, but the very thought of it became impossible so I avoided it, as it certainly wasn't something I could process all by myself. I lived in a robotic state, some days forcing myself to leave the house when all I wanted to do was to crawl into bed and die. I simply went through the motions. Holidays came and went, and my smiles were all forced, phony. I was running on empty, as I put on a brave front so people wouldn't worry.

After six months into that first year without him, I lost our beautiful and young dog Buddy to cancer, too. The day I returned to my house, after having no choice but to let him go, everything stopped. I spent months in bed. I kept remembering my beloved being so sick, and then losing our sweet Buddy, all of it playing over and over in my mind. It was so unfair, and I was angry, especially because my husband had worked so hard all of his life for our future and all the new memories we looked forward to making. His life was cut short while the world kept spinning for everyone else around me. It was a confusing time, and I shut down. I tried so hard to reason with all of it, but to no avail. Unbeknownst to me, the grieving process was another thing I was avoiding. I didn't know how to move forward; I merely existed in limbo from day to day.

Once cancer came, it was the beginning of the end of our world as we knew it. I really don't understand a whole lot about this disease, the different types, and their individualized treatments, but I don't know a living soul on this planet who hasn't been touched by this cruel disease in one way or another. One might imagine that science would have already learned how to obliterate it once and for all, especially with all the progress we have made in so many other different areas. And yes, I personally do question whether or not it has to do with the pharmaceutical industry, aka Big Pharma, having a financial hand in keeping it alive. But, what do I know? My belief is that our doctors and scientists are doing the best that they can to fight this disease, however, their progress is limited to the resources given to them. Drugs, as well as knowledge shared publicly, are spoon fed to us, controlled, and what frightens me are the powers behind them, those who are complicit, unaccountable, and who have skin in the game. We humans are literally the only species who would fuck each other over for a profit, and that's a fact. Hey, these are just my personal thoughts. I don't keep a tight lid on filtering my opinions, and as you can clearly see, I don't mince words.

This infuriates me, especially because I believe that money comes before a person's life, no matter how young or old they are. My husband received very good care; those relentless doctors and nurses who attended to him are heroes. However, I remain sad, and solemnly a tad bitter, as I am just another statistic left alone to grieve without having had any say in how someone, somewhere, somehow failed us and everyone else defeated by this war, which is driven by the powers that be and their defalcation.

At the beginning of my husband's illness, I recalled the people I knew who were lost to cancer. They were mostly all acquaintances, except in the case of my own mother, who I had lost seven years prior. I had little to no experience when I was first personally introduced to cancer, and I learned a lot when my mother was diagnosed. Initially, they said she had stomach cancer. This was a totally different type of sickness than I had ever had to help her deal with. The "C" word had entered the room. It was actually here, in my own immediate family, and it stopped me right then and there. I immediately knew it was my absolute duty to take the greatest care of her, as she had finally moved back from Florida to the New York area where I lived, and I was close by. I surmised that with the best doctors and the right treatments she would live through it, and at first she did, but a few years later it returned with a vengeance and she was then diagnosed as having stage 4 lung cancer, and it was terminal. She wasn't a regular smoker; she sometimes snuck one in the bathroom at night before bed, thinking she wouldn't get caught by her kids. She never wanted to set that kind of example for us. She'd leave the bathroom window wide open, whether it was summer or winter, but she always left her drowned cigarette butt floating in the toilet, then would forget to flush it; a telltale sign of her naughtiness. Sometimes she grubbed one from my father, back in the day when friends gathered to sip cocktails, trying to appear chic. It just wasn't something we ever expected. None of it made any sense to me at the time, but I did learn how cancer cells can lie dormant and undetected, and that it is during that time that they gain strength. When they wake up, they spread quietly and become strong enough to do incredible damage.

For the longest time, I held myself accountable for dropping the ball when her stomach cancer was deemed cured. Should I have been more diligent in following up during the next couple of years and kept on top of routine testing? I kept questioning all the "what ifs." What did I miss, where did I go wrong, or what if I had taken her to a better treatment facility? In actuality, it was no one's fault, as the proper follow-up care was indeed given. But, now I was just incredibly sad to know that I was going to lose her, so I played the blame game, and targeted myself.

Finally, at this stage of my life, the time had come where I realized how much I adored my mother. She was such a sweet soul, and during both of her illnesses I made it a point to spend a lot of time with her. Truth be told, when I was younger, I never saw eye-to-eye with this woman on anything. We were polar opposites from different planets. Dad worked a lot, so he was hardly ever around, which left her solely responsible for raising four children on her own, 100% of the time. All of it proved overly stressful for her, and since I was also a pretty rambunctious child, who was always getting into mischief, she was constantly reprimanding me. She needed my distractions like she needed a hole in her head.

Sadly, I can honestly say that I remember only two times where my mother was able to give undivided time to me. The first time, I remember sitting alone, outside on my block one day, swinging on a low chain-link barrier which blocked a parking lot at the end of my street in the Bronx. I saw my mom walking down the street and immediately became scared, thinking "Oh boy, what did I do now?" I was always such a nervous child. Instead, she said she had a fun surprise for me, took my hand, and we walked several blocks over to Broadway where there was a theater that was playing a Disney movie - Sleeping Beauty. I absolutely loved it! Having her by my side, talking and laughing for a full couple of hours, with her attention focused solely on me, is one of my dearest memories of us together.

The second time was when my mom started making clothes for my Barbie doll. They were so beautiful to me. She made them from scraps and remnants from old clothes that were being discarded. I was out of my mind with happiness! The next day I asked her to make more, but that was when she shut me down and said she didn't have the time. It's sad when one can only remember two specific incidents from their childhood where their parent made them feel special, and separated them from the herd of siblings.

As much as I begged, my dad never had any time for me. Actually, I don't remember him having any time for any of us, including my mom. Oh yes, promises were made to me, and in all sincerity at the time, but were never kept. His work always seemed to interfere. He would apologize, tell me to be strong, and always told me, "Weakness is not attractive on such a pretty little girl, so please don't cry." If he wasn't working, other conflicts would arise and our plans would always head south. A child accepts it, acts out in different ways that they're not even aware of, and always convinces or blames themselves that everything is their fault. I became a master of disguise, holding in all of my sadness and never allowing anyone to see my pain. I remember times when my mom spanked me for doing something wrong, but then would feel so frustrated with me because I would never cry. Then, she would purposely spank me harder, and for longer, just to try to get a rise out of me. She never could though, as I trained myself not to allow physical or emotional hurt to cloud my facade. It's crazy how you think instinct protects you when all it does is delay the inevitable. All I wanted to do was scream. Scream for attention. Scream to be heard. Scream to be seen. So, when I did cry, I did it alone, and often, but always on my own terms.

It wasn't until later in life, when I was a young adult, that my mom and I began to have long conversations and actually started liking and respecting each other. By that time, both of my parents had retired and moved from New York to Florida. I would fly down and stay with my parents for a couple of weeks, go shopping with mom during the day, and then play gin rummy in the evenings with my dad, who was a real card shark. They both made time for me. I was also old enough to finally realize they were pretty nice people, hard-working, finally having earned a beautiful home, with great neighbors and good friends surrounding them. They were relaxed, and the three of us had at last found kinship. Still, at that time, I truly didn't know everything about my mother, and she wasn't about to divulge specific portions of her past, at least not with my dad still being alive and within earshot. As they say, a woman's heart is as deep as the ocean, and hers held many secrets.

One secret wasn't so confidential, however; the story of where my sister was born, Scotland. The beginning of my parents' marriage was a bit turbulent, to say the least. Dad had a wandering eye, on top of several other vices, and when mom was well into her first pregnancy, she left him behind in New York and went home and delivered her baby there. My sister was born in Glasgow, Scotland, the only sibling born out of the United States. After a few months went by, too many pressures from my mom's family made her return to her husband; the main one being the fact that my father was a Catholic, and my mom was a Protestant. Her family didn't want her to leave him. They felt it would disgrace him in his family's eyes if she were to divorce a Catholic. So, my mother returned to New York and to show her commitment to their marriage, she converted to Catholicism. Their marriage held together and it produced three more children. My mom forgave him, but found it difficult to forget at times. Their marriage lasted 50 years.

However, she did share lots of funny stories with me, and never realized the potential impact some of her tales imprinted on my very impressionable mind. To make matters worse, she also had a habit of repeating them. Often. She was unconsciously funny, and one day while she was sitting in her chair in the living room, sipping her before-dinner gin and tonic (I was nearby preparing dinner), she proceeded to tell me the story surrounding my conception and my birth. Again. She never ate a lot of food, so I was a little worried because I knew how long this story would take, and she was processing alcohol on an empty stomach. She asked me, "Did I ever tell you about the time when you were born?" I replied, "Yes mom, I've heard it." I thought, "Oh no, she's gonna tell it anyway, please God, make it stop!"

In her light, Scottish brogue, or rather *burr*, she smiled and continued, "You were conceived from a night of very passionate love making with your dad." I sighed out loud, "Well, good to know it was *him*, but still gross." My dad was sitting on the couch and looked at me frowning. She continued, "I looked undeniably beautiful that day, more so than I usually do. Even my bitch of a mother-in-law, who always hated me, commented on my beauty." I thought to myself, "Didn't you guys make up a long time ago?" She looked at my father, "Jimmy, why was she even there that day?" She started thinking out loud, "I'll bet it was to check up on me, to see how I was dressed, or if the house was clean, or if I was catering to her little prince hand and foot; I never could win that witch's approval!" I thought, "Oh God, here we go again." "She was jealous!" she yelled, nodding her head. Then she looked towards my dad who got up off the couch, shaking his head while walking towards the family room to watch his golf on TV (after all, she was talking about his mother, and was most likely the millionth time he had heard it).

Looking right at my dad's back she pointed towards him and continued, "I don't remember how you did it, but you made her go home, and that got me in the mood, you were great!" Then she looked at me and just kept talking, "Your father noticed how good I looked, which is why he got rid of her fat ass faster than you could say your name!" (Note: I was named after my Nana, Greta). Adding to her story, "Then your dad whisked me off to the bed where we accidentally made you, the most beautiful wee slip of a girl, because I looked stunning that day!"

There is nothing like being reminded, again, of how you were an accident. Lost in her thoughts, she started humming a little song. I stopped setting the table and quickly looked around for some bread, crackers, anything to stop the gin-soaked wisdom that was flying out of her mouth. I said, "Mom, please, eat something." She waved the food away with her hand and continued, "You were my last-born child, and you were so determined to come into this world. You had such a sweet, wee mind of your own!" Then she took a few more sips from her glass, and muttered something about cutting something off, or a shop being closed down, and how a party was over. Now softly crying, she said, "I was in labor and had to pee, so I hobbled to the bathroom, then started screaming! Had it not been for that nurse putting her hand over your head to hold you inside of me, you would've been born into the toilet!" She continued, "Halfway out of me, you were, but she raced me back to the bed!" I wondered, "Maybe it was Jack LaLanne, did he teach Kegel exercises too?"

So, I thought to myself, "This sweet wee slip of a girl almost slipped into the plumbing? Interesting." I said, "Thanks mom, you've got one incredibly mighty strong squeeze box there." She picked her head up looking puzzled, then nodded and smiled at me, as I gently took her empty glass and placed it onto the end table next to her. She mumbled to me, "Who squeezed a huh, what?" Isn't it ironic how all us at one time or another during our lifetime feel as if our life is going down the toilet, and mine actually almost did? When I glanced back, she was sleeping. Dinner was ready, and I lowered the lights near her, and then brought dinner into the family room just for me and my father. We ate off of folding trays watching golf in a very awkward silence. For the first time in memory, my dad didn't ask for seconds in fear of one of us passing through the living room and waking my mother in order to get to the kitchen. One story was enough for everybody that night.

I remember that every single time I would pack my bags to go back home to New York, after having had a wonderful time with my parents, my mom would always pick a huge fight with me, completely out of the blue, and totally unexpected. I would fly back home, and as I sat on the plane, I would ponder what in the world I did wrong. It was years later when I finally realized why she picked the fights. It made it easier for her to say goodbye. It's painless for some people to part this way instead of just honestly saying what is in their hearts. Well, that was my mother. Defensive, guarded, hurting, but forever stoic.

The years went by and my dad died at age 72 from coronary artery disease. He had suffered many years with this ongoing battle. His wishes were to be cremated, with one strict stipulation: He told my mother "Don't put me in an urn, put me in a cardboard box, then leave me in your nightstand drawer. I don't want to give those rat bastards at the funeral home a dime more of my hard-earned money; I want you to have it all!" My father was very outspoken, just like his mother.

My siblings and I flew down to Florida one at a time to comfort her when my father's condition grew grave. My brother Jim was the first to arrive while dad was still hospitalized. He stood by her side and also took great care of all of the paperwork that needed to be handled. Dad passed, and I was the second to arrive on the scene. After a few days, my mom received a call from the funeral home telling her that my dad's body had been cremated and his ashes were ready to be picked up. I drove my mom over there. That was a bewildering few moments, to say the least, and I couldn't wait to get out of there! Entering the undertaker's establishment, an older woman greeted us in a very hushed tone. She whispered, "I'm so sorry for your loss, please follow me." I wondered if I was in church, as the atmosphere was dimly lit and somber, with low, depressing music playing in the background. I quietly said to my mother, "Why isn't there any sunshine in here, it's so pretty outside, and what's with that music?" She nodded in agreement with me. It sounded like it was piped in from the Julia Robert's movie Sleeping With The Enemy, the 5th movement of Berlioz's Symphonie Fantastique titled Dream of a Witches' Sabbath. Talk about unsettling. If that's what they were aiming for then they achieved their goal, as it perfectly depicted the dark, disturbing vibe of this mortician's tomb.

My mom and I were led to two chairs, and sat silently across from each other, a small coffee table separating us. Another, younger woman walked around the corner holding what looked like a little shopping bag from Bloomingdales. She centered it on the table and placed her hand on my mother's shoulder, offering her condolences, also in a low and subdued voice, as my mom sat there staring at the little bag in disbelief. Wide-eyed, my mom whispered to me, "How in the world did they fit your father into that little bag?" I acted quickly and said, "Oh God!" Then I snatched the two handles of the bag, grabbed my mom, and hurried past the older lady who was holding the door open for us. At the same time, that same woman had the nerve to try and sell my mother an urn, you know, for her husband's dignity's sake. I don't know why, but I started laughing on my way out the door. The woman shot me a dirty look. Now I understood exactly what my dad was talking about. He felt it was all about money, and he was right, for dying is a business to them after all.

I got my mom into the car and placed my dad onto her lap. I said, "Here ya go, you hold him; he'd get pissed off at me if I did while driving." He always said, "Both hands on the wheel, 10 and 2, like a clock." This is what he taught me from the beginning when I first learned to operate a motor vehicle under his supervision. He had been a NYC firefighter and had instructed many young firefighters on the methods of piloting those huge fire trucks, and also taught all of my siblings and their friends how to drive. I was his last student, and he constantly reminded me, "I have never had a failure!" Suffice it to say, I passed my first and only driving test with flying colors. Yeah, no pressure there.

Mom remained living in Florida after dad's death, and eventually sold their home and moved into a gated community for older adults where she remained until our family moved her back to New York, as she was alone and started to need a lot more help.

Sixteen years had passed since we lost my dad. Mom was now much older, and sick with terminal cancer for the second time around. The doctors gave her six months to live. My siblings and I once again stepped up to the plate. I was also now presented with an opportunity. The clock was ticking, giving me a very small margin of time, and I finally wanted to get to know the *real* her, adult-to-adult, and I was determined to make that happen. I had tried a few times before, but it got me nowhere. I knew there were still some secrets circulating around in her pretty little head.

So many years had now gone by, and even though we had become close since she came back to live in New York, it wasn't until she got sick for the second time around that I started to pry a little harder, and she finally gave in. She knew that I would understand, as it was pretty clear how I had grown up and looked at her without judgment through older, and now, much wiser eyes. She opened up to me and I listened to her life stories, and what her life had really been like. I began to understand her more clearly, and I finally learned the art of keeping my mouth shut and just listening. I learned so much from her, especially how when I was little, I would drive her crazy with my non-stop talking. She could never get a word in edgewise. She confessed to me "You drained me, you were always a wee chatterbox, even your first word was a paragraph!" I laughed, as I actually remembered the non-stop garrulous conversations which annoyed her to no end. Through this time with her, there was so much remorse on her end for actions never taken, time she didn't spare, and accountability for wanting to do it all over again, the right way. I found forgiveness, I believe we both did. Unfortunately, this window of time, this glimpse into her past, was short-lived.

Life was not easy for her and it broke my heart to hear her many stories of growing up in another country; stories which carried the fondest of memories mixed with ones of shame, sadness, spending years without a father, and struggling, as they were very poor. She was courageous and left her homeland of Scotland alone, along with everything and everyone, to travel by plane across the ocean to America at just 19 years of age, to marry my father after WWII ended. It was never easy for her. There were many roadblocks, but she managed to keep her family intact through the years and find pockets of happiness along the way as her life progressed. I think her years of marriage to my dad eventually reached a comfortable point, and aging together mellowed the edges of their relationship, smoothed the bumps in the road. Although she forgave my father for his many vices and indiscretions, she never forgot.

Cancer is so sneaky. It doesn't just take one's life at the end, it also slowly pulls your loved one away from you during the process. There were times when my mom would just sit there and stare when I was talking to her, as if she were somewhere else. Sometimes, while we were watching old-time classic movies, which she taught me to love, I would catch her glancing away, again lost in her own thoughts. I only started noticing a quick decline towards the very end. She was slowly drifting away from me in the last two months she had left before she died. That was the hardest part; losing her before I actually lost her. She didn't talk much anymore, and forced half smiles when I cracked a joke. This strange, very unfamiliar social distancing gave us no time for reminiscing anymore; it left me constantly trying to catch her attention and snap her back into the moment just so I could hear her voice, or perhaps a tiny laugh.

My beautiful mother was slowly disappearing into the midst of dementia. Our bond became linear, a one-way street, the polar opposite of the kind of reciprocal love which was tangible at one time, and I desperately wanted the last part of her life to be extended so I could somehow bring her back into the here and now, to be able to hear more stories and just listen to her speak in words that made sense. For many, dealing with the grief cancer brings becomes a lonely, chronic, daily experience, continually challenging our courage to remain strong in front of our loved ones, as the loss builds before it actually comes.

I found cancer to be beyond cruel, as those precious and special moments I so desperately wanted with her were robbed from me. It was emotionally exhausting, and at the end I was left motherless, and with so many unanswered questions. Still, I followed through with her plans exactly as she wished. Sometime during her illness, she reached out to my brother Paul to change her plans from cremation to burial. My father had prepaid for both of them to be cremated while they lived in Florida, but my mom changed her mind when she came back to live in New York. My brother honored what she had asked of him, and made final arrangements for her to be buried in a beautiful veteran's cemetery, Frederick Loescher Veterans Memorial park, located in Spring Valley, NY. She was happy with my brother's choice, as dad was a veteran of WWII. But, she secretly made me promise that dad's ashes would NOT be placed into her casket. She wanted her final resting place to be her own. She made it clear that the emotional impact and lasting effects of the painful events from parts of her marriage became indelible scars, leaving behind memories permanently etched into her psyche. I made the promise, and agreed that I would take dad's ashes home with me to stay.

Mom died on June 10, 2014, exactly three months after she turned 87. Some would say that's a ripe old age, but for me it still wasn't enough time. I miss her off-beat sense of humor, her sweet naïve nature, her crazy and overly-repeated stories, our conversations (or rather gossip sessions, but all good), her advice, her wisdom which was beyond her years, and especially her kind words and finally, yes finally, her beautiful and unending parental love. I find it hard now remembering all the arguments and absent hours I experienced with my mother, as I've chosen to keep her in my heart, and recall only the good moments I shared with her. I know that if she had it to do all over again, she would, and with the best of intentions. Yes, she was unique, I'll give her that, but for better or for worse, she's still that voice in my head that is always pushing me to be better, to always challenge myself, respect what others think, to put myself first instead of always standing at the back of the line, and to never accept anything less.

After her services, I received a call from the funeral home. There was a problem. The director told me in no uncertain terms that she could not stay buried in that cemetery without my father in the same grave with her. Oh boy, "What do you want me to do," I asked him? He offered to take part of my dad's ashes and have them placed into her grave; otherwise, she would have to vacate the premises. Wait, what? Leave? Raising my voice I asked him, "You're going to exhume her?" There was no way I would allow that to happen! I promptly drove over to the funeral home with my dad's ashes, told the director to make sure he scooped out only the good ones, (he laughed), and to put the remainder into a beautiful, wooden urn carved with the fire department's insignia on it in order to honor him. I thought, "Enough with this ridiculous cardboard box, my father deserved much better than that." It was a done deal, and his ashes would be buried on top of my mother's coffin within the next few days. At least he wasn't inside her coffin with her; he was sort of within reach, but beyond grasp. Perhaps mom would be ok with that.

I then visited her grave and remember it being very overcast outside. I placed a new arrangement of fresh flowers, as all of the beautiful ones initially left there from her wake and funeral Mass had already been cleared away by the groundskeeper. I asked her for forgiveness in breaking my promise, made my point that it was either put up with his better half for eternity, or she'd be exhumed. I firmly told her while standing on top of her grave, "I swear to God Mom, if you don't finally forgive him, I can't promise where you'll end up. If I have it my way, I'll change you into a red dress and give you a Viking ship burial!" That would surely change her mind, as all of the beautiful jewelry that she had willed to me would go down in flames with her. The Vikings believed in burying their deceased loved ones in a ship, then torching it, along with all of the dead ones accompanying treasures; it's a symbolic final journey. I was pretty sure that would change her mind, as nobody burns Winnie's jewelry. The sun came out. I smiled and walked back to my car. I took it as a sign. I think I speak for everyone here when I sum up the mother/daughter relationship in one word: Complicated.

All kidding aside, and when all was said and done, she left me with a broken heart, not to mention countless casualties of war, friendships that got fractured along the way, family members arguing, and then losing touch. Cancer cheated all of us. It won our time, our energy, our patience, our stability, our hopes, and the memories that we still wanted to make. It spread fearlessly as it validated its presence.

One of the best kept secrets of life is how none of us really feels all grown up until specific events happen. We experience milestones in our lives as we climb our life ladder at a steady pace, marking our achievements and turning points, e.g. that first day of school, learning and finally mastering multiplication, and in my case, my first bra, a first date, high school graduation, first real job, and then living with someone, and marriage. But, then we are faced with the realization of our parents' mortality. Some people have learned to accept this natural progression, as the older generation typically leaves before us. Still, it can be life altering, as it doesn't make it any easier, but for some reason there's this built-in human coping mechanism when a parent's death occurs. It doesn't matter whether your parent was loved or resented, whether the relationship was warm and close, or distant and conflictual. Even your age doesn't matter, or how old your parent was at the time of their death. People feel emotionally adrift when they try to understand death and sometimes begin to question their own identity. The recognition of parental death is a decisive point in one's life, as you become aware of how vulnerable each new day is. Death embeds a deep knowledge of your limits. It can transform an adult child's life and crazy enough, actually feels like the beginning of maturity.

CHAPTER 4

AJNA CHAKRA

(My Paradox of Illusion)

AFTER MY MOTHER DIED, LIFE continued on for me, albeit I was grieving. Around a year or so later, I woke up from a beautiful, emotional dream I had been having about her. I was crying, and as I climbed out of bed, I couldn't shake my sorrow, for I missed her terribly. I went downstairs with our dog (Roscoe at that time) to let him out for his morning walk, and I remember it being a beautiful, blue-sky morning, without a cloud in the sky. I stood on our patio and asked my mom why she hadn't given me a sign like she had promised she would, to tell me that she made it home and that she was happy and with God. Something told me to look up, and when I did, above my head was the largest and most brilliant cross I had ever seen. It was crystal clear; a cloud formation against a bright, blue sky that had happened in an instant, and without my knowing. My tears turned joyous, as I had finally gotten my answer. This was her message to me, telling me that she was home. I've picked up on many signs throughout my life, but this one was the most significant at that time. It brought me great comfort knowing everything would now be ok.

Just a few days later, an actress named Roma Downey, who once starred on a show called "Touched by An Angel," was being interviewed by Kelly Ripa and Michael Strahan on their live weekday morning talk show which aired from New York City on ABC. Ms. Downey recalled how she was trying to tape a brand new religious show in Rockland

County, New York a few days prior to her live appearance with Kelly and Michael. Unbeknownst to me, her cast and crew were set up on location not even one mile away from where I live. Rockland County contains very beautiful and historic landmarks and has film crews constantly scouting and filming throughout the year. It has become commonplace to see film sets in our area several times a year, even on my own block, with large cables blocking off streets, police activity, and lots of detours. Her entire set was shut down early that morning before they even started rolling because they spotted a very large cross in the sky, a sky that had been crystal clear up until then, and they all took it as a sign from God. I knew exactly what she was talking about, and the timing was perfect, for it was the cross that was over my home. Coincidence? I think not.

Synchronicities, or acausal connections, have happened to me all throughout my life. In classical physics, all events are believed to have a cause, while acausality suggests that some events might occur without a preceding cause. If you read Carl Jung's Theory of Synchronicity, it explains everything on a much deeper level, and how random coincidences in our lives can have meaningful connections relating to a person's inner thoughts, or their psychological state. He believes there is a deeper connection between the psyche and the material world, thus indicating they are different aspects of a single, unified reality. His theory of phenomena suggests that the universe can be understood as a unified whole, whereas events are not isolated incidents, but rather interconnected through a deeper principle, and are not subject to the usual rules of cause and effect.

My mother taught me to try to construe signs optimistically, as she believed they should always lean towards a desirable, and positive outcome. She encouraged me to take advantage of my idiosyncratic perspectives. Unfortunately, most times my pendulum swung towards negativity. I use the pendulum metaphor to imply my constant oscillation between my fluctuating opinions, because as they say, as hard as I tried to find the sunshine in the storm, the outcomes were not favorable. It wasn't my fault, or because I was drawn to pessimism, and I certainly wasn't biased when these signs occurred. I was in my younger years, and just too many predictions of tragic events materialized. No matter what efforts I made, not a single positive aspect could be found in any of them, and truthfully they frightened me. But, I have made significant progress over the years which I believe is attributable to not only my personal growth, but also the process of self-actualization, realizing a deeper understanding and connection to life. I learned to fulfill my potential, talent, and capabilities. To sum it all up, thank goodness that with age comes personal evolution, heightened awareness leading to increased intuition, and much wisdom.

I had an opportunity to have a reading once with a real-life medium when I was in my early thirties, with a woman named Rena. She was very well respected, and known around the area as being an insightful occultist, unprecedented in fact. She only worked out of one place; a bright, purple-colored gay bar located in Nyack, New York. It was rumored that she also lived in the small apartment on the top of this bar.

People said she would only use tarot cards, that the reading would last one hour, and that she wasn't expensive at all. I was forewarned, however, that she was extremely temperamental, not to challenge her, and just to be a good listener. They said it was her entire world, and it was never about money, so it was taboo to dispute her fee, 'cause she'd throw you out on your ass if she heard that you did. Cash was always paid in advance to the bartender, never put directly into her hands. Talking about money in front of her insulted her capabilities, as she was content living the meager life she led. She was an unpredictable, dark-haired bohemian gypsy, and lived and breathed every second of her life around this kind of mystical practice.

So, I booked an appointment with her one afternoon. The man who took my reservation told me her fee over the phone, and everyone was right, as I felt she was dirt cheap. It didn't take much to drag my sister-in-law Barbara along with me, as she was also very curious about the occult world. We just wanted to have our fortunes told, and maybe get Rena to give us the correct numbers so we could hit the lottery. But, unbeknownst to Barbara, I wanted to ask Rena privately about multiple signs I had received in my life. I hoped that perhaps she could offer insight. When we arrived, Barbara was a little timid, "You go first," she whispered, as she literally pushed me into the reading room where Rena was sitting and waiting.

So, I went in, and was determined to keep my face blank, so I showed no emotion. I thought, "If she's as good as everyone says, then she won't have any problem cracking my poker face." I sat down at a small, round table, and we exchanged pleasantries, and briefly began chatting. I think she was trying to get a good read on me, actually. I felt intimidated by her immediately, as there was something about her eyes, and she had a very strange aura. Then she began to shuffle her cards. She explained to me that tarot cards are tools used to connect with spirits, offering insights into your past, present, and potential future. She then placed one card at a time, laying them face up. I don't recall exactly how many, but then she spread them out, and began the reading. I have to admit that it started off very generic and could have applied to anyone. She pressed on and then told me I had two children, one born from my mind, and the other born from my heart. Two sons. Ok, now she had my attention. But, she also saw that I had three children from another lifetime, sometime in the early 1800's where I was a wealthy, strong, independent woman who had just left her husband. That was strange. Two or three other insights were then made, which she was also right about, but there was another intuition where she saw many windows surrounding me. That gave me a strange feeling. In actuality, two weeks later, the large corporation I was working in switched their computer platform over to a new operating system called "Windows." So, what do you know!

The reading paused for a moment. Rena then looked up at me, smiled, and asked, "Are you aware of the Ajna chakra, a concept in the Hindu tradition, the third eye?" I shook my head as she proceeded to go into great depth about it to me, how there were seven chakras within the system of energy centers, the third eye was the sixth out of the seventh associated with intuition, something about it being located in between your eyebrows, yada, yada, yada. I kept wondering, "Where was all of this going? Land your plane Rena." She stopped, realizing by my expression that I wasn't quite keeping up. Finally, she explained it was somewhat of a portal to a higher consciousness; the ability to see what is beyond the physical world. I responded, "No, I never heard of a third eye." She clarified it for me, "Miss Greta, you have an extremely strong inner vision; your awareness is strangely heightened; you have instinct without logic." Oh, ok, now I knew exactly what she was talking about, but I never put a label on it. Still, I refused to flinch, as I wanted her to go on, because now she actually knew a few tidbits about me before I even had the guts to ask her.

Another few moments passed, she stopped, and then very pensively asked me, "Can I please have your hand?" Her entire demeanor changed; I thought she only used tarot cards, but she shoved them to the side very quickly. So, I replied, "Which one?" She said, "Both." So I offered her my left hand first, and she turned it over and looked at my palm. She studied it, and focused on my lifeline. She told me that it ended ¾ of the way down, with no continuance after that. I asked her, "What does that mean, that I'm going to die before my time?" She wouldn't say anything other than, "Lost energy." There was another line she showed me which ran parallel with my lifeline, but it didn't start where my lifeline began, as if it would join in sometime during my life. She then said, "Oh, two souls, not one!" She sounded very surprised. I assumed she was talking about me and my husband, because I was wearing a wedding band.

She explained that usually that second line means vitality, a person's inner lifeline, but this was not happening in my case, as it was somehow crossing over where it shouldn't. That second line had ended at the bottom near my wrist, yet it clearly had a break. She wouldn't explain anything further.

She then immediately asked for my right hand, and examined its palm. She was having difficulty with this one, and she bent my hand open further, and stretched it as she rubbed her thumb against all of the lines to redden them. "I need to get a more detailed reading" she explained. She was really serious about this stuff! I remember her frowning, as if stumped.

This time she said my lifeline was interrupted at the ¾ point in my life, exactly like my left hand was, but this one had a gap, where it then picked back up, and continued until it forked. She asked me, "Is this your prominent hand?" I replied "Actually, I'm ambidextrous, but yes (gun to my head) it is the one I favor a little more, and the one I prefer to write with."

That second line next to my lifeline was exactly the same as my other hand; however, this time she said that both lines had a very odd pattern. Shaking her head, she reiterated about two souls. She then showed me a third line intercepting and crossing through the second line ¾ of the way down. She said, "This is extremely rare, very unusual; you have a third line that is not supposed to be there and it cuts through the second line, dividing it." She looked seriously concerned.

I looked closer at these two lines, which were right next to my lifeline, and I saw exactly what she was talking about, and asked her, "What does that mean, more husbands?" She said "Your lifeline is your soul, the line next to it is a supportive, yet separate second soul, which is meant for you. It intercepts into your lifetime twice." I was puzzled. She raised her voice, "Look at your lifeline, look at the gap. It continues after the gap. It means time will pass. Then, your lifeline will be intercepted at the bottom by this odd, third line, right at the fork, and the fork is pointing down!" I thought, "What in hell's bells is she talking about? She had mentioned there were only two souls!" Again, I asked her if the third line represented another person. She shook her head and explained, "It means a soul interrupted, yet is still here in this same lifetime, and it is meant to be with you always." I thought, "Interrupted? Interrupted how?" She then muttered something about a "negative shift." I replied "Negative how?" She ignored me. What did she mean about time going by after the gap before it gets intercepted?

Then she let go of my hand. I didn't understand what she was talking about, and I could clearly see that she didn't want to elaborate any more. She immediately retreated back to her tarot cards for another few minutes. Honestly, I really wasn't paying much attention anymore, as I was concerned about what she saw. It was all I could think about, and I felt too afraid to push her buttons any further. What did she mean when she said my lifeline had a gap, then picked back up, with an odd third line intercepting it at a negatively shifting fork? What did the gap on this right hand mean, and why did my life fork down? On my left hand, my energy ends, yet my right hand shows it picks back up, then something very bizarre happens. It was so puzzling, and clearly she didn't want to discuss the matter anymore. Then the reading ended.

I thanked her for a very well-informed reading, and left the room feeling confused. She wasn't. She also went well over the one hour time limit. I got up and walked away as my sister-in-law Barbara entered for her turn. I remember looking back at Rena, and she was staring at me. Her crazy eyes were glued to mine with a hurt look, like she felt sorry for me or something. I didn't know what to make of it, I got chills and I felt spooked, and I knew I would never return to her.

If memory serves me right, my sister-in-law Barbara did go back to Rena a couple of times with a friend of hers, so I guess Rena didn't scare the shit out of her like she did me, and she only used tarot cards with Barbara and her friend. She never read their palms. Why mine? Sitting in the waiting room, I thought about what she told me, "A soul interrupted, yet is still here in this same lifetime, and it is meant to be with you always." Hmmm, that was surely something to ponder. I also thought that I had to give her credit, as she was right about my having had two children, one born from my mind, and the other born from my heart. I cover that later, as she was 100% spot on.

Sometime after the reading, however, I did have a very unearthly, anachronistic dream of time travel. I had left my husband with three children in tow. I was sitting in a stagecoach readying myself for a long journey. I was a high-society lady with two of my children sitting next to me to my left, and one other small son, perhaps seven years old, sitting opposite me, crying. He was wearing dark-brown knickerbockers with a matching suit jacket, tweed cap on his head, beige knee-high socks, and dark brown shoes vaguely resembling those of Buster Brown Oxfords. His little feet didn't even touch the floor. I distinctly remember telling him, "Michael, stop crying." He was breaking my heart, as I knew he felt lost and confused. I was wearing a long-sleeved, high-necked, empire-waisted, dark-brown dress that had a fitted bodice which was made from very heavy cloth, it felt like wool, and it had a pattern on it with little black flowers, along with a flowing ankle-length skirt. My hat was a large, and Edwardian-style adorned with a few silk flowers, and was tilted slightly to the left side of my face. I wore my hair swept up, and sported black boots on my feet, but I couldn't specify which style. The two children to my left were a blur.

Most people forget their dreams upon waking, but this one stayed with me for the rest of my life. Every aspect of it felt so real, as if it actually happened in another lifetime. It could be that Rena simply planted a seed, but this fleeting moment into my past, from another time in history, was something I cannot let go of. I smelled the horses, how it was a cold day, the dust swirling up from the street, and the light scent of my perfume; roses. There were two drivers, one of which had a shotgun strapped to his shoulder; working men bustling around us loading our suitcases onto the top as I watched through a long, oblong window. Everything was so colorful, and I felt emotional, with all of my senses acutely intact. I was really there feeling sentiments of determination, and anger from a betrayal. It was surreal; or, all of it could have been just as simple as a seed that was planted, and would one day grow into a dream.

CHAPTER 5

INSIGHTS GAINED, POSSIBILITIES EXPLORED

Synchronicity entered my life again. It was in August 2024, exactly one year after my husband died, and it brought me the clarity I had been lacking and desperately needed. It came out of nowhere, and when I least expected it. Immediately after it happened, I wasn't sure if I should share anything about it, as it contained areas of my life that I wasn't yet ready to reveal. Yes, people knew I was grieving, but most didn't quite understand the depth of what I was experiencing. Therapy had been a real challenge for me from the get-go; so many significant difficulties were manifesting in me up until this turning point. I remained guarded and struggled with very private thoughts that I kept from the outside world. After this sign, I knew I wanted to write about what happened, but I wanted to do it on my own terms, not bring anyone else into it, because I didn't believe that someone would have truly understood what happened. I surmised that rational people would immediately cast poor judgment upon me, or even worse, laugh at me and deem everything I experienced as insignificant. It wasn't.

After a lot of self-reflection, I finally gave in and shared it with two extremely close friends whom I've known for most of my life, and who know me, my character, and my heart better than anyone. These friends have always had my back, as well as my best interests for all the years I've known them. If both of them were worried that I was losing my sanity, they would have reigned me back in immediately and insisted I hesitate. Instead, they listened and believed, for they already knew about the gift I had. They were truly heartbroken when they learned how I had suffered alone in silence for so long. Their worry turned around as I explained how it all guided me and showed me the way back to my life, so they took me into their arms, cried with me, and encouraged me to tell the world. It was as if God had finally turned a light on.

Everyone I know describes me as a strong, intelligent, independent woman, but inside I am really just a gentle soul, a romantic, shamelessly sentimental, and a spiritual dreamer. I crave balance, harmony, and peacemaking; I suppose I fit perfectly into the zodiac sign of Libra. We are ruled by Venus, and embody creativity, elegance and charm. Our energy is known for its artistic expression which only a true Venusian can emit.

I have often questioned if all of our fates are predetermined for us. Are we all made for just one person, or does our fate shift alignment as we navigate through this realm while being steered by something much greater than us, something that knows *all* as our lives change course through our existence? The way I once felt, about a man the night I met him, was as if I had loved him from a previous lifetime. Farfetched, perhaps, yet I cannot dismiss this concept of soul recognition, and for that matter, déjà vu, for I strongly believe in both.

What if the stars really do align at just the right moment, in just the right place, and guide us towards our destinies, no matter how many times in our lives, no matter how joyous or how tragic the journey? I have always felt too wise and much too restless to just settle for a mundane, compatible mate to share my life with. My personality's unique configuration is sincere, honest to a fault, trustworthy, and loyal. I'll always tell you if you've got spinach in your teeth, and I've been described as someone you can always depend upon to be there in your time of need. I am truly respectful of others, and one of my greatest traits is my open heart. I remember one night in a posh, fancy restaurant where I spent three hours in the ladies room because I liked the attendant's company; so much more than that of the company I left at the table. I don't hold airs, never did, and never will.

I have busted my butt to get to where I am today. I have always yearned for more in my life, and finally feel I have earned distinction.

From when I was young, there were many along the way that I spent my time with, and talked myself into believing I might have loved. But, at one particular moment those stars did align, when the universe guided me towards a center point where my soul was awakened, and my life rewarded beyond imagination.

I truly believed that we would have forever. In hindsight, I have found myself pondering that famous poem written by Alfred, Lord Tennyson: "*Tis better to have loved and lost, than never to have loved at all.*" I did question whether this was all for naught. Why did it happen, what was the reasoning behind it all? Was there some great lesson I was supposed to have learned after living through such a catastrophic ending? Was it the right decision to have opened myself up so completely to this beautiful man? Or, had I known the outcome, the unbearable and tragic heartbreak, would I have chosen to walk away for my own sanity, for my own protection?

The truth of the matter is that I never had any choice, as I fell in love with him the instant I saw him. His soft eyes, his smile, everything about him was genuine. He was my best friend, my keeper of secrets, my protector, the one who was always there for me, to make sure that I felt wanted, understood, safe, secure, and above all, deeply loved. So I stayed, and yes, it was the right decision for me, despite the fact that in the end, he broke my heart. But, you see, a heart can only be broken if one has deeply and truly loved. Our hearts are not complete until there's recognition when loss invades it, shatters it, and for those several moments in time, it stops its beat.

I am someone who always accepted the idea of my own demise, but placed the idea of ever losing him as nonexistent. I suppose I subliminally thought I'd be the first to go, or hoped I would be, as the thought of losing him didn't dare cross my mind. I wouldn't allow it, as that would have been unfathomable, so I dismissed it. But, it did. It happened, and, I endured, and survived. I can honestly tell you that this type of loss is dark. For me personally, it created three years of a blackout period in my life where all I could see, all I could remember, was sickness, hospitals, nursing homes, disabilities, wheelchairs, therapies, countless medications, and struggling. The list goes on and on.

This was until the day that I received that sign, which allowed me to finally trace the breadcrumbs back and go behind that wall. It was difficult to break through the barrier I had built in my mind where all I was doing was scrambling, as if I was watching our life as a sad movie. I felt so disconnected, numb, and detached. Those few years had washed over me like a tidal wave, where I felt adrift in a sea of doubt, then swallowed up under a shadowy abyss that eclipsed our once happy life. But, somehow I did it. I can't tell you how many times I kept wishing I would spend the rest of my life with him. Yet, after fate intervened, the universe decided that it would be only he who would spend the rest of his life with me.

Is it easier to drift through this life and never get to experience this kind of deep tie with another human being? Or, if we do find this type of love, do we all only get one pass, one opportunity to experience a great love such as this? None of us can make any promises as to how our next chapters will read. I can say for certain that now I'm finally trying my best, I have faith in myself, as my beloved wouldn't have had it any other way. In fact, he told me so right before he died. He said "Find love again, I want that for you. I will always watch over you until we meet again and I promise that I will wait for you. So for now, just remember how I loved you before I met you, I love you now, and I will always love you." Those were his final words to me, the words he said to me countless times during our life together.

I carry this hope that people speak about and try to somehow find the strength to move ahead while protecting that small light within myself, that light which drives me to keep the will to live, to put one foot in front of the other. If we allow our loved ones to live on within that vulnerable, delicate light, then in actuality, they remain with us for all of eternity, for we humans are designed to have the ability to forever hold that beautiful love which they gave to us unconditionally when they existed in this physical realm. That can never die, and should not ever be forgotten, no matter where life leads us on our new path. But, can living with this kind of grief be made easier if we can somehow learn how to shift the balance of damage in the end? Is there a proven method to use as we try to pick up the pieces after our beloveds leave us? Where do we start? How do we begin?

Like all of you walking on this lonely path, I try my best every day to rise, move forward and just grab on with both hands to any little bits and pieces of happiness when they present themselves. I've learned to keep busy and not isolate. I keep surrounding myself with good friends, those who love me, those who feel my pain and really listen to my sorrows when I have a weak moment. When I'm asked to go somewhere, I always say yes, whether I want to or not, because I've found that when I'm surrounded by laughter, the weight of the world seems just a little bit lighter for those few precious minutes. It doesn't last long, as it's only a distraction, a healthy escape, a therapeutic pursuit to healing. So, I use deductive reasoning, as I'm quite afraid that they will stop asking if my answer is "no." But, as time goes on, it has brought me a source of comfort and relief.

I'm taking risks and stepping well out of my comfort zone, that's for sure. I especially appreciated the select few who championed me, ones who never offered defeating words such as "You should have been over it already," or, "You should have been feeling much better by now," or, in my opinion the worst one, "They're in a better place." *They are in a better place?!?* Talk about exacerbating the rain that was already heavily pouring over me. Comments like these leave you nonplussed as to how to respond, especially when some individuals continue to ramble on, persistent in their incessant chatter, with some even equating it to when they lost their pet.

Yes, losing a pet is painful, unimaginable, I know that firsthand, but it does not compare to losing a soulmate. No one should offer unsolicited *wisdom* to another person grieving on this level of cruel solitude. It's not their right to do so, and their unfamiliarity creates a blind spot; limited experience results in a narrow view and biased comparisons. If the nonbereaved are going to say anything, then perhaps they should offer "I'm sorry for your loss, do you want to talk about it?" Give me recognition, allow me to respond. When someone hurts from the pain of grief, they need to feel that the pain is being validated. Tell me how much this person I loved impacted your life. I have suffered a great loss; I don't need to feel judged, dismissed, or misunderstood by people who want to *solve* my grief problem. I'm not looking for an answer. There isn't one.

Simply put, please, just comfort me, sit with me, walk beside me, and stop treating my grief as if it's some kind of disease that can be cured quickly. Some things cannot be fixed; they can only be carried. So, to all those who've never experienced what it's like to sit in the front row at a funeral, or to have gazed into your beloved's casket and wanted to crawl in there with them, I'm truly glad that you haven't been there yet. Hopefully, that day doesn't come knocking at your door for a long time. But for now, as they say, you don't get to hold the mic.

It's always the sting of well-meaning comments, those who offer up advice and cause us to question if it really is us, e.g. "I'm worried about you; you're not grieving the right way." Were they somehow insinuating that I wasn't able to process pain in an intelligent way? And, it's usually more than one person. To me it always felt like they were either derisively mocking my mentality, or offering well-intentioned phrases, but they were ignorant, empty condolences, and something I certainly didn't need. For some people, *the less said, the better* is a good starting point. At times, I was actually able to smell the smoke that was coming out of my ears from the thousands of gears grinding inside of my head.

Don't adopt the group mentality and think that it's you, because it's most likely not. People should use discretion before speaking. Walk away, and focus on what really matters, because you need time to find out who you're supposed to be, and how you are supposed to feel. Find a way to listen to that little voice inside of you, self protect, and in the end, forgive those who have hurt you. Don't carry their weight around on your shoulders.

There are always going to be those acquaintances who drop out of our lives when we move through a loss as profound as this. They are people who either don't want, or know how to stay within our circle. We need to recognize this and stop looking towards those who don't look for us anymore. But, we should also be realistic, and stop posturing ourselves where our needs can't ever possibly be met. Instead, we should try to be more flexible as not everyone understands what you're going through, because it hasn't happened to them. But, sometimes our true necessities do fall on deaf ears by the people who never try to understand our feelings. It doesn't pay to seek validation from anyone, because your worth is never determined by someone else's ability to acknowledge it. You must do what feels right for you, what is good for your soul. There's no reason to ever second guess yourself, as your intuition is hardly ever wrong; sometimes it just gets a little skewed from the noise of other's opinions.

Initially, therapy helped me sort through the emotions I couldn't deal with on my own, but just a tiny bit, as those sessions happened much later than they should have, nine months later, in fact. I had been sinking into a deep depression and didn't know it. Still, to this day it never cured that never-ending, aching pit in my stomach, this aching I have for him. But for me, therapy at the time was much-needed counseling, the beginning of an agonizing process of self-discovery, albeit I hit a crossroad right before I received that sign. But, nowadays I do believe that from time to time, you may feel as if it's a good idea to step back into therapy to fortify the tools you've learned, as grief can sometimes come out of nowhere and sneak up on you when you least expect it. You can rely on that person with whom you share your concerns, and who helps to keep you centered. There's nothing wrong with admitting you can't handle certain things, as it's all a part of the process of letting go.

From a realistic standpoint, eventually you're going to have to learn how to walk on your own two feet, whether you like it or not. And, you're going to have to learn how to build all of your roads on today, because tomorrow's grounds are unsteady, uncertain, and are promised to no one. That's life. Personally, I still step back into therapy, as sometimes I need a little positive reinforcement when I find myself slipping into funks that I can't sort my way out of. I'm only human. They say that behavior can be learned and we can either strengthen or weaken it, that it's entirely up to us. It is so true. If we remain feckless, irresponsible, then we'll never understand the root cause of our procrastinations, we'll never challenge our negative thoughts, focus on our strength's, recharge, and finally recover. I am a living, breathing example of wishful thinking. I am committed to dismantling my misery mask, and finding ways to cope with challenging emotions when they arise. I wake up hoping that each new day is just a little bit better than the one before. You can look forward to the day when you will feel whole again, instead of being afraid and fearful of the future and wondering where we go from here, or basically, just waiting for the other shoe to drop.

As we forge on, we should ask ourselves if we've begun to expand who we include within our inner circle as we move forward. Will there be new people whom we'll meet and eventually allow into our lives? So many transformations are about to take place as our new life begins to reshape. I believe that anyone who stimulates our senses, and encourages us to move ahead, can remind us that there is still life to be lived. We should seek to find the exhilaration we once knew, and benefit from it if we find more. Perhaps we will even find another person with whom we feel we can intimately love, someone we allow deeply into our heart to give our lives new meaning and depth. Or, perhaps it will just be someone who will walk with us in this darkness who helps us rediscover how to make our light a little brighter; someone who grasps the nature of our pain, and who cheers us on as we reconnect with life.

For some of you, the thought of having another intimate love hasn't yet crossed your mind. Maybe you can't, or won't, ever do this, or even contemplate the idea. The decision is yours. It's not a replacement of your beloved, I can assure you of this, but perhaps it could be an enhancement of your spirit. I only ask that you think of it as just this, a possibility, one in which there will be new beginnings to embrace, and if you do, be sure to engage fully, give it everything you have. Don't hold back, or close yourself off. My friends, if you choose to open your heart again, then the potential for happiness and connection is always there. It's an act of courage, yes, but you may also be giving yourself the gift of possibility for a richer, and more fulfilling life. If you choose not to, you can find new purpose and meaning in friendships, family, or personal endeavors. You can discover that love takes many forms, and you can focus on nurturing those relationships. Whatever your dreams, always keep your aspirations intact, even when there are setbacks. Uncertainties are common feelings, but we should be open to opportunities where we can grow and discover possibilities. Let's not fixate on the final destination just yet; instead, let's put our focus on the process of exploring and learning, and I guarantee that along the way, you'll find that there will be many new prospects waiting for you on the horizon.

CHAPTER 6

ALLOW ME
TO INTRODUCE MYSELF

My name is Greta McNeill-Moretti. I'm just an ordinary girl who came from very humble beginnings. I was born in New York City near Second Avenue, and was the youngest of three other siblings; two brothers, and one sister. My family started out in the projects, then the six of us moved into a very small, rented house in the Kingsbridge section of the Bronx, New York. Location wise, we were approximately three blocks south of Gaelic Park, which is located at West 240th Street and Broadway. Gaelic Park is primarily known as the home of the New York Gaelic Athletic Association (NYGAA) and is a cultural hub for New York's Irish community.

In this tiny house on Irwin Avenue, my brothers, Jim and Paul, shared one bedroom. My older sister Marlene (eight years my senior) and I shared another bedroom. She was very pretty and popular, and I admired her greatly. However, the eight-year difference had a significant impact on our relationship. Bluntly put, I was just her pain-in-the-ass little sister. I knew it, and so did she. I remember once when she and her boyfriend were babysitting me. I had a potty mouth and started causing trouble, all for attention. My sister quickly nipped it in the bud by jamming a huge bar of soap in my mouth. That tasted horrible! Good'ol Ivory soap, which is 99.44% pure, where the sodium chloride in it is considered the life of the party. To this day, I cannot stand the smell of Ivory soap. Just writing this, the back of my throat has that weird feeling in it from the memory! Point duly noted, dear sister. She felt awful right after she did it, especially when she realized I then suffered from diarrhea all night long. Thankfully, we became much closer over the years, as time does have a way of putting us all on the same page.

My father was of Irish decent, born in the U.S., but he was brought back to Ireland as an infant and raised there. He returned to America after WWII, and began his career with the New York Police Department, eventually switching over to the Fire Department of New York, Engine Co. 73, Ladder Co. 42. He was a proud fireman who worked very hard, and over his lifetime he achieved the rank of Captain, along with the respected title of "Big Daddy," which was bestowed upon him from the admiring brotherhood he served alongside. He adored opera, and our house was always filled with music when he was home. Because I was a little kid, I tolerated most of his choices, but secretly developed a very deep love for La Boheme which, in English, translates to "The Bohemian." This refers to someone who lives an unconventional and artistic life, and disregards social norms. No wonder I loved it so much; the song felt tailor-made for me, as if it were written for my soul.

All I ever wanted was to spend time with my father. He was very handsome, fun to be around, and so full of life. However, he spent many hours at the firehouse and also worked odd jobs on the side, mostly painting houses, just to make extra income. From time to time he would make promises to me about places we would go, just the two of us, but they never came to fruition. I don't think he purposely meant to ignore me. He was just trying to keep food on the table and a roof over our heads, and there's only so much time one can fit into a day. Suffice it to say he was practically never home. Back in those days, that was the norm for some families and was never questioned, unlike today, where most parents are very hands-on and spend a lot of time focusing on their children. I blamed his absence on myself most of the time, and I believed I wasn't good enough or that maybe I was a mistake since I was the youngest of the children in the family. I wondered that a lot. As the final one, I can say for certain that I wasn't spoiled like a lot of last-born children are. Quite the contrary, I was totally unexpected, and my mother did the best she could, to put it lightly. And, to be very frank, most times I felt abandoned by everyone. I struggled with insecurities, feeling unloved and less valued. I was (or felt) invisible and insignificant, and was *"put up with"* from a mom who was losing a lot of her patience.

One time, when I was playing make-believe, I decided to marry myself. So, I found the white veil from when I made my first Holy Communion, clipped it to my hair, picked up a small, steel bolt that I found lying in the dirt in our backyard, put in on my right ring finger (what did I know), and turned it three times ceremoniously on my "digitus annularis," and just like that, I pronounced myself married to me. As I proceeded to consummate the union, I then kissed my hand, and rubbed it onto my cheek. When I passed by a mirror, I noticed that my face had blood all over it. I looked down, and it was my finger that was bleeding from turning this rusted, sharp bolt three times. My parents couldn't get it off of me because my finger had started to swell. So, what did my father do? He called his buddies from the firehouse. Before I knew it, a huge fire truck pulled up in front of my home, and all these young firemen circled around, fussing over me. I just loved them, they were so handsome, and so cool! They pulled out a hacksaw, one of them distracted me, and before I knew it, I was divorced. To this day, I wear the scar that proves it. Unfortunately though, the alimony I paid was a very painful tetanus shot in the ER.

I found myself getting into trouble often; I was always looking for mischief, solely to gain attention, and I always felt like the runt in the pecking order of siblings. I was self-conscious, and very nervous much of the time, so I spent many days isolating myself in our backyard shed where I felt safe in my own thoughts. Alone there, I would belt out songs, put on shows, and dance for my dolls, safe in knowing that no one could hear or ever find me. It was my emotional safe space, my private haven, surrounded by all of my dad's paint cans. Yes, it was a lonely solitude, one that no little girl ever have needed to find, but it was the best place to go to cry alone, because there, no one could see my weakness.

My mom was a housewife who emigrated to NYC from Glasgow, Scotland at 19 years of age when she fell in love with a boy, my father. It was the end of the war, and they met at a place in Glasgow called The

Locarno. This ballroom was regarded as one of the city's top dancing venues for many years, and held special memories with all of the social Glaswegians and was also popular with the American servicemen during the Second World War. My mom was especially beautiful and quite a dancer. Prior to meeting my father, she had won three beauty contests, one of which was judged by the actor Michael Rennie who said it was her smile and her spirit that captivated him immediately and placed her above all the rest. She had always prided herself on her strong resemblance to the actress Elizabeth Taylor. I have to say, it was pretty close. When she wore makeup, it was always applied flawlessly and her eyebrows perfectly matched those of Elizabeth's.

My mom was the type of woman who was always prepared from the moment she got out of bed. There was never a day that went by where she wasn't wearing the most stylish attire for any occasion. Even during her downtime at home, her hair was immaculately styled, along with expertly applied makeup, and she always wore her finest, but understated jewelry, as she favored a minimalist approach. She had a slender figure; lithe and delicate, and possessed a strong sense of style, although not a materialistic woman; just a lady with a keen eye for quality, a refined taste. She had class, that's for sure, and people definitely noticed. She always told my sister and me, "One must always be prepared for the possibility of an uninvited guest." We always wondered if that was why her refrigerator was constantly well-supplied with chocolate and goodies. Her motto was, "Keep the pantry stocked for unforeseen visitors." Yeah, right. Everyone knew about her huge sweet tooth, so the excuse about uninvited guests was a thinly veiled attempt to hide her milk and dark chocolate secrets.

Growing up, I was this skinny, scrappy little tomboy, playing stick ball on the streets of the Bronx with the boys. But, at the same time, I was also a girlie-girl. I loved my Barbie dolls, hopscotch, jumping rope and being part of the "cool girls club," playing around with hairstyles, wearing tons of makeup and sporting white go-go boots. We looked like nine-year old hookers. Thank you Nancy Sinatra, who released her single "These Boots Are Made For Walkin'" in 1965, and inspired the sexy boot trend.

My hangout buddies were Gloria, Monica, Susan, Paula, and Lillian. Gloria was the popular one who always led the pack. Monica and Susan were both very sweet and followed the crowd. Paula was very kind, a good soul. She was the one who missed me the most once I moved to Yonkers. One day, she walked, all alone, for well over an hour, from the Bronx, crossing over the line into Yonkers, just to see me. I will never forget that. Lillian was my very best pal, and we were practically inseparable, maybe even raised in the same playpen. We did everything together. Even our moms were close. Lillian put up with a lot from me, as I was just a tad older, and I often loved to take charge. I would tell her what we were going to play with, and how things would be done. Because she was very gentle and good natured, she would always go with the flow. She lived in the house behind us, and it was very hard for me when her family decided to move back to Ireland, as things just weren't the same without her anymore. Eventually, she came back, and to this day, we still keep in touch. She's still sweet, funny, and outgoing. She's a personal trainer, and has a body that won't quit. Maybe it's good that she lives over an hour away from me now, because if she were any closer, I'm pretty sure she'd be dragging my lazy ass to one of her classes. She's still an awesome human being and beautiful, both inside and out.

I'll always cherish my childhood memories, those days of skinned knees, bruised egos, and earned licks. In the afternoons, carrying quarters in our pockets, all of us would run as soon as we heard the Good Humor ice cream truck's jingle ringing up the street. I always picked the same ice cream on a stick, a creamsicle, vanilla on the inside, covered with a cool coating of orange-flavored sherbet; it was my favorite, well, after chocolate, of course. While we played, some of us would end up dropping them on the sidewalk, kiss them up to God, and ate them anyway (our mothers couldn't afford to give us another 25 cents for a new one). Childhood. Although mine was fun a lot of the time, you still couldn't pay me enough money to rewind the clock on that one.

What I miss most of all, are the long summer days playing in the neighborhood until it got dark, with my mom calling out the window for me to come home. My very favorite holiday was always Christmas, tons of tinsel on the tree, and Mario Lanza's hymns and carols playing on the phonograph, on repeat. My mom would decorate the tree with these big colored bulbs that had liquid inside them, and when they heated up, they bubbled. They fascinated me, as I thought they were magic (in actuality, they were plugged in and my mom flipped the switch when I wasn't looking).

My childhood was a playbook of trouble; I was a naughty and spirited little prankster. I have to say, I'm pretty lucky to be alive, especially after some of the stunts I pulled, like climbing very tall trees that were growing in the middle of concrete playgrounds in the Bronx, as there certainly were no safety nets in those days. Or, when I got a little older, my friends and I would hike up very unsteady, rocky cliffs that overlooked the Hudson River. I guess I had no fear back then. Today, I can't even stand on a chair without getting dizzy. Even when I attend a Yankees game, I can't sit in the nosebleed section due to my incredible fear of heights. Or, the times when we placed pennies onto the railroad tracks so they got flattened when the freight trains ran by. My friends would call for me to join them, as they jumped onto the side for a twenty-second ride. Not me! That's where I drew the line, for I knew that was downright stupid and dangerous, and a lot of times I ended up walking home alone, but at least I had my pennies.

Over the summers, my family would vacation in Montauk Point, Long Island. My dad had a fireman buddy who owned a large portion of land surrounding the beautiful Lake Montauk. It took this man several years, but around 1960 he and his friends and family managed to build over fifteen small cottages and bungalows. He would rent them out to families, and he always gave my dad a break in price. It was two weeks every summer, when my entire family was together 24/7, and those moments remain frozen in time, as they were the most special memories of my family that I will always carry in my heart. We took lakeside swims during the day, and while my sister sunbathed, she would watch the owner's handsome son water skiing on the lake. I think he was showing off for her. They dated for that brief spell; I'll call it summer love. He couldn't take his eyes off of my sister from the moment he met her. How could he? She had a body that wouldn't quit; I was actually embarrassed at how big her boobs were; mine were as flat as pancakes. Not to mention, she had legs that went on for miles. I was too young to understand their chemistry; it was sizzling. But, I remember that as soon as we returned home, she moved on and was dating someone else before she even unpacked her bags. She changed boyfriends like she changed the channels on the TV.

After mom and dad cooked (yes, they actually joined forces, collaborating in that small kitchen), we would all eat dinner. Well, most of us; I was so picky, or so I was told, because most nights they served the catch of the day. There was no one on God's green earth that could make me eat fish. I wasn't about to sprout gills and swim with the other sea creatures surrounding the dinner table (referring to my two brothers and their armpit-farting contests). I was turning green from the smell, and my cookies were about to explode all over the floor. Suffice it to say that most nights I embraced the gooey goodness of macaroni and cheese, alone, outside sitting at the picnic table enjoying the beautiful breeze, sans the pungent, briny aroma of cooked fish. It was like enjoying a warm hug in a bowl.

But, I did love watching my dad and brothers surfcasting, and fishing in the ocean near the lighthouse. But, that only lasted roughly an hour most times, as we girls would get bored, depart, and walk around the quaint town to take in all the sights that Montauk had to offer. We'd window shop, buy little souvenirs, and post cards that we'd write out during the quiet spells, those short intervals of stillness, a.k.a. the "lull" of the maritime doldrums.

My sister would wear these gigantic rollers in her hair. That's what the young, attractive girls would do to give people the impression that they had a hot date that evening. In actuality, most times she did! I took long walks with my mom during the evenings on the beach collecting seashells, then all of us would take pictures in front of the lighthouse. Some nights we would catch a movie at the local, and one and only, theatre. I remember watching Casino Royale in 1967 sitting on a folding chair. The theatre was actually a large auditorium, and they didn't offer cinema seating. The chairs were set up before a movie played, then dismantled and stored away when it ended. You should have heard the loud gasp my mother let out when Ursula Andress had an intentional nip-slip. She actually showed some nipple! It was so risqué at that time, and my mom tried to cover my virgin eyes, but too late, ha ha. Suffice it to say, my father elbowed both of my brothers, as their male eyes stayed glued to the screen, each sporting silly, cheeky grins on their faces. My sister just rolled her eyes.

Some days while my dad fished, my family would picnic on the beach, sunbathe, and relax. I'd go off on my own, and loved jumping all the way to the end of a nearby jetty; large, wet, slippery boulders that spanned far out into the ocean. When I could go no further, I would sit there in solitude and ponder life, while concurrently watching the relentless waves smashing against the riprap under my dangling feet. I loved the feel and smell of the spray from the ocean. I was in awe of the beauty of God's gentle brush strokes on his canvas, the seamless blend of a magnificent sky that fused with a never-ending ocean on the horizon. To me, it was like a gaze into heaven; I never tried to reason with it, as my young, wide eyes simply and purely absorbed all of its majesty. It became a part of my soul. I never heard the yells coming from the beach, as I was always too far out. That was when my family actually realized I was missing. My father would hear them, then catch a glimpse of me out of the corner of his eye, and quickly shove his fishing rod into a beach spike, and cursing all the way, he would crawl out to get me, hanging on like a spider.

I remember another time when I was young; I quickly slipped far under the water at a public pool which was slanted. I sat there, submerged, until an adult came along, grabbed me, and yanked me out, only to hear my mom screaming for dear life. I was blue. I had been under the water for a couple of minutes, because I decided I was going to hold my breath just to see how long I could. I did wonder why it was that people were swimming all around me, above me. Shouldn't their feet have been touching the ground next to where I was sitting? I was too young to grasp the concept of depth perception, nor did I think much of it. I did, however, feel ethereally peaceful. Unbeknownst to me (someone who hadn't yet learned how to swim), I had slipped into the deep end of the pool, so standing up wasn't an option. Meanwhile, my poor mom was having a conniption fit.

I was on the cusp of turning ten years old when my parents were finally able to buy a very small starter home in Yonkers, New York, approximately 30 minutes away by car from the neighborhood I loved in the Bronx. For me, Yonkers was like a cold, alien planet. I missed all of my Bronx friends terribly, but over time, and as difficult as it was, I made new ones. While in grammar school, I loved acting and always secured the lead in any of the plays I tried out for. I was a natural and could remember pages and pages of lines without a hitch. I was never nervous on stage; in fact, I craved the attention and always gave it my all. I never had stage fright, and I still don't. Performing in front of strangers never bothered me, as they didn't know the real me. I was a character, and if I flubbed my lines, I'd adlib, as I was never at a loss for words.

Technically, it was a performance; I had nothing to hide, nothing to prove, and certainly nothing to fear. I loved interacting with a live audience, and even thought that perhaps I'd make it to Broadway one day. Hit your marks, say your lines, and break a leg. Yes, I had the talent, but after a few years, I lost interest and decided to take up another extracurricular hobby; twirling.

I never had the confidence, or felt that I was pretty enough to be a cheerleader, and twirling seemed to come very naturally to me, so I learned. I advanced rather quickly, lead all the local parades, and eventually won the championship of 1969. I remember firmly telling my family not to come to the competition that day. They were shocked when I muttered something about how it was fixed so that my arch nemesis would win, since her mother was involved in everything.

This woman basically meddled into everybody's business and always got what she wanted for her spoiled rotten little girl. However, I may have bent the truth a bit. I did indeed have an arch nemesis who gave me real competition, and always kept me on my toes. Unbeknownst to everyone, however, I intended on giving it my all that day, and if I lost, I knew I couldn't bear to see my family's disappointed faces. That would only have validated and supplemented the low self-esteem I carried around like a weight. I was flawless, and won the competition and the coveted title of "champion," but because I told my family not to be there,

I had to walk a long way home alone, carrying a trophy almost as tall as myself. Strangers driving by me were honking their horns, cheering and clapping, and yelling congratulations. In the end, my family was thrilled, offered some nice words and proceeded to remind me how it would've been nice to have had a ride home had they been invited. Talk about egg on my face.

I could even twirl two batons simultaneously (I believe this is where my ambidexterity proficiency was advantageous, instrumental in that regard), and occasionally at tournaments they were lit on fire, aka fire spinning. My teacher was the one who always entered me, as I was the leader, her most hopeful. When it was my turn to "batter up," she would stand on the sidelines holding her breath, while simultaneously sweating bullets, pacing, and biting her nails, worried sick that I'd go up in smoke, as I never listened to her, so she never knew what to expect. She would have already presoaked my batons in some kind of lighter fluid thoroughly, so as to give them enough time for the performance. Regular batons and fire batons both are measured in length for the individual user, and are evenly weighted on both ends. Regular batons are made for routines containing tricks and rhythmic gymnastics, and each end has rubber stoppers. Mine were always autographed by my friends.

Fire batons are more geared to artistic performances; they emphasize artistry and creative expression, rather than prioritizing speed or precision. They're primarily used to create a captivating, optical spectacle with fire, art tools designed to mesmerize the audience through the visual appeal of the flames. Each end is made of a high-temperature Kevlar material with rolled wicking heads. Each of these ends are wrapped in aluminum foil or plastic to preserve the liquid before lighting. I would always deviate from the bland routines she taught me, and she knew it, because I felt that I had more creative moves, and I was way too fast. She was always telling me to slow down in fear that I'd drop the batons and the fire would extinguish. From the sidelines, right before my routines, she would yell "Flips!" This meant I should spin the batons rapidly to shed excess lighter fluid. (I think my teacher mixed camp fuel with kerosene, I really don't know and never asked her; I surmised she knew what she was doing). You would have to quickly turn the batons, as this ensures that the fuel doesn't drip down their shafts. She had already squeezed most of the fluid out using rubber gloves.

Next, she would start with her usual contributions, or rather, heckling, "No elbow rolls, that's too slow, and watch your hair!" "Did you remember to spray yourself down with water?" I was confident enough in my craft to think I could escape that fate, which I always did, but good thing she did remind me with her prompts, because the only equipment she had to extinguish the flames was a wet towel. She never carried a fire extinguisher, and the places where competitions were held didn't provide anything either. You had to come prepared. I won many trophies and medals using my own artistry, and I made her proud.

My team (we were called The Sparklettes) almost made it onto a reality show called Ted Mack & The Original Amateur Hour. We came very close, but alas, we didn't qualify, and of course, I blamed all of them. It couldn't have been me, you know, that lunatic who auditioned while throwing fire into the air, with her long hair coming within a quarter inch of being ignited when it came down. I was warned to tie my hair up, but this rebel wanted to look sexy on TV and showed up with it flowing freely down her back. The fire touched my very flammable sequined costume countless times during our performance; good thing it was already sprayed down, but it's anyone's guess how it didn't burst into flames. My team was afraid to stand close to me, and our uniformity was out of whack; we looked completely out of step. I felt I could pull off the routine with grand aplomb; I was wrong. I eventually took the blame and apologized to my peers. I took a lot of chances, I really did. I had no fear, but if anything really did go wrong, I would have soaked up as much attention as I possibly could. Firemen would've needed to show up to put me out. I remembered those firemen from the "wedding ring" incident. Think about it. You know, those guys who look like they work in Chippendales? Yes, I was barely 13 and definitely coming of age and beginning to realize that there was a big difference between boys and girls. Real big!

As I matured, I learned that if I put my mind to anything, I would succeed. All I needed to do was try. However, a huge neurosis of inadequacy always followed me, controlled me. I was hypersensitive and had a very low opinion of myself which I hid under a facade of strength. It hindered many other dreams I had, at least until I started high school. It was there where I found my confidence, my spirit, my tenacity, and my individuality. I discovered that I was actually very pretty, indeed. I never quite knew it, merely hoped, but now a lot of guys started paying attention to me. Even though I shed a few of my emotional deficiencies, unfortunately there were still certain patterns I struggled to break. I wasn't quite able to completely let go of them, and simply learned how to hide them better.

Initially, my goal in life was to go to medical school. I had a very strong calling to be a doctor, and an incredible love and respect for science, and I certainly had the grades. I still have a picture of myself at Christmastime with my little doctor's bag and my trusted holiday assistant by my side, a doll Santa brought me that was almost as tall as I was. That was the Christmas where my entire family was poked, prodded, vaccinated, and transfused. All hearts were monitored, tongues were depressed, and people gagged. Chiclets gum was prescribed because everyone was running a fever. Sadly, no temperature checks were allowed, as they were all too pissed off at me after I told them to turn around and bend over. No one escaped Dr. Greta that day, not even my poor little teddy bear, Pip, who successfully recovered from open-foam transplant surgery.

My little Pip was named after David Lean's 1946 film adaptation of Great Expectations. It's definitely considered an epic. It was one of the great transformations to film of Dickens's literary work. I believe it was Anthony Wager who portrayed Pip as a boy, and John Mills who portrayed Pip as an adult, but please don't quote me on this. The story was about a humble orphan boy, Philip Pirrip, and took place circa 1810 in Kent, a tiny county located in the south of England. Pip was given an opportunity to go to London and become a more refined and well-mannered man with the help of a benefactor he didn't know. He was quite a character who evolved from a naïve little boy into a gentleman. He was ambitious, romantic, and idealistic, but also made mistakes. As a little girl, I watched it, but I didn't understand much about it at that time. However, I immediately fell in love with him anyway. I also prayed to God that I'd never end up like Miss Havisham, whose heart was broken when her fiancé Compeyson abandoned her on their wedding day at the altar! She was left humiliated and heartbroken, withdrew from society, and remained in her wedding dress for the rest of her days, as if forever frozen in time.

Unfortunately, my father firmly elucidated that I wasn't allowed to attend college, as there was never enough money. Student loans were not an option either, because he would not cosign. His opinion of my indecisiveness between medicine and the arts had him scratching his head. He said, "How can you not decide? They're two completely different occupations!" But, I couldn't. So, I was forced into studying business, just like my successful sister before me, at a local business high school, and to also get a part time job at a little TV repair shop to earn money to help contribute to our house's income. This wasn't necessarily a bad thing, just not my dream.

It also meant that I would need to be transferred to a special, different high school. However, I did gain life-long skills, and it taught me responsibility. My typing was clocked in at 140 words per minute with the same for my Gregg shorthand. My father always told me I had great fingers, as I could fix anything that was broken. No wonder I did well at twirling! Still, I so wanted to be a surgeon. Or, maybe I could have starred on a TV show as one.

When I was 19, my parents retired and decided to move to Florida. This is when I truly found my independence. I shared in the responsibility of paying the rent for the house they left behind in Yonkers with my two brothers, as my parents had a difficult time selling it, because it was located on a steep hill, and decided to turn it into a rental. It was a win-win. I had a boyfriend, a good job, and great friends. I would make it a point to fly down and visit my parents a couple of times per year, and as the years slowly passed, I took a lot of college courses paid for by the companies I was employed by, but only business curriculum modules. Working full-time during the day, while attending college classes sporadically at night did present challenges. At first, it appeared it would be easier to fit in night classes, but they only met once or twice a week; too many potential drawbacks if I were to try and obtain some kind of degree, and it just seemed like it would take forever. It was all good, for I later realized my true passion was geared more towards artistic ventures, such as marketing, advertising, and especially writing, so the courses were advantageous. I had always loved to write! Medical school, which I initially thought was my "dream," became a distant memory.

I've been told that I have a knack for getting to the heart of the matter. I've written tons of short stories and speeches for people who needed help finding the right words to say at special occasions. Basically, I'm someone who can fill in the blanks. I've also won awards for advertising slogans when I worked for Kraft Foods Corporation, prizes actually, but it made me feel special when my coworkers recognized that I had talent. It was only recently that I decided it was finally time to write about my own life, although it was a personal tragedy which became the driving factor. My husband always encouraged me to live my dreams, follow my compass, find my passions, but especially to return to writing. Time after time he told me, "One day Greta, you're going to make your mark, and I'll be right behind you, but you won't need my encouragement to help you shine, because to me, you always have, and you always will."

I'm a curious type of person, open to new experiences, always searching for new ideas, and learning from my failures. I'm not one of those moody, creative types by any means; in fact, I'm always upbeat. Well, on the surface. Deep down, I tend to be a bit melancholy. That's the tortured artist inside of me, I suppose. I'm the clown who wears the mask, a facade of humor; the person who conceals a trail of tears hidden behind a painted smile.

Many people describe me as an emotional floater, a common expression used for one who drifts through varying mindsets, often *appearing* as detached, aloof. But, in actuality, my brain is working on full throttle under the surface; it just shifts from one state-of-mind to another without a clear reason. I know what you're thinking; no, I'm not bipolar. I look at it as more of a type of freedom that allows me to observe, and then compartmentalize events I've experienced in my day-to-day living. You see, once I connect, I dive deep, then fully and passionately commit. Sometimes, I'm a good observer, and catch a lot of subtleties that most people miss. Other times, things fly right over my head because I'm daydreaming.

I've worked very hard most of my life, mainly in the corporate world, for large, well-known companies, transferring from one division to another. I succeeded to the highest grade-level that I could without the formality of a college degree. It honestly would have been too much to handle once I started raising my family; I just didn't have the extra hours to put into that type of commitment. So, I continued in my capacity of Senior Administrator, supporting different branches and units, occasionally having the opportunity to fill in as IT support, which I loved.

My strengths lie in organization, and I enjoy delving into demanding projects, but I've also always had an artistic side that constantly pulled at me, but was always sidelined. I loved writing, and even did return to acting much later on, but try paying bills with those skills unless you're related to someone famous who can give you a leg up. Where is nepotism when you need it?

When I was a young girl, I wrote tons of poetry into my diary every day. At that time, I was oblivious to the fact that my father was also a writer. He wrote many love letters to my mother and was very poetic. As I read between the lines, I think a lot of them were subtly apologetic, for later in life he felt deep contrition for neglecting or unknowingly hurting my mother. Right before she died, she gave all of them to me as a keepsake. Some from his collection featured poems that were remarkably singular, with some holding a lingering, beautiful quality. Perhaps one day I'll get some of them published in my father's memory. All I knew about him was that he was a fireman, a scratch golfer who enjoyed spaghetti and meatballs after a good game, always worked additional odd jobs, was obsessed with opera and British TV shows, and was great at cards. It wasn't until recently that I discovered that he and several members of his family were writers and painters, all of whom were very artistic in nature.

I also discovered that there were artists on my mother's side of the family as well. Mom had a biological half-sister (they shared a father) who was a very accomplished folk singer in her day who lived on the Isle of Man. I cannot divulge her name for legal reasons, as she may actually still be alive. She was someone who would be comparatively famous nowadays on the same level as Taylor Swift. Yes, she was pretty huge in her time, so I suppose my love of the arts is genetic. She was highly educated. She attended both music and drama schools, where she trained in singing before getting her big break in the media after a highly successful audition. It is a fact that she was, without a doubt, one of Scotland's biggest ever female singing stars. I even have one of her old cassette tapes that my mother gave to me, and on the cover is a picture of her when she was young, which is a mirror image of my mom.

Unbeknownst to my mother, I eventually contacted this singer through a radio program where she was scheduled to give an interview. I told the DJ conducting the interview that my mom, her half-sister, lived here in America and was dying from cancer. I also passed along a picture of their father. This singer denied any relation to my mother. She knew, as I'm sure her entire family did, about her father's many indiscretions. It was a pity. My mom was ignorant as to what I was trying to do, for I knew if it worked out, that all she really would have wanted was just to be a tiny part of her sister's life, to get to know her and learn more about the father they shared for just a small instant in time. Nothing else. It may have given my mom the credibility she craved and deserved. I guess some secrets are meant to remain as just that. Private affairs.

Since she bore his surname, my mother thought that the man my grandmother had once been married to, whose name was Colonel Webley, was her biological father. But, in actuality, he wasn't. I don't even know his first name; her family never spoke much about him. My mother was born in 1927, the youngest of three siblings. My grandmother met Colonel Webley sometime in the latter part of 1910, introduced through family members, who encouraged her to allow the relationship to develop and consummate in marriage. All of the family viewed her like some sort of wild filly, way too spirited; one that needed to be rounded up and tamed. When my mother grew up she discovered who her real father was: A very wealthy, influential businessman who owned a bank, a paint store, and several other businesses in the area. He was already married with children, one of whom was that famous singer. He was a member of high society, belonging to The Royal and Ancient Golf Club of St Andrews, originally known as the Society of St. Andrews Golfers.

Grandma had conducted a few brief affairs during her marriage to Colonel Webley, which was an unhappy and stringent union from the get go, and she felt stifled under his strict rules. She was a happy-go-lucky soul who craved her freedom, but in those days divorce was scoffed at. In her eyes, this wealthy businessman was a true love affair; however, he was more driven by primal instincts. He moved on with his life and ended his relationship with my grandmother when my mother was only a few years old. Colonel Webley was aware, but stayed in the marriage anyway, for he truly loved her in his own peculiar way, however, he certainly had anomalous ways of showing it. He took great care of their four children as if all were his own, although just one son and one daughter were biologically his. As for who the father of the other daughter was, well, you'd be rolling the dice on that one. To this day, none of us know.

Yes, my grandmother led a very colorful life. She was a captivating beauty, matched only by the sweetness of her nature, which was expressed through her love of dancing and singing. She also had a wicked sense of humor! She had a stunning figure, and always used it to her advantage by dressing very stylishly, although her frocks were frugal in price. Naturally, men flocked to her everywhere she went, and my mom had what she referred to as many "uncles." She was a lady of character and charm, and certainly embraced a very vibrant life for her time. Before he departed, that very married, high-society gentlemen secretly gave my grandmother a little money to take care of my mother and herself. In the meantime, another "uncle" came along and sweet talked her into poultry farming, so she took that money and invested all of it into a chicken farm and hid it from Colonel Webley. Now, don't get this confused with a chicken ranch; that's a historical brothel in Texas, ha ha.

No, it was a real-life chicken farm that was well run in its heyday, but had been left run-down and a bit neglected, which was why the price was right. She thought this little farm would make money eventually, even though they were only starting out with one chicken coop that housed two full-grown female chickens, and an assortment of approximately 20 little chicks. The guy she entered this endeavor with had sweet talked her into thinking he knew everything about running it properly. Alas, he didn't, and unfortunately she naïvely allowed most of the responsibility to fall onto his shoulders. He didn't care about the farm; he was also fully aware there wasn't a rooster in sight. He cared about the large difference he pocketed when he lied to my grandmother about the sale price of the farm. So, beyond being a thief, he cruelly deceived and took advantage of her trust by entering her life and intimacy under false pretenses. But, the one thing he overlooked was the fact that he couldn't steal her heart.

My grandmother was very optimistic; her glass was always half-full. She assumed that once the little chicks grew up, a lot more little chicks would be born if they all mingled, and she found the whole idea hilarious, so she set them all free. Hawks and jays were always circling, and grandma fed them every day too. Yes, these warm-blooded vertebrates with feathers had more food than they knew what to do with, and grandma wondered why some of the chicks never came back. Every day, one or two of them went missing. She wondered, "Where'd they go?" At first, the poultry farm seemed like a good idea, but for someone who didn't know a thing about chicken farming, especially when she later learned how roosters play a significant role in reproduction, it was short-lived, and so was her affair with that "uncle" who also took any money made from egg sales and ran for the hills. In the end, he may have emptied her purse and robbed her blind, but her heart remained full and untouched; something he was never able to capture.

Her one and only true love, a local tavern keeper, was unfortunately a married man who stole her heart when she was a young woman. His priority was his wife's well-being and needs, so he remained committed to their marriage. He couldn't abandon his obligations, as his wife's disability was a major factor in his decision to stay.

So, my grandmother remained in her marriage to Colonel Webley for a couple of more years until his untimely death, which became the most joyful day of her life. For her, it was a much-needed relief from the dead-weight nuptial of unhappiness she had been chained to, and the day in which she happily and dearly departed, literally dancing right out the funeral home's door, and into the arms of yet another "uncle."

My uncle Bertie remained single and lived with my grandmother for many years after Colonel Webley died and took the very best care of her as she aged. Grandma passed away at the ripe old age of 96. As she drifted into eternal sleep, her mind's eye held the vibrant yet arduous memories of her past, an extraordinary one imbued with both exceptional triumphs and significant hardships. One in particular was during World War II, when Glasgow and the surrounding area, particularly Clydebank, were significantly affected by air raids, carried out by The Luftwaffe, the German air force. Clydebank is very close to the greater Glasgow area in Scotland, where my grandmother lived, and is located just outside the city boundaries, about 6.5 to 7 miles northwest of Glasgow's city center. The two are so close that a train journey between them takes barely 21 minutes.

Clydebank was the most devastating raid, known as the Clydebank Blitz. The German's targets were the Shipyards on the River Clyde, and industrial facilities like John Brown & Co shipyard, and the Singer Corporation factory. Clydebank, a shipbuilding and munitions hub, suffered extensive damage, with only eight out of 12,000 houses remaining undamaged, and 4,000 houses completely destroyed. It resulted in approximately 1,200 deaths and 1,000 injuries, and over 35,000 people were left homeless. Although Clydebank suffered the most significant proportional damage, Glasgow had a higher overall number of fatalities during the raid. They experienced a significant number of casualties and widespread damage, with at least 11 air attacks, including five major raids. One particular evening, I remember my mom describing to me an air strike that took place on either March 13 or 14, 1941. My mom was 14 years old. The air sirens went off, and my grandmother grabbed her children and they made a run for the nearest air raid shelter; a simple, brick structure located a few blocks away on the street. People were laying flat on the ground, too frightened to move. A bomb exploded yards away from them, leaving my mom almost deaf in one ear; she heard nothing but a high-pitched ringing for days. She was terrified, crying. My grandmother was hit by shrapnel, small fragments from exploding ordnance made from metal, which penetrated her body from her head to her feet. With blood dripping down her face, she never stopped holding my mom's hand and kept running to safety.

She was an amazing woman, one who lived through a war and survived, trusting her intuition and relying on her inner strength, even in the face of fear. She didn't merely exist; she lived with an insatiable passion and vitality. Her heart was always an open book, and she danced with life's rhythm, shaping her own path with unwavering conviction. It was truly a life well-lived, a beautiful narrative filled with purpose, strength, and unbridled joy.

CHAPTER 7

THE ONE

It was September 6, 1974 when I met him at a college mixer which was held at Manhattan College (now Manhattan University), located in the Bronx, New York. He was set to begin classes in just a few days and had aspirations of achieving great success studying Civil Engineering, along with dreams of conquering most of the female student body along the way. He had been very shy around women for most of his life and felt that now was the time to spread his wings and fly boldly. Unbeknownst to both of us, that dream was about to get clipped. The new freshman class was starting in a few days and the administration encouraged its students to mingle and get to know each other before studies took off. The college had formally been predominantly male, but had begun accepting its first undergraduate female students just one year prior.

I was very familiar with this college and frequented it often with my girlfriends whenever special events or dances were going on. It was our stomping ground, and the guys we met there were older and cool, suave. Hey, they were in college and had their own dorm rooms! There was also a local tavern a few blocks away called The Greenleaf, where college students and people from around the area hung out, and where I met many good friends, thanks to my fake driver's license. I always got along better with older people; I just related more on their level. Man, we had such crazy fun!

I remember it being one of those horrible, never-ending, dreary, and miserable rainy Fridays in New York. I had no interest in going out that evening, fearing my hair frizzing, but my friend Stephanie insisted upon it. We went everywhere together. She was stunningly beautiful; tall, thin, blond, green eyes, big boobs; your basic nightmare, but, I just adored her. I was her best friend, and we were always laughing. We never had a problem attracting the opposite sex, that's for sure! Stephanie had this aura about her; she looked like a professional model and shined like a star wherever she went. Men would gather around her the moment we entered a room. I always held my own, as I was also quite pretty, though not as tall. I was a different type; I had long dark hair, hazel eyes, and really nice boobs too, but I was certainly not Cosmopolitan magazine material like she was. However, it was nice knowing that I'd never go home without someone asking for my phone number too. Being a wingman does have its perks.

Stephanie and I grabbed a couple of beers as we walked in. We stood there amongst an overflowing crowd of people and blended in as we secretly hunted for cute guys. Then I saw him. Oh God, he was gorgeous, with long, thick dark hair, a strong and prominent nose, soft brown eyes, perfect lips, slight build, but not too tall. I felt like I was standing in the middle of that old song "Some Enchanted Evening," the score from the play South Pacific, because we kept staring at each other from across the crowd. How cliché, seeing each other across a crowded room, but it happened, and I was immediately drawn to him. I remember how the feeling hit me like a lightning bolt and how it went way beyond just physical attraction. My whole body was in shock, and it left me completely unable to say anything to my friend. I went numb, and my legs were going weak. Stephanie tugged on my arm and said something to me, so I turned away for a brief moment.

A few seconds later I felt a tap on my shoulder. The guy standing there introduced himself as Steve. He was tall, dark, and handsome. He reminded me of a male model, straight out of the pages of GQ. The guy was just too pretty, too perfect. Standing next to him was that other gorgeous guy, the shorter one I had been in a staring contest with. Steve introduced him to me saying, "This is my friend Larry and he wants to meet you, says he knows you from somewhere." Then, he proceeded to explain how Larry was too shy to approach me on his own, immediately swung around, and very self-assuredly introduced himself to Stephanie. Next, he grabbed her arm, and off went the Hollywood couple to score more beer and make out in a dark corner.

That was the last I saw of my friend Stephanie until much later on that night. Larry and I had also started talking and meandered off together through the crowd to find a place to sit. We talked about why he had chosen to attend Manhattan College, and what he would be studying. He told me where he lived, which wasn't far from where I lived, and how he recognized me from a year or two back when he worked as a roadie for a very popular band, whose keyboardist I had been dating at that time. We were amazed to find out that we would both be turning 18 in one month, October, and that we were both Libras. He asked if I was currently dating anyone, and I said "no" faster than a New York minute! For this guy, I was definitely free.

Truth be told, I was always dating someone. I started right before age 13, and would have started sooner, but parental supervision always got in my way, not to mention two older brothers who were always ready and willing to kick some ass if I snuck out and got caught with a boy, which actually happened once; lesson learned. I remember my first French kiss. My mouth and nose were literally sucked up into this gigantic, wet, slimy vacuum as he slobbered all over my face, and I couldn't figure out how to break the seal. Luckily, he didn't leave a hickey on my nose. I didn't know any better and just wished it would stop. What a disgusting mess. Even my hair got wet, and it was leaking down my neck! I told my friends about it, and everyone laughed at my stupidity, but the more advanced girls took me aside to inform me he was an over-pouted, fish-lipped schmuck who didn't know what he was doing. Still, I shied away from French kissing for some time after that, too repulsed and afraid that the next one would puke in my mouth, or something even worse. Then, there were the guys who thought they knew everything and acted cool by blowing smoke circles after taking a drag from their cigarette. They told me to catch their smoke circles with my tongue.

That was their explanation of French kissing. Idiots. No, I wasn't stupid enough to fall for that one.

They say there's a theory that throughout our lifetime, we will fall in love three times, at three different stages during our life. I think they're right. There were many guys along the way, too many to count, all insignificant and most short-lived, and I told all of them that I loved them. Yes, I lied, but none of them held any real importance to me. They were all just for some fun for a few short dates, and then I'd be on to the next victim. I'll call this the first stage of thinking they loved me, puppy love. Ah, youth.

Over time, I learned the true art of French kissing. I found out a lot along the way, including what going to second base was. Then, along came that middle guy, a musician (keyboardist), when I was going through my second stage of love, someone with whom I experienced a feeling of intense obsession. But, it was more of idealizing and admiration, mixed with lies, betrayal, and emotional damage. He was that slippery stepping stone, a guy that was a year older than me, and our involvement was more of a romantic infatuation than anything real. It lasted approximately eight months, and then he cheated on me with my best friend at that time (no, it wasn't Stephanie), so it ended. I was actually contemplating going all the way with this romantic Valentino, I was still a naïve virgin, and my so-called best friend was giving me pointers one night on how to actually do the deed. She was also a year older than me, and very experienced in the art of intercourse, well, actually all matters of the flesh. Meanwhile, behind my back she was actually already doing the deed with my boyfriend.

Man that hurt! I was only 16 years old at the time, and I lost who I thought I was in love with, along with my best pal, my closest confidant. But, it was the best thing they both ever did, as it made me stronger as an individual, and really opened up my eyes. Thank God I didn't lose my virginity to him, something that was so very precious to me, as I wanted to share such a significant and beautiful turning point in my life with someone I deeply loved and trusted. I was a child, a fool who romanticized the notion, and fancied the possibilities of a future with this snake who could never fulfill that role.

This was definitely the relationship where I grew the most; however, it also fed into my inferiority complex. He broke up with my ex-best friend eventually, and both wrote me letters of apology. He even tried to win me back; he didn't succeed. However, for a year after that I did put up walls, and became extremely protective of myself for any future romantic endeavors. I became suspicious and careful, but I also knew exactly what I wanted going forward in a new relationship. Trust.

Then, along came Larry, the third stage of love. The one that dropped into my life when I least expected it; the one whose eyes I got lost in, and all I could see were flawless imperfections. I found that deep attachment and commitment, not to mention that he was the best kisser I ever had. To me, his kisses were more like transformative experiences, so there were lots of make out sessions in the backseat of his Buick Electra classic car which produced many steamed up windows. Almost one year after I met him, both of us now 18 years old, his Buick was the place where we lost our innocence to each other. We were alone in the middle of a golf course. It was a quiet, magical, clear evening under the vast, silent canvas of stars, where we crossed that threshold, leaving a part of ourselves behind. As he held me so tenderly in his arms, it evoked a sense of renewal and metamorphosis, and I cried for what was, but more so for what was yet to come. We were so deeply in love.

The rock band at the mixer that night was so deafening, that Larry and I had to huddle close, practically shouting in each other's ears just to be heard. We discovered that both of us traveled in the same circles, knew the same people, yet somehow, I had never known about him. He always blended into the background, remaining unnoticed among his friends. He told me how he would watch me from afar, and how he felt that I was unattainable. At first, I took it as a compliment, yet I remember my face feeling quite flushed, as I didn't want him to get the wrong impression of me. Yes, I was very pretty, but what most others didn't realize was that I also still dragged around the inferiority complex that I hid so well. So in actuality, I was embarrassed that he believed I was out of his reach. That was the last thing I ever wanted him to think.

Sitting there together, we were getting along very well at this point, and I remember staring at his lips, his eyes, and the way his hands moved while he talked. He had beautiful hands. He caught me looking, and he explained it was because he was Italian, and that Italians speak with their hands a lot. I laughed. Everything about him was alluring. He was so funny and easy to spend time with. Every so often, I would catch him staring at my lips when I looked away. Our attraction was undeniable. I kept thinking that perhaps we did know each other after all, because there was something that strongly pulled me towards him, like that first moment when I saw him across the room. We talked long into the night, and were practically finishing each other's sentences. He made me laugh so hard it hurt, to the point that words would no longer come out of my mouth. He was silly, had such a great sense of humor, and a fun personality. He was overly, and irrefutably attentive towards me.

The live band drew a crazy-fun crowd there that night, and the house was rocking to great music, but I noticed how he waited for the slow songs to play, for it was only then when he would take my hand and pull me close to dance with him. Later, he confessed to me how he desperately wanted to hold me and that the slow songs were an excuse to be able to do so. When he did, I remember how tightly he put his arms around me, how close I was to his body. I loved the way he smelled as I laid my head on his shoulder, how soft his long dark hair was, how he felt, and how he moved. Everything about him triggered an immense fire within me, and I knew I was protected and safe. A strange familiarity took hold of me, as if I remembered him from another lifetime. I had found such comfort in his arms, and when the mixer ended, we walked for a couple of blocks down to The Greenleaf Tavern. It was still raining, and he put his denim jacket over my head. We draped our arms around each other as we walked. Neither of us wanted the night to end. As we entered the bar, we bumped into the Hollywood couple who were still making out. We crashed their party and hung out with them until the place closed down.

Eventually, he took me home and we stayed together, talking on my front porch, just the two of us. We were finally alone, and he insisted on enveloping me into his jacket, holding me because it was so cold. The rain was beginning to let up. It was as if time stood still. We found ourselves wrapped in each other's arms, bodies close. As he looked into my eyes, he gently tilted my head back, took his hand and caressed my cheek, then ever so gently placed his mouth on top of mine and kissed me deeply. My heart was beating so fast; I had never felt this way in my entire life. Good thing he put my back up against the wall to shield me from the wind; it was something stable to hold me up; otherwise, my legs would have given out. We stayed together until the sun started to rise. This was an intense connection, not only physically, but also as if our souls recognized one another. We both fell hard, quickly; we were crazy for each other. From that moment on, we were inseparable.

I remember as a young girl that I used to keep a diary. I would write poetry, then enter what I did each day, the many guys I had dated along the way, how long we were together, and everything I could pour my silly heart out over from a day's events. I knew I was long overdue in putting the diary away, but the morning after I met Larry, as I lay in bed, I opened it and wrote his name at the bottom of the list. Under it I inscribed "Larry Moretti, Mr. Right, The One, The End." Then I drew a line under his name and closed it. I never opened my diary again, and from that day forward, it has been forever kept within my safe keeping.

CHAPTER 8

A TAPESTRY OF CULTURES

When a new relationship begins, each person brings along a history of their lives, generational familial memories, and traditions. Some of us are weighed down by our past experiences and carry emotional baggage and scars. Personally, my "travel needs" were crammed with concerns of suspicion, jealousy, worrying that a partner might leave me for someone else which was driven by my insecurities. I also harbored traits of possessiveness, but mostly I feared abandonment. I projected the pain I felt from that previous relationship onto Larry; my eyes viewed him tinged with skepticism, anticipating the day he'd inevitably walk away. In hindsight, I should have been a much more discerning bellhop, as there certainly were a lot of things I could have made a better effort to have removed from the luggage I carried before unloading them onto him.

Whatever our past, it contains mental souvenirs from living within our individual family dynamics that stem from our nationalities and family of origin. As our new relationships evolve, we consciously or unconsciously try to recreate our family dynamic from our early lives. Some of us believe that our way is the best way of doing things, so conflicts of interests enter the picture and can sometimes become a power struggle.

It certainly impacted Larry and me. He came from Italian decent with a warm and loving family. He only had one older sibling, a sister named Barbara, who embraced me right from the get-go. I liked her immediately and thought she was incredibly beautiful. She had the same crazy sense of humor I had, and everything made us laugh, so we had a lot in common. Both of Larry's parents were born in America, but their parents had come from Italy. Larry's family were wonderful people and loved spending as much time together as possible. Sundays were especially great, as that was always their day to relax; the day they reserved for unwinding together as a family unit. Delicious aromas, from his mother cooking gravy all day, always filled their home. So many pasta dinners with wine, along with laughter and great conversations were always present at their dinner table. Sometimes a baseball game would follow and there would be yelling at the TV, and they always cheered for the Yankees. One particular Sunday, when Larry and I had only been dating for a few weeks, he brought me to his home to meet his family. To all of them, it was a sign that he was serious about me, as I was the first girl he ever introduced them to. His mom fussed over me like I was her own daughter. It was there where I felt invited, comfortable, and more at home than anywhere I had ever been in my entire life. Although I felt sheltered enough in my own home, this place was just different, and I never felt insecure there. His entire family purposely made the time to get to know me, and accepted me for all that I was, or rather, all that I would allow them to see.

Larry and I did everything together. We especially loved picnicking at Jones Beach on Long Island, New York. When wintertime came, we relished the beautiful, and cold, sunny days under the sky while snuggling together under a heavy blanket, seagulls circling, surf pounding the shore, with not another soul in sight. It was just the two of us, lost in our own little world on miles of empty beach. He would sing songs to me, make me laugh at his silly jokes, and talk about his future dreams. It was amazing to me how we had lived so close to each other, yet hadn't met until now. I kept thinking, "Where was this gorgeous, funny, and intelligent guy all of my life?"

We often rode out to the beach in his Buick Electra 225, a classic. It was all electric, and had a huge back seat, and on one particular day, we took full advantage of it before even starting our trip out. We were together for almost a year now, and I loved being with him. I always felt safe, and Larry thought himself a great driver, which he bragged about often. Although, I did wonder, but never questioned, where all of those small dents in his car came from. One day, his best friend, Bobby Mac, confided to me that he thought that Larry was the worst driver that had ever lived. He hit everything in sight because he drove too fast and took chances. The fact that he didn't see well probably didn't help matters either. One time, while he was driving a taxi to earn extra pocket money, he inadvertently missed a turn and drove a little old lady down the front entryway of her church. She made it to Mass, early in fact, although her little hat flew off her head from bumpily descending all of those church steps. I think she prayed her rosary more than one time that morning! Still, to me, the sun and moon rose and set around Larry, as I thought he drove greater than Mario Andretti. Yes, he took chances, but he was cool, adventurous, and no one could talk him down to me.

But, on that particular day, as we were nearing the beach, I felt he was going a little too fast for my own comfort. I warned him to slow down, or pull over and I'd drive. We were on Ocean Parkway. He took his hands off the wheel, kept driving, took me at my word, looked right at me and said "Go ahead." My stubbornness trumped his, and although he was now only cruising at 10 MPH, both of us were locked into a staring war as we drifted into the nearest tree. We were both headstrong and had heads like granite. We crashed, but it wasn't hard, we looked at each other, and all I remember was both of us laughing uncontrollably. A new dent. Then he pulled me into the back seat (like Rose did to Jack from that scene in the movie, Titanic), and before I knew it, we were right back where we started. This most certainly got no argument from me. ☺

I loved listening to his stories of growing up. He was born in October 1956, into an Italian/American family in the Nodine Hill section of Yonkers, New York. His sister Barbara, who was eight years his senior, excitedly awaited his arrival, and doted on him like a second mother. She had insisted for the longest time that her mother have another baby, and actually guilted her into having one, as she so wanted a baby brother. Larry was their only son, and last born child, and his parents were overly protective of him. He forged strong friendships with other boys he met, starting in the third grade at Public School No. 23. There he met his very best friend Bobby Mac, followed by Bob Bailey. In the sixth grade he met Mike Losco, and then in the seventh grade, John Donnelly and Joe DeNardis. All of them became "the gang." Naturally, around seventh grade, they all discovered girls. They'd make chain-link jewelry out of Wrigley's gum wrappers, which had to be the same height as the girls they had crushes on. If the girl accepted their tokens of love, they were considered to be "going out" which only lasted a few days, but during that time it was well known to everyone that they were an item, and the guys felt like superheroes.

At home, he was a dutiful son and very close to his mother, who was a seamstress. His dad worked for the post office and left for work very early in the mornings, so when he got home at 4 p.m., dinner was served like clockwork. Larry enjoyed watching westerns on TV with his dad, fishing for bluefish or bass in the Hudson River with Bobby Mac, and playing gin rummy. Back in those days, whenever you went somewhere, you walked, so he and his friends would enjoy watching baseball games from the stands while playing cards at nearby Fleming Field on Prescott Street, where his dad and his father's good friend Charlie were always nearby. On weekdays after dinner, his mom and Charlie's wife Molly would sit on folding chairs in the front of their building and chat, while his dad and Charlie would sit a small distance away from Larry and his friends keeping a watchful eye, while also enjoying the games. The older men would then depart early and walk down a few streets to the local bookie where they placed small bets on the horses before they walked home. This was their daily ritual, the good 'ol days, enjoyed during much simpler times.

In his youth, Larry felt awkward, and was probably a little more sensitive than most, as he was often referred to as "goofy looking," by the gang. Eventually, he took it in stride, as he knew it was only in jest, and he let it roll off his back. They all busted each other's balls in one way or another. He definitely had way too much hair, and earned the nickname "Barney Google" because of his thick glasses. He even wore braces on his teeth, both top and bottom. In those days, everybody had something dippy, ditzy or goofy going on, and each relentlessly teased the other about it; it was just a part of growing up. Every single one of them were good kids who came from families who loved them, and raised them right. All the parents knew each other, and most all lived within the same neighborhood or area, so everyone looked out for one another. It took a village.

Attending ninth grade at Benjamin Franklin Junior High School was a turning point for Larry as far as his physical appearance went, and his friends didn't break his chops so much anymore. In the next couple of years he started morphing into a young man; shaving, losing the braces, graduating to contact lenses, and growing his hair stylishly long, but they still ribbed him about his prominent nose. When they turned 16, he and Bobby Mac began placing small bets on harness racing at the Yonkers Race Track. They also enjoyed golfing together, and just like the old series on TV "That Seventies Show," the gang would occasionally hang out at Mike Losco's house playing basketball, then retreat to Mike's basement to smoke funny cigarettes. They had such great times, their laughter enveloping into a cloud of thick smoke, wafting up the stairs, and via intercom, Mike's dad would yell for them to take it down a notch.

After Benjamin Franklin Junior High School, Larry attended Saunders Trade & Technical High School, where he became interested in Civil Engineering. It was there where some of his friends founded a very popular local band they named Lime Rickey, with Bob Bailey as the bass player, Mike Losco as the drummer, Bobby Orlando as their lead guitarist, and with that keyboardist I used to date (he'll remain nameless), along with Larry and John as two of their roadies. These same friends would watch him run track in school (he was a very fast runner), and they took advantage of his legs whenever they played football in a local field against other guys from different areas. When high school ended, everyone either went on to college, or started jobs.

Everyone moved around, had careers, or married and started families. They didn't go far though, and the gang always kept in touch.

I saw all of them not too long ago, as I wanted to return some letters a few of them had written to Larry when he worked overseas. They were deeply touched, and they all reminisced about the good old days.

I remember Larry's mom once telling me a story of when she was pregnant with him. Everyone was watching the 1956 World Series held at Ebbets Field in Brooklyn, New York at Dodgers Stadium. It was October 10, 1956, during game 7 of the New York Yankees vs. the Brooklyn Dodgers. She announced that if Yogi won the game for the Yanks, she would name her child after him. Catcher Yogi Berra went 2-for-3 with 2 HR's and 4 RBI's. He then homered twice to help the Yankees keep a 9-0 win and the World Series championship! Larry was born three days later at Professional Hospital in Yonkers, New York, and as promised, his mother named him Lawrence Peter, after Yogi.

Later in life, Larry and our youngest son Lawrence Peter, Jr. (whom we call Pete), actually got to meet Yogi Berra in person at a little comic store named "One If By Cards" that one of Larry's friends owned in Hartsdale, New York. Larry described the shock on Yogi's face when he told him he was named after him. He had never seen a human being run for the bathroom as fast as Yogi did in all his life because he thought Larry was trying to tell him that he was his illegitimate son! There they both were, the son Yogi never knew he had, along with another namesake, a bonus, a grandson. It was hilarious, and I don't think Yogi ever made it out of the men's room.

Then there was my Celtic heritage, which was a bit confusing, to say the least. My dad was of Irish decent and my mom was Scottish with a little bit of English sprinkled in. Yet, I was only exposed to limited Irish traditions during my life, for my mother's side of the family lived in Scotland. I loved visiting my paternal grandmother's apartment in the Bronx for Sunday dinners. Nana cooked pot roast with Yorkshire pudding, then my siblings and I would hang out with my many cousins watching the weekly Disney special on her small black and white TV in her living room. All the adults would then treat themselves to after-dinner drinks, cigarettes and poker games with lots of shouting, cursing, and tons of laughter. It was all in good fun.

Nana had a very unique personality: Unfiltered, a tad abrasive, blunt, unshakable, and definitely a rule bender. No one ever needed to guess what was on her mind. She was a proud matriarch who had borne seven children. She loved family gatherings and possessed a wicked sense of humor. She was someone who always commanded attention, spoke her mind, and was blessed with a strong, capable arm with great aim. She proved it once when her third husband abruptly got up and walked away from the poker table after being caught stealing in a small change game. This guy was so cheap, he was cheating in a penny-ante hand. As he walked into the living room, all us kids watched as a glass ashtray flew through the air and clocked him right in the back of his big, bald head. Nana was the dealer, literally. Nobody had ever really liked this guy anyway. He was tall and thin, creepy, and just too quiet. The huge, thick, black glasses he wore made his pupils look like pinpoint dots. Nana dropped his suitcase outside the front door faster than he could say his name, which she also dropped when she served him divorce papers.

I loved getting together with my cousins, and I have to say, there was never a dull moment. Picnics in James Baird State Park in Pleasant Valley, New York, where all of the family would get together, were the most fun, as we listened to bagpipe players and watched Irish step dancing. This was the same park where I got scooped up out of the deep end of that pool! Those were good memories and fun times with great people, but then everything stopped when I was about ten years old. A rift occurred within my father's family which caused my siblings and me to lose contact with my cousins, aunts, uncles, and even my Nana. My siblings and I never questioned anything; we just abided by our parent's wishes to cut all ties. We didn't know any better. We also didn't realize how being without them would deeply affect us as we grew older, but we knew to keep our mouths shut and not to ask questions. Parents can be quite intimidating. They make mistakes and poor decisions without owning up to the consequences of their actions, and it is the children who suffer in the end. Later in life, I reconnected with my father's side of the family, and now, all of the cousins keep in touch. There were so many lost years, but I'm grateful for the renewed connections and to have them back in my life.

Since my mom's family all lived in Scotland, the 3,200 miles difference between us dashed any hopes of establishing strong and lasting ties with her Scottish roots. Mom missed her family dearly, so her mother would come and visit us here in America from time to time, for a few weeks at a clip, until she grew too old. She would only travel by ship, as she had a great fear of flying. We all felt very close to Grandma. She was such fun; loving, affectionate, naïve, and sweet. She was unconsciously funny, and whenever she cooked, the arms of her robe would always catch on fire, and she'd be patting the flames out as she continued singing, never letting it faze her.

I always wanted to meet all of my family who lived in Scotland, and I finally had the opportunity to do so. I was 12 years old when my mom took three of her children back to Glasgow, where I was introduced to my extended family. Even her favorite sister Celia had traveled from Norway with her son, my cousin Finn, so we could all be together there. Finn taught me a few Norwegian words, which I still remember to this day, and he always caught me bluffing at cards. It wasn't hard to catch my "tells." My face would turn beat red and I'd have this ridiculous grin on my face, not to mention that my neck artery looked like it was ready to burst. He was a bit older than me and treated me kindly, so I had a tiny crush on him, as puberty was calling my name. I was starting to become a young lady who was definitely no longer interested in playing with dolls.

Everyone I met there; aunts, uncles, and many more cousins, were so different than what I was used to. Some were very talented singers and piano players. They were all very warm, funny, outgoing, and playful. I remember thinking, "Ok, this is where I finally fit." While visiting, my mom's aunt pulled up the bench in front of her piano, sat and began to play Edelweiss, a song from the movie, The Sound of Music, which was released in theatres on May 2, 1965. It had become my very favorite movie of all time, and remains so to this day. The song was very emotional, and my aunt's voice, and her rendition of it were incredible. She truly brought it to life for me. I silently sang along with my aunt while tears ran down my cheeks, for I wanted this special place to be my homeland. I was beginning to feel like I was a part of this beautiful country and so connected to these talented, artistic and warm people. It was as if I had always belonged there, and I didn't want to ever leave.

My mom had one brother, Herbert Webley, who had been a decorated soldier, having served on the Island of Gibraltar. Uncle Bertie, as we called him, had his heart broken when he was young and chose to never marry. He was such a sweet and kind soul, and very handsome. I loved him the moment I met him. He took to me very quickly as well, and I'm sure it was because I looked exactly like my mother did at my age. I must have brought back fond memories of when he stepped in and took on a fatherly role in raising my mom after Colonel Webley passed away. He spoiled my mom rotten and was always there for her. Mom's name was Winifred, and he referred to her as his wee Winnie.

I would often perform my twirling routines for all of them in the backyard, and everyone cheered me on from the second story back window of my grandmother's apartment. Everyone fussed and fawned over me, and I soaked it all up like a sponge. Another audience! It was an amazing feeling, as they celebrated my finely-tuned routine with cheers and applause. I did my best so as not to disappoint them. I was still the typical Greta, always looking for recognition in any way, in any place, and at any time I could get it. I was a born performer.

Uncle Bertie took me everywhere and one day he made sure I got a front and center seat on the second tier of a double-decker bus. I was thrilled, and I will never forget that day. I felt like I was Superwoman, sitting up so high, as we sped down Buchanan Street, one of the main shopping thoroughfares in Glasgow. He treated me to lunch, and I ate their traditional fish and chips dish. We each indulged in an ice cold refreshing glass bottle of Irn Bru, which is a carbonated soft drink that originated in Scotland in 1901.

When I finally got back home to America, I wrote a long letter to my grandmother and Uncle Bertie thanking them for everything. I remember crying as I wrote it. And, in all seriousness, I began to write, "What is this bittersweet reality, this painful truth that I feel? Why must distance be the price of loving so deeply, and why is the ache of absence, the measure of a love, so vast?" Then I explained how each page of my letter was stained with my tears, and that I was going to run away, far away, to my homeland, and to be on the lookout, 'cause here I come. Oh, the drama of a 12 year old girl going through puberty. They probably sat down, looked at each other, and rolled their eyes, laughing, knowing that this little child will one day likely write a novel, a future Nobel Laureate, as this wee twirler was nothing short of a mind filled with a mental maelstrom of ideas. They probably also agreed, "She needs Ritalin."

Growing up, I would not describe my immediate family as warm and fuzzy people on the exterior. They were more stoic and proud, which portrays a seemingly cold front. But, I assure you it masks very tender hearts with good intentions beneath the surface. People of Irish, Scottish, and English decent are some of the most generous, kind and sentimental people you will ever meet. It's that stiff upper lip and mindset surface that you have to scratch past. But, when they let you in, the rewards are amazing.

When I was a teenager, there weren't many sit down dinners in our house. It wasn't intentional; the adults worked long hours, younger kids attended school, then hung out with friends afterwards, sometimes eating dinner with their families, so no one had any time or energy to discuss the day's events when they finally arrived home. There was never a set dinnertime. We all sort of went our own ways, like a bunch of ships passing in the night. Holidays were what always brought us together, so most of my childhood memories remain focused on those, especially Christmas. That is the one holiday which has always been deeply embedded in my heart, with Thanksgiving being a close second.

Familial memories and traditions certainly became integrated into the dynamics of Larry's and my relationship. After four years together, and with Larry now holding a college degree in Civil Engineering, he embarked upon a great career. He landed a job at Tonis Raamot's company, located in New York City. They immediately sent him overseas to work on a project located in Algeria, which lasted several months. At the time, it was a good break for us, as we were starting to bicker more frequently. We both matured a lot during our four years together, and our evolving perspectives on different subject matters often diverged, leading to conflicts that strained and tested our relationship. We began to raise questions about the direction our relationship was going in, and our compatibility in the long term.

We certainly lived our lives with passion and enthusiasm, but we also irritated the hell out of each other at times, debating, arguing, and fighting. However, while doing so, we never called each other a cross or insulting word, and we certainly never engaged in any physical conflict. As much as we disagreed over some things, we still had the utmost respect for each other. There were issues to be smoothed out as our relationship was developing, shifting towards a more mature and realistic understanding of what we were building. For our relationship to endure, more than just superficial lust was needed. It was about building a house, not just pitching a tent.

There were definitely times that each of us wanted to change some aspect of the other just to make things easier, yet we never did lose sight of what we actually had, which was magic. We were simply growing up, but wanted to grow together, not apart. Larry asked me numerous times, at different stages during our relationship to marry him, as he was convinced we were meant to be together forever. Teasingly, I would always first say yes, pause, then add, "I'd really like to think about it, though, as I need more time." I was lying, he knew it, and he would always laugh.

There were many outside interferences which always seemed to get in our way, but one of the main problems was my trust issues due to my insecurities. Larry was always very self-confident about himself and our relationship. At times, I interrogated him for things he didn't even do, all stemming from suspicion; my main worry being other girls looking his way. He was faithful to me, but I wouldn't give him a break. I was still young, and at times very self conscious, as he was a gorgeous-looking guy and other women certainly noticed, all the time! He also had a great personality, was funny, witty, charming, intelligent, and a true gentleman; women gravitated to him easily, as he was extremely sexy, but didn't even know it. My doubts always crept up and interfered, and the poor guy had done nothing wrong.

While he was working in Algeria, the distance between continents, over time, brought us closer. I was working for a very large company at this time, which was located on Third Avenue in New York City, and was surprised I never lost my job, as most of my hours in the office were spent writing letters to him, as he was all I could think about. We started to write letters to one another, and it was through those letters that we actually fell deeper in love, as we were astonished by how much we discovered about each other. I wrote him lengthy, voluminous correspondence, on their readily supplied paper, and used their mailroom for free postage and fast expedition to where my boyfriend was. My good friend was the main phone operator there and would accept collect calls for me from him. I got away with murder, and yes, I still kept my job.

Months drifted by. It was such a long summer, but we finally woke up, and it dawned on both of us, how we deeply regretted not recognizing the value of what we had before it was too late. We needed that break; it allowed us to give in to each other, accept each other for who we each were, where we came from, and where we wanted to go in the future. So, we learned to bend, and I tried as hard as I could to show him my trust. I have to admit that he demonstrated remarkable patience and resilience and took all of my bouts of envy in stride; he never gave up on me, whereas other men would have walked away, because it was too much drama. But the fact was, that we were crazy for each other, and nothing, or anyone, could ever come between us. He saw the real me when I couldn't, and when you've got that spark, it's a force of energy that's impossible to relinquish.

So, when he finally flew home we reconnected, and the next day he and his best friend Bobby Mac headed straight for the diamond district in New York City, where Larry spent all of the money he had made in Africa on a ring. He then called my father, who lived in Florida, who again said "No" for the one hundredth time. But then, my dad let out a big belly laugh, gave his permission, and promptly told him "Good luck pal, you picked the wrong sister; this one's gonna keep you on your toes, you can have her!" So that night, while we were in the middle of, shall I say, fervid lovemaking, Larry asked for a final time if I'd marry him, and I quietly said "Yes." He stopped, purposely looked into my eyes, expecting the usual, funny *"but, I'll think about it"* quip that always followed, and questioned me again, "Yes?" Seconds went by in silence, and then we both cried out *"Y E S!"* Simultaneously.

So, in the fifth year of our relationship we were married in a Catholic church by a Franciscan Monk, Fr. Fred Hill, on October 20, 1979. We wanted more out of our relationship than merely living together. We wanted to experience a deeper spiritual bonding, one made in the presence of God, and one that would be blessed to last the rest of our lives. Whether we would be fortunate or not to have children, we left that fate in the hands of a higher power; first and foremost, we wanted our souls to be united ethereally. I remember it being just about us that day, and he gave me the wedding of my dreams. It was a beautiful sunny day, surrounded by great friends and loving families, and certainly one worth celebrating. Larry always gave me everything, and would do anything to get it. Although I was not needy; he spoiled me anyway. We both knew that material things were temporary and didn't truly matter. What meant the most to us was to give each other our hearts, our spirits. On that day he gave his name to me, and I knew I was his forever. The band of gold was certainly a sweet token, a symbol of our union, but it could have been a Wrigley's gum wrapper for all I cared. His name was what meant the most to him, and I was honored as I proudly took it.

We both truly believed that we came from what great novelists have written about all throughout history; destined lovers who searched and managed to find each other through any and all obstacles throughout time. It sounds so corny, but that's honestly how we felt. The physical chemistry we experienced was scorching hot, and whenever he looked at me, I felt as if I was lit on fire. It was mutual. It was so pure; just absolute love. It reminded us of a love letter which was once written by Ludwig Van Beethoven, a German composer and pianist, to his beloved in July 1812. The letter was never sent, and its recipient's identity remains a mystery:

> *"My thoughts go out to you, my immortal beloved,*
> *I can only live wholly with you, or not at all.*
> *Ever Mine, Ever Thine, Ever Ours."*
> —KIRKLAND, JOHN, C., "LOVE LETTERS OF GREAT MEN"
> - VAN BEETHOVEN, LUDWIG, PUBLISHING HOUSE ERSEN AND
> HAINAIM PUBLISHING CO., LTD., MAY 12, 2008

Many people have asked me for our secret. I would always tell them they were overthinking everything, because there really was nothing to figure out. For us, it was meant to be, it was fate, our destiny. All we ever wanted was to simply spend time with each other. Neither one of us had an ego over the other, ever. Neither of our jobs interfered. Yes, there were brief periods when we were apart. Let's face it, HUGE fights (remember, we were both young and very passionate people), and long-term romances can be challenging, but suffice it to say that when we did finally reconnect, the walls shook. I won't elaborate, as I think you get it.

Larry had a way about him of being able to calm me, assuring me that I was his only one. He had a smooth and quiet way of talking, yet always sincere. I loved the sound of his voice. I don't believe he ever lied to me, but even if he ever attempted to, it would have been written all over his face and I would have caught it immediately, as he was such an honest man, to a fault. You see, the one thing he always gave me was his whole heart, and over time, I finally trusted it. It took me a long time to grow out of most of my insecurities. And although I still carry elements of them to this day, it was Larry who saved me, who showed up at the right time in my life and taught me my value, and how to see myself for who I was. He was a strong man with a very persuasive and cogent way of thinking, and was determined never to give up on me. In his eyes, I was the most beautiful woman in the world, inside and out. There was never an event that we attended throughout our entire life together where he didn't turn to me and whisper, "I have the most beautiful girl in the room."

Yes, life threw many curveballs our way. There were countless ups and downs, but not enough to ever separate us, as we wouldn't allow that to happen. We learned from our mistakes and became two compelling characters who embraced each other's emotional depths; we had a true love affair, and it withstood the test of time. We also both tremendously enjoyed each other's senses of humor, and were constantly cracking each other up with the guilelessness and simplemindedness of two innocent kids. Over time, we gained an immense trust for one another, and always wanted the best for each other. Our greatest moments were simple and happy ones. We struggled financially many times along the way, but I would have lived in a shoebox with this man. Giving our entire hearts to each other was the greatest fortune either one of us could ever ask for, and we knew it.

CHAPTER 9

BLOODLINES FROM LOVE, BLENDED WITH LOYALTY

WE DECIDED TO TRY TO start a family, and were thrilled both times to welcome healthy sons. Our first was Nicholas Joseph, named after Larry's father. He weighed in at a **RIPE** 10 lbs, one quarter ounce, after I endured 36 hours of grueling labor, eventually ending in a cesarean section. When Larry entered the operating room, he saw all the bright lights, tubes, abundant staff, and the reality of it all made him turn and run for the nearest exit. He literally bumped into my surgeon who was walking right behind him, and who yelled for someone to grab him. The nurse then guided my husband into the chair next to me. He made it through, as I think he kept his eyes closed most of the time. After Nicholas was born, I was so glad it was finally over, especially after finding relief from all of the God-awful heartburn I had endured every day during the last six months of my pregnancy. I only gained 31 lbs. in nine months, and it was pure baby. I was really looking forward to having bigger boobs, but I didn't get that lucky. If you viewed me from the back, you'd have never even known I was pregnant. I looked like a basketball twice its size had been stuffed under my shirt. Everyone said it would be a boy because of how I carried, and they were right. They also told me that heartburn meant that the baby would have a full head of hair, just like his dad, yet this basketball bounced into the world as bald as a billiard ball. My parents had traveled from Florida to stay with us for a few weeks to help out with the baby. So, that evening when my parents visited me, I was lying in my hospital bed, flying high on pain meds, and my father, thinking he was a comedian, handed me a blue-bottled parting gift of Mylanta, topped with a bow. My mom stood alongside him, congratulating me on having a cesarean because all of the Hollywood stars did it that way. She exclaimed "You're still a virgin!" "Yeah, ok, mom," I replied. Then she promptly asked me why I wasn't wearing any makeup. She said "Elizabeth Taylor always puts her best face forward." Rummaging around in her pocketbook, she quickly pulled something out, leaned over me, and before I could say a word, I was wearing her lipstick.

Six years later, our second son Lawrence Peter, Jr. (whom we call Pete) arrived, weighing in at 8 lbs., 2 ounces and was named after Larry (or, Yogi Berra). This time I thought I'd give natural childbirth a try. There was a large gap between both children, and my doctor said it would be safe, so, I never scheduled another section. Labor set in, and I bravely arrived at the hospital. One hour later, intense pains came swiftly and jolted my memory. I announced that I had changed my mind, and that I'd like another section. But, there was nothing that the staff could do, as all of the operating rooms were occupied. So, many hours later, and still without pain medication due to all of the anesthesiologists being occupied in all of the OR's, in a cold and sweaty mess, I was finally prepped. The nurse forgot the blanket I had asked for, and left me draped in only a light hospital gown that was ten sizes too small, with strings that didn't even meet. It left my backside and everything else open to anyone's guess.

As I got wheeled into the operating room, panting, I was placed, half-naked, onto a table looking like a beached whale shivering under all the cold, ultra-bright lights. My hair was drenched in sweat, and every pore of my body exposed. Not my best moment. Suddenly, I watched as the youngest, greatest looking male staff ever entered the room, as if they all walked directly off the set of the soap opera, General Hospital. Each one had miles of Colgate-white perfect teeth, long, thick, sexy hair tied back under their scrub hats, and six packs bulging out of their surgical shirts. Nothing fazed them; they were used to seeing everything. Naturally, it was the best-looking one out of the whole bunch who approached me immediately. He cheerfully asked, "Hey beautiful, how would you like a cocktail?" Translation: Epidural. He was the anesthesiologist. I mean, how old was he, 19? Most likely not, but he looked it. Blinded by his teeth, I replied, "Sure, I'll have a margarita with salt, and bring Jimmy Buffet with it!" "Anywhere but here," I thought. How I would love to be wastin' away again in Margaritaville, instead of lying on this cold table. He laughed, then warmly blanketed me and any shred of dignity I had left.

Larry timidly entered the room shaking, sat down next to me, and right before our second son was born, he passed out. One of those handsome "actors" jumped on queue, caught him, and cracked opened the smelling salts, just as everyone yelled "It's a boy!" Larry woke up to find a beautiful and perfect little baby. So with an ear-to-ear, embarrassed grin on his face, and me just happy he was awake, we both realized that this was far better than nibblin' on sponge cake, and watchin' the sun bake.

I think we had the greatest children anyone could ever ask for; such beautiful and thoughtful human beings, not to mention, both are extremely handsome, just like their dad. Yes, I am biased, but, then again, who wouldn't be? I'll never forget Larry's relentless trips to the store for diapers and formula, returning to a tired, worn-out new mom, running her a warm bath, and while exhausted himself, would then put on his "dad" hat to take over.

Make no mistake about it, both of our children were carefully planned. When Nicholas was born, his dad proudly grabbed a hold of him, for he had a *son*, and he never let him go! Growing up, Nick was very attached to his father; he was literally wrapped around his leg, as they say. Just like that medium Rena had once told me, Nicholas was indeed the child who was born from my mind. He was our first; a very meticulously well-thought-out child, and I became pregnant with him faster than a speeding bullet. The first three months were difficult; every day was unending nausea. The moment I entered my fourth month, it became a smooth, and uncomplicated pregnancy that culminated in an unexpected birth; he certainly wasn't the weight my physician guessed he would be. He didn't just bake in the womb, he fermented. When he was born, he emerged, or rather *launched* into the world . . . with extra ballast fully formed and ready to take on society. He arrived with the weight of a small toddler!

Pete (Lawrence, Jr.) on the other hand, was a very different story, as I had a lot of trouble conceiving him; it took a long time. One day, however, he popped up rather unexpectedly on an ultrasound. During work one day, I dropped everything I was doing and literally ran to my gynecologist's office after experiencing severe stabbing pains on one side of my lower abdomen, with spotting. I wasn't expecting my next period yet, so I knew something was definitely wrong. I was in fear of an ectopic pregnancy, something my friend had recently suffered through, as I had all of the same symptoms. It would have broken my heart if I was pregnant and needed to lose the baby.

Larry met me at my doctor's office for moral support. A blood test revealed that I was indeed pregnant, but further testing needed to be done immediately. I was terrified, and very emotional. Countless tests were performed, uncomfortable to say the least, but after all was said and done, my doctor confirmed what he believed was a "zygote." I asked, "A what?" Beaming, he explained it was a pregnancy at its very earliest stage of development! A teeny-tiny dot was discovered within an amnionic sac that was located attached to my thickened uterine wall.

In the context of pregnancy, a thickened endometrium is a normal and essential part of the process, as it prepares the uterus for successful implantation of a fertilized egg and supports early fetal development. This was a dead giveaway, and he was dumbfounded in what he believed he viewed. It wasn't in my fallopian tube, and my doctor was quite impressed with himself for finding it. He explained that ultrasound technology, especially in the early weeks, has limitations, and that something like this is not usually visible, but his best educated guess was that this microscopic structure was exactly that, a pregnancy. All the other tests also pointed in that direction.

Got to be kidding! How in the world can someone find a human a couple of days into development? Doctors are brilliant, and even this one felt amazed at how my pregnancy was only a few days old, not even a week into its gestation. He kept grinning, shaking his head. There was no other explanation. Larry and I looked at each other and laughed, knowing full well where, when, and exactly how it happened. No wonder Pete has such a great sense of humor; his conception resulted from a deliriously fun night. It could have been either the Reverse Cowgirl, or the Upright Doggy Pull-Back. Then again, the very reliable Camel Ride might have also done the trick. Those certainly were the good old days when this little Gumby was stretched beyond her imagination, and, all in the name of love.

I connected with this little baby boy from the second I laid eyes on him. I remember the nurse wheeling him into my hospital room; he was wearing this silly little yellow hat. I don't know what it was, but he just stole my heart right then and there, and he made me laugh so hard looking at the crooked, stringy little pom-pom on the top! Yellow became my favorite color after that, with blue coming in at a very close second. Yellow just makes me feel happy, while blue calms me. Growing up, he was very attached to me, and literally wrapped around my leg. Just as Rena had said, he was the infant who I thought I would lose, who was destined to become the child who was born from my heart.

I remember all the vacations our family used to take, they were great, but too few and too far in between. We always seemed to be struggling financially. After our children grew up, finances became more stable, and Larry and I loved taking road trips and traveling to different places alone, and one of my favorite ways of getting around was cruising. He only tolerated them to appease me. There was always a give and take, something every relationship needs. He didn't care for cruising, as ships bored him; it limited his possibilities in as far as what he could do. Not to mention that he wasn't a fan of all of the deep miles of ocean surrounding him, since he couldn't swim. Everything got very old, very quickly for Larry; he was always looking for excitement, and being that we were stuck on a ship, no matter how big or how small, to him it felt like a prison where there was no escape. Nothing bothered me wherever we went, or whatever we did, so I admit that most times I just went with the flow, and let him lead the way. But, I liked that he always wanted to steer the ship. He liked being in charge with his lady love always by his side. Oh, there were plenty of times I flipped the tables on him when he least expected it, and, it turned him on. It turned us both on.

We loved doing everything together, even fishing, sometimes catching, but with me, always releasing. I threw my line out once trying to impress him and accidentally hooked a bird which he laughingly reeled back in and set free. We were both animal lovers, and during wintertime we'd feed the wildlife surrounding our home. It never ceased to amaze us, the nature of the deer, so beautiful and amazing in their quiet grace. The very best times were the two of us in the kitchen, cooking together, often ending in playful food fights that he would always win. It was the little things too, like his keen knack and impromptu patience for untangling my necklaces, or, teaching me how to play cards so I could win against my dad. I especially loved Valentine's Day, when he would make homemade pizzas that he would fashion into the shape of hearts, just for me.

Larry's greatest hobby was motorcycles, and only Harley Davidson models. He loved riding with me hanging on the back, until I stopped due to a fear of falling off the bike and eating dust. Still, he traveled to many places within the United States with various friends, all of them riding their H.O.G.'s. The breaks were good for us, as they gave us time to enjoy our independence. I would hang out with my girlfriends drinking wine, eating lavishly, and we would all gossip about our men. It gave him time to see new cities, eat and drink at very questionable establishments, and vent to the guys about the crazy lady he lived with.

Neither one of us was perfect, that's for sure. As two separate people, Larry and I had very different personalities, though often juxtaposed when we were together in our daily interactions. We created a unique contrast, like light and shadow, opposites attracting, and it forged such a close connection. We definitely complemented each other. I was the logical one, stubborn to a fault, a bit puzzling, always wresting with decisions, tenderhearted when trying to see all sides of a story, and forever vulnerable. Larry was so confidently strong, decisive, stubborn yet yielding (always to me), a bit impatient at times, but unwaveringly sincere. Perhaps we sound-boarded a tad off of our parents' marriages, with both sets lasting over 50 years. They definitely were good examples, and certainly were cut from that "old school" cloth, with mindsets tuned into "you stick it out no matter what." Yet, there were only a few comparisons between their marriages and ours. We wanted so much more. But, there are consequences when one deviates from established and proven methodologies that define success and strength in a marriage, or collaboration, if you will.

We decided to hold no secrets, confided everything to each other, and initially accepted our slip-ups, of which there were many; our stubborn resistances, defensive viewpoints, sometimes poking and scraping at one another as we pushed each other's buttons. Yet, we always seemed to return to that middle ground that remained steadfast and stemmed from our mutual respect for one another. We never accepted looking the other way, and decided not to ignore indiscretions, should there ever be any, in order to live comfortably as compatible partners, like a lot of marriages or relationships choose to do, to "make it work." We also decided that our union wouldn't be something disposable, something that would run its course, then get thrown away because one party wouldn't bend on a dream they had for themselves, as neither one of us was selfish in that respect. If self-seeking entered the picture, with one coveting a desire they believed would bring them fulfillment, an intention that would completely impact our aforethought life path, we knew we would be empathetic and stand behind each other to support this yearning. We always embraced each other's aspirations. We felt that we had built a solid connection, one that was nurtured by years of love, and we didn't want it to ever succumb to vanity, lust, or ambition.

The words "split" or "walk away" only once entered into our vocabulary, but we crossed over that bridge and detoured, determined to find our way back. Lots of couples contemplate this at one point or another in their relationship. Divorce. Show me a perfect marriage, and I'll show you when purple cows fly over three moons in the sky. The two of us never believed in walking away just because it seemed easier, but it was tempting when things got really hard. We weathered that storm and didn't abandon ship when real trouble once found us.

We thought the beauty of our love was resolute, because we always committed to the effort of hard work in order to gain longevity. But, there was a turning point that was extremely painful; a critical period which could have radically shifted the dynamics of our alliance, but ended up being a learning curve. It was undeniably, deeply hurtful. But, it was the one that made us stronger, and helped us to move on in forgiveness, for we couldn't live without one another.

We decided to leave it behind us, heal, and somehow grow from it. Life has a way of tempting you, yes, whispering better options into your ear, especially when times get hard, but they're just illusions trying to pull you away from the bedrock of your relationship. External temptation skews our perception of reality and plays a role in how susceptible a relationship is to outside interference. But, if you are transparent in all aspects of your alliance, and you're sharing a life built on trust and truth, it empowers you and brings you an emotional safety net. It creates an environment where you feel safe being vulnerable with your partner, sharing your true thoughts and feelings without fear of judgment. This emotional security allows you to address issues openly and work through challenges together. It gives you the strength to fight for one another, to persevere through tough times and to find ways to repair any ruptures, and that's exactly what we did, and we never looked back.

Larry always pushed me to challenge myself, to risk uncertainties, and to test the boundaries. We lived mostly in a state of harmonious bliss, mixed with our ridiculous, and often silly fantasies of euphoric utopia. When we were younger, heated discussions sometimes led to incendiary explosions of external combustion, in a metaphorically good way, of course. The afterglow was always great, if I say so myself. Most definitely, we were fated for one another. When he fell short of his expectations, whenever he doubted himself, was stressed out, or suffered from anxiety, or panic attacks, I protected, safeguarded, and shielded him. When my insecurities manifested, deeply-rooted from my past, he lifted my spirit, defended my principles, and solidified my value. No, we weren't perfect people, but in essence, the balance we found was an ideal synergy.

One thing I loved about Larry - he was a dreamer. He had big plans for himself and our family, and he was anxious to open his own business. So, he utilized his skills and founded a geotechnical/environmental drilling company. He also brought an enormous amount of contacts he had made during his tenure working at different engineering firms, and his drilling company flourished relatively quickly.

Through business dealings, Larry found a really great friend, Tony Burgio. They worked together on many projects, and it was inevitable that the two of them would become close, as they had much in common, and really enjoyed spending time with each other. They were like two Italian Stallions. Through the years, they visited many casinos where they loved gambling at the tables, experienced road trips together riding their Harleys all over the country, and going up north to a country cabin owned by another good friend, where Larry did most of the cooking for everyone. It was a fun place where everyone gathered after a hard work week. After dinner, all the "boys" would retreat to play cards and smoke their cigars. It became pretty evident to me that Larry and Tony were inseparable, they were practically Siamese twins, two peas in a pod, yet also like an old married couple. I couldn't resist, and one day I decided to jump onto the tabloid bandwagon and humorously nicknamed them "The Laronys," short for Larry & Tony. I took a page from the Hollywood stars like "Brangelina" for Brad Pitt & Angelina Jolie, or "Bennifer" for Ben Affleck & Jennifer Lopez, and let's not leave the silent film stars out, "Pickfair" for Douglas Fairbanks & Mary Pickford. I can assure you though, that both Larry and Tony were very much cut from the heterosexual persuasion. They always laughed at the crazy title I came up with for them, and took it in stride.

Bert was one of the many drillers Larry had, and a great one at that. He's who we would refer to as "Our brother from another mother." Sporting the nickname "Bertie Boy," one couldn't miss him if they tried: Inordinately tall, long blond hair, rugged and wild looking, beer chugging, rock-star lookalike, funny as all hell, heart of gold, and boy could he sing too! And, really well! He's also a plumber, very smart, and if you ever needed to know something about nothing, he's your "go to" guy; the true, one and only original trivia king. We never could figure that one out. He nicknamed Larry "Harry" after that heroic character Bruce Willis played in the movie Armageddon, and, fittingly so.

Larry had full charge of his staff of drillers, all very skilled, whom I always referred to as "The Island of Misfit Toys." Drillers are a rare breed. They are a unique, tobacco chewing, F-bomb throwing, chain-smoking, dirty, crazy looking, scary bunch of derelicts that look like they stepped out of a prison. Some of them got paid from the office manager on Friday afternoons, and then made a beeline for their local shady-lady establishments. There, they would get very intoxicated while raining their cashed-out paychecks onto their favorite G-string gladiator who was hanging off the nearest pole. Their ex-wives and trouble always seemed to chase them, and Larry spent countless Monday mornings bailing some of their asses out of jail just so he could put them back to work, except for Bert that is.

No, Bert was the one Larry fired at least eight times, and always for a good reason. Bert reminded me of that character, Kramer, from Seinfeld. If the world was getting hit with asteroids, Bert would be caught in the middle of it unscathed, weaving and dodging while directing traffic, saving lives, then falling into a crater and getting caught on the ledge hanging from the seat of his pants. That guy is filled with true and insanely-wild stories that are cringe worthy, yet have you laughing so hard your stomach hurts. I'll give you an example:

Once when Bert was 24 years old, he and a bunch of his friends were in a pub, not too drunk, but suffice it to say each had more than a few shots under their belts. It was around 1 a.m. and the bar was starting to empty out a little. Bert spied an expensive sports car pulling up to the entrance. Suddenly, an older woman emerged from the vehicle with her maid in tow. She was wearing an all black, flamboyant, antiquated ensemble which had exotic fringe and feathers. It complimented her curves, and the dramatically-applied makeup she wore was as if it was baked onto skin bearing the marks of time, thin, wrinkled. Yet, she was stunningly attractive, and carried the remnants of a faded echo of striking beauty. She appeared oddly eccentric, and was overly glamorous. There was an undeniable and captivating elegance about her. Everyone noticed, but most especially Bert. The bar's dim interior provided the perfect shroud for her initial approach, and she certainly didn't lack confidence in her encounter.

She extended her hand to Bert and introduced herself. He realized she was an extremely famous old-time silent movie actress, 92 years old in fact! She told him he looked like a good little German boy (wait, Bert little???), and after both of them threw back a few Jack Daniel's shots, which the lady insisted upon paying for, she licked her lips, and very straightforwardly asked him to accompany her home. Ninety-two years old, and this sex symbol from that bygone era in cinema history was still honing her seduction skills, and was out and about cruising for some nookie. Bert, being the ever consummate gentleman, felt it was his duty to oblige the lady. So, the two of them, along with her maid, drove a short way towards her mansion, while all of Bert's friends, also "gentlemen," invited by her maid, followed in their cars.

They all gathered into a very grand sunken living room that was overlooked by a large, baroque, architecturally theatrical-designed balcony, and started partying. Hard rock-n-roll was blaring in the background, with everyone having a great time drinking and getting high. After a few minutes went by, the music and lights lowered on cue, and all of a sudden Van Halen's song, "Hot For Teacher," began to play on full blast. A door opened behind the balcony, where a bright light emanated from a large bedroom. Everyone looked up, and there was the spotlighted actress, slowly sauntering forward making her grand entrance wearing a simple, completely see-through robe, effortlessly using her body language to convey her mood for a hot and steamy, erotic night. The backlighting perfectly captured every single curve of her body. She scoured all of the gentlemen's eager faces, then gestured right towards Bert, beckoning and yelled "Hey, David Lee Roth, get up here!" Bert flew up those stairs faster than greased lightning!

The actress and Bert swiftly retired to her boudoir, and just like the golden age of Hollywood, their scene faded into a visual metaphor, and waves started crashing onto the rocks. As for her maid, well, she got friendly with all of Bert's very naked and very appreciative gentlemen friends in the pool. Two extremely wild women with absolutely no boundaries. But, ya gotta hand it to Bert. I mean, who else do you know that's still young and alive today that was able to carve a notch into their belt by sleeping with a woman who was born in the 1800's?

The next morning, the actress tried very hard to bribe Bert to stay. Bert woke up with a massive headache, and glanced over towards the nightstand where $400 in cash was laying there waiting for him. The overly-satisfied actress heard him stirring and entered the room brushing her hair with a smile. She offered him an even greater package if he would stay with her, but Bert liked his just the way it was, and said he was late for work. She drove him, and even walked him in so she could bid him a proper farewell. As she turned and walked towards her car, Bert spied a true ingénue, who displayed a muscle-memoried gait, still heavily relying on visual storytelling, with movements that were graceful, melodramatic, and highly exaggerated.

All of the workers laughed and teased Bert about his "grandma." They all knew him too well and laughed so hard that they were crying. Bert laughed too, scratching his head, as he watched this enchanting woman, who had once been America's sweetheart in her heyday, walking away, leaving him with memories of some of the most unexpected and surprising sexual positions that he never even knew existed. She turned once more, looked at Bert, blew him a kiss, and with a dramatic wave of goodbye, was never seen or heard from again. She lived to 99 years of age, starred in more than 100 films, and I'm pretty sure she lived each and every one of her days to the fullest.

From time to time at work, Larry and Bert would get into an argument about something that happened on a job, which always led to a screaming match in the office, with Bert storming off, cigarette hanging out of his mouth, chug-a-lugging his 32-ounce can of Colt 45, while angrily stuffing his last paycheck into his pocket which Larry personally wrote by hand. Red faced with his wild hair flying behind him, Bert would fling open his Ford F-150 door on his truck, spitting mad. This old truck had portions of the floor missing; he could see the road under his feet. It was like something out of The Flintstones, and he actually liked it that way! It was always over-packed, everything, except for the kitchen sink, was in that truck. I swear to God that if you looked hard enough it was probably buried under the radiator; don't forget, he was also a plumber! It looked like something out of Sanford & Son. But, he always had whatever anybody needed in a pinch.

Even when he had the money to fix this truck, I think most often the priority of funds was to first make sure that his daughter had what she needed. Second, would be bills bearing extreme consequence, meaning, it either got paid or lights were turned off. Then, naturally next came beer, followed by cigarettes, and I suppose you could even throw in a good porn mag for good measure. He knew his priorities. He'd slam that door cursing, and backfire all the way home.

This was the truck that Larry bought just for Bert, that same truck Bert never parted with, as broken down as it got through all the years. It wasn't until 2025 when Bert had no choice but to finally junk it, for it was literally on its last foot. And believe me when I tell you, it broke his heart to give it up. It wasn't the truck itself which held sentimental ties, it was the memory of the man who gave it to him, his brother from another mother; his "Harry."

But, after a while it became pretty clear that Bert wasn't ever going to leave. Like clockwork, he'd always show up hanging off the drill rigs bright and early the next morning smoking his cigarette, drinking his brown-papered bag of *coffee*. Yea, let's call it that. It was his early-morning jolt brew, something that would probably knock most people off their feet, but to him, it was just a little liquid nerve wakeup call, that shot of adrenaline he enjoyed as his day got started. And throughout the day, that boost blast had many friends neatly tucked away in his cooler. Don't forget, the guy's huge and stands at 6' 5", so what would probably make you comatose, simply refueled his battery; it was like water to him. There he was, waving, and wearing a huge, stupid grin on his face. Larry would take one look, laugh, shake his head, mutter under his breath what he always called him, "Puddin Head," then walk back into the office where he'd find Bert's ripped-up paycheck on his desk. I've got to say, Bert grows on you like an atopic dermatitis. He goes away, but guaranteed, he always comes back, and we were so grateful that he did, because he was the one who became a part of our family. And, while the majority of Larry's other drillers weren't the brightest bulbs in the box, I've got to say, these street-smart thugs sure could drill! Although, it would have been more fitting had Larry named his company Armageddon.

After a few years, the recession hit and business dramatically slowed down. Times were hard for everyone, and people everywhere were losing their homes. It hit Larry's company hard, receivables stalled, and drillers started becoming nervous and began to look elsewhere for employment opportunities, eventually quitting. Everyone that is, except for Bert. He was loyal and stayed, and worked hard for long hours alongside Larry for many months with no pay, just trying to get the company out of its dire circumstances. Company funds started to become unaccounted for, so Larry turned to his office manager who offered no explanation. The next day, she left for lunch and never returned. No one could reach her.

We came to find out that the last check she had written was to herself, along with a nice, juicy bonus. She had cleaned out whatever remaining funds the company had, and then opened her own drilling business literally down the street from Larry's company. She had already enticed, and took, one of his main drillers, who became her business partner, along with one other driller, a helper. She also attempted to steal all of Larry's contacts, software templates (which I had designed), and assorted office supplies. Only one client out of hundreds gave her any business. She applied for minority-owner status so her company would have the edge and be awarded projects in lieu of Larry's company. We were stunned. During the time she had worked for him, she wasn't just doing her job; she was learning the ropes, fully intent on becoming his competition. What made it so much worse was that she was a single mom whom Larry had helped as much as he could from the moment he hired her.

I remember walking into Larry's office and finding nothing but chaos. Paperwork had not been filed in months, their destinations clearly marked, all thrown haphazardly into an old, empty filing cabinet at the back of the office in a dark corner. Some were thrown into the trash can next to it. The main reception desk was in total disarray. When I started up the computer, it was as if a child had been sitting there for months pounding on the keyboard like it was a toy. Nothing made sense, everything was illogical. Information technology was another little skill I had picked up along the way through college courses funded by the many companies I worked for, but even I couldn't decipher her methodology. Eventually, I figured everything out and created order. My heart sank deeply for Larry, such a good man who had treated her so well, trying to help in any way he could, and who trusted her with the business he had worked so hard to build. I stayed and silently took over. My goal was to get his office up and running again, and I never left.

Larry's company, like many back then, never did recover due to uncollected receivables, and we got tired of negotiating what they owed. It was a great company in its heyday, and had one of the best reputations in the business. Sadly, however, there comes a time when you have no choice but to walk away, chalk it all up to experience, learn from it, and start over. Larry put more effort into saving his company than I've ever seen anyone do in my entire life. He was a man who never gave up. But, in the end that's exactly what we did. We closed the company down, and we brought Bert with us. Another drilling company contacted Larry immediately, and asked him to take over their geotechnical division. Larry agreed, the salary was good, and Bert acclimated quickly into their existing team of drillers. Actually, he led them. All drillers know each other through previous job sites, not to mention their common thread; their crazy wavelength of eccentricity. They're all bound together by their mutual understanding of chaos. But, like I said before, man, these guys can drill! Especially Bert; he was the best. It worked out great for all, but especially for Larry, because the pressure eased significantly once responsibility for overhead shifted onto someone else's shoulders.

Although we would never wish any harm on a person who was as cunning and deceitful as that office manager had been, karma decided her fate a few years later when Covid-19 hit. We came to learn that she died young, leaving behind her son who grew up and proceeded to sue her business partner, taking most of his money. I guess what they say is true, "What goes around, comes back around." Life carried on for us, as nothing outside of our world ever jaded us, or our relationship.

The world kept spinning, and life moved both of us forward, those two, crazy, die-hard romantics. Years had passed in our marriage, and he would still leave little love notes on my pillow when I least expected it, sometimes flowers, just "because." There was this little piece of paper he gave to me once where he drew a heart with a bow through it, put the date on it and wrote "I love you." I then took that same piece of paper and wrote something back to him with the date. I would put it where he least expected it. This went on for several years, that same little piece of paper, back and forth, where we would both add something, then hide it in a silly place, knowing the other would find it. Different dates, different little love quips. I still have it.

The best time I ever spent with him was in Cold Spring, New York. Cold Spring is a village in the town of Philipstown in Putnam County, New York. It was a weekday in 1990, and Larry called me at work to tell me to get off at Metro North's Yonkers Station, which was not my usual stop going home. He said he had a surprise date night planned for us. Once together, we boarded another Metro North train to Cold Spring, where he pulled out two champagne glasses and a bottle of Moet & Chandon to toast to "us." We were the only ones on the train amongst many other commuting passengers toasting to a million "nothings," kissing, laughing and snuggling all the way to Cold Spring. People looked at us like we were nuts, either that or two alcoholics who couldn't wait out a simple train ride to reach the next saloon. No, we were crazy in love.

We got off the train and walked through the small village which was packed with intimate little art shops. Local bands were playing on the street. He knew how much I loved little villages filled with artists and musicians, and we held hands while walking to a local pizzeria. It was, at that time, the only brick-oven pizza restaurant around. Larry had heard about it and wanted to share it with only me, knowing that pizza was my favorite food in the whole wide world. It was a simple moment in time, like this beautiful date, that I will always cherish and remember for the rest of my life. It's the little things that take precedence over the monumental milestones. It was always that way for us.

CHAPTER 10

THE SHAPE OF LOSS

CANCER CAME OUT OF NOWHERE in July 2021, in the form of a brain tumor called Glioblastoma, and it set its sights on Larry. We fought this disease hard for a little more than two years. It was aggressive, and deemed terminal from the get-go, as it slowly disabled him.

There were absolutely no definitive telltale signs prior except for one, but by then it was too late. That's how this disease presents itself. Silently it grows, until it rears its ugly head. Larry had begun cat napping often, but we dismissed it as something that came with the territory, as he had been working long hours. It's not something one learns from a routine physical, nor is it something one can find immediately when complaining about a headache, which Larry never experienced. Due to insurance restrictions, a lot of times MRI's are not readily prescribed. It seems that nowadays a person needs to have an awfully good excuse to warrant an MRI, and insurance coverage varies, depending on one's specific plan. Even if this disease is accidently found early, it's still the same prognosis. Oh, you may be lucky enough to fight it early with treatments, including surgery, which will undoubtedly buy you more time, but it's never going to go away. Estimates indicate that approximately 90% of patients will experience recurrence within two years of initial diagnosis, and that is primarily attributed to the aggressive nature of this disease, and its ability to infiltrate surrounding brain tissue, making complete eradication extremely challenging. It's also not the type of cancer that metastasizes to other parts of your body. It only stays and grows in the brain and spinal cord. It is defined due to a combination of factors, including the origin within the brain's supportive cells, the tendency of this tumor to spread diffusely, the presence of the blood-brain barrier, and the tumor's ability to hijack neural signaling for growth and invasion.

The tumor first made it presence known when Larry was at work. He called me to complain that he was keyboarding gibberish; everything he tried to type appeared distorted. All of his keyboard strokes were nonsensical, even the words he was reading, and the sentences he was trying to verbalize. I asked if he wanted me to come to pick him up, but being that he was so far away in Jersey City, he adamantly said no, and that he felt he would be fine to drive. As usual, he was being overly protective of me. But, I was worried because I had given him a dose of NyQuil the night before to help to ease the symptoms of a sinus infection he was fighting. I thought it would help him sleep, and I did ask him not to go into his job the next day, but nothing could ever convince him to stay home from work. I don't think he missed a day of employment his entire life. We both thought it was the remnants of the NyQuil that had him feeling fuzzy and out of sorts.

He finally left his headquarters to come home, and after only one block into his journey, he crashed (and totaled) his car when he hit a double-parked car. Thank goodness he was fine, and nothing was broken, but when EMS arrived at the scene he refused to go to the hospital. He just wanted to come home to me. The police allowed him to call for an Uber, but he was feeling confused, as he always thought he was a great driver and didn't understand what had happened. What caused the crash? At home that evening he had no appetite, and during the night, tossed and turned a lot, and completely unaware, he elbowed me in my face with his right arm. **Hard.** The next morning he had no balance, and the entire right side of his body was weak; hence, the elbow snafu. I dialed 911 for an ambulance, as I knew something was very wrong and thought it might be a stroke. It was when he didn't argue with me that I knew it was serious. It became our turning point.

Initially, he was diagnosed as having had a mini-stroke, but they were wrong. They kept him in the hospital, as further testing was required. The next morning, after a neurosurgeon was called in for consult, the results revealed a large mass, a brain tumor. We learned that he blacked out while driving home which was the cause of the accident and the first telltale sign. A biopsy was immediately scheduled to determine what type of tumor it was. I began to research all the various types of brain tumors, cancerous and noncancerous, and came to the conclusion that as long as the type of tumor he had didn't start with the word "glio," we could go from there. We would get the proper treatment and deal with it. The prefix "glio" fundamentally meant a death sentence. Everything I read about it led to the same fate.

After the biopsy, Larry's surgeon told our family he had determined it to be cancer, yet he was unsure of which kind. I prayed he was wrong, as I was still in denial. There was a 48-hour window of waiting until the results would come back, and it seemed like an eternity. I tried to calm Larry, told him it would be benign, but I was lying. I didn't want him to know what the doctor had said, I knew it would scare him, but he reminded me how his grandmother had died of brain cancer. For the next two days he was quiet, thoughtful, and nervous, as everyone was. I was alone and sitting by his side in ICU when a neurologist walked in to speak with us. Larry was sleeping. She solemnly whispered to me, "glio." I insisted we go into the hallway to talk. Even with treatments, the doctor told me that he would live for a year. His Glioblastoma was graded WHO 4, which refers to the World Health Organization's grade 4 classification for brain tumors. This organization uses a grading system to categorize brain tumors based on their aggressiveness and the appearance of the tumor cells under a microscope, and only 25% of patients survive more than one year with treatments. Without treatments, survival is typically three months. Glioblastomas represent 15% of all brain tumors. About three in 100,000 people develop the disease. While this rate is specific to the United States, Glioblastoma is also a global health concern, with an overall global incidence of less than ten per 100,000. The average age at diagnosis is 64, which was Larry's age, and the disease occurs more commonly in males than females.

The doctor told me it wasn't my responsibility to tell him, that I was to leave that burden to her. I couldn't breathe. Truth be told, I needed to compose myself if I was going to walk back into his room at all. I didn't know how to tell him, I couldn't. Larry had a strong intuition, and my expression certainly didn't help. Immediately, a few more doctors entered his room to discuss the findings and their recommendations to start with radiation treatment. I sat there numbly, holding his hand, encouraging him to fight. I believed that there would still be a chance that he'd be the one who would make it, as the thought of him dying was not an option. I questioned myself over and over as to why he couldn't be the first one in history to survive this. I prayed so hard that somehow, somewhere there was a panacea for this disease, a silver-bullet cure. He was young, strong, a fighter, and I was determined to make that happen.

I felt as if I was losing my mind as I spent many countless nights researching this horrible disease that I had never even heard of. The news hit both of our grown sons incredibly hard. They were shocked, as this staggering, incredulous news was mind boggling. Their dad was their rock, best friend, mentor, their entire world. They couldn't fathom how this disease chose him. I could lie and say how all of this initially brought our family closer together, but in reality it drove my children and me into defensive corners. I tried to handle it all on my own, and our oldest son struggled, questioned my decisions, and sought more answers, as he rightfully should have. There were also many other pressures outside of this tragedy that fell onto our younger son's shoulders, which are simply too personal for me to share. Suffice it to say that the three of us, over time, were able to work through it all, but the process to achieve that goal, for me, was arduous and fraught with challenges. I felt like I had been put through the emotional wringer, but I also discovered a reservoir of resilience I never knew a human being could be capable of.

When true tragedy hits, no one can predict a person's behavior when they're trying to survive a storm. However, both of our sons truly did step up to help in any way that they could, and spent time with their dad every moment that they were able. It broke my heart to see their lives so disrupted and taking a turn in an entirely different direction, one they would never choose for their father to walk. For the first time in my life, I couldn't find any words to comfort my own children. I found myself wanting to lean on them for support, but I couldn't. I felt that all I did was create animosity and confusion, which will always be the biggest regret of my life. I was trying so hard at the time to make all of the right decisions, and it was exhausting trying to pull it all together.

Everything was being destroyed, all of our plans, all of our dreams. No matter what doctors tell you to expect, you still freak out and scramble to find some shred of normalcy. I felt as though I was losing my mind, hoping there might be errors they didn't catch, or mistakes that could somehow be reversed. Simply put, my family's world was crumbling. As much as I was in denial, our sons were also researching this disease and approached their father's diagnosis in a much saner, and more rational way than I ever did, despite being broken-hearted. Acceptance of this kind of fate is impossible to comprehend for anyone, but our two sons ended up intrinsically strong for our family. Dire circumstances lead you to discover what you value most, where you find unexpected strength within. The human spirit is truly astonishing. I knew that behind closed doors they were both reeling in pain, but they put on a brave front and encouraged their dad to stay strong, and the three of us finally found a common ground to fight this battle for him, together.

I went to work quickly and sought out only the best doctors and surgeons to take care of everything and anything that could possibly save Larry. He endured 30 rounds of external radiation, and chemo failed each time, even after several attempts were made. At first, they told us surgery would not be an option, but I wasn't about to listen. I found the absolute best, the brilliant and top elite Chief of Neurology at Westchester Medical Center in Valhalla, New York, Dr. Simon Hanft. Whenever I found encouraging data, statistics, or new trials, I quickly contacted his office hoping for a miracle. Although he cautioned all the risks to us, citing his years of familiarity with this disease, he also offered complete honesty, his personal time, true compassion, and his steadfast support. We never gave up. Larry's tumor was approximately four inches in diameter, a solid mass which hadn't yet spread deeper into his brain. Dr. Hanft said he could remove it, but that in time it would grow back, as this type of tumor always does. The surgery would be what he referred to as a "Hail Mary." It would be extremely risky, difficult, and with a low chance of success; but it was our last-ditch effort, especially since Larry had already begun radiation treatments. If another tumor emerged, we would cross that bridge when we got to it.

It was a lengthy, complicated surgery, but Dr. Hanft successfully removed the tumor, although it had damaged healthy brain tissue surrounding it, leaving it necrotic, which left Larry with permanent right-sided weakness and partial peripheral blindness. But, it was finally behind us. We knew it was a small fix, buying us just a little more time. There were complications brought on from additional radiation, internal Gamma Tile seeds, which were immediately placed into the void where the tumor was removed. Larry fought hard and powered through each hurdle. He was strong and wanted to live, and we convinced ourselves we could fight it.

Financially, our insurance covered most of the bills; however, we were still responsible for the cost of the uncovered parts, like transportation. Because he was disabled and required a wheelchair, these were out-of-pocket expenses, to and from the radiation/oncology building which was located 15 miles away from the nursing home he was then living and rehabilitating in. The debt was mounting, and rose well into the thousands. These costs accrued over five days a week for six weeks straight. There was no more savings; we were running on empty. His closest friends banded together and formed a GoFundMe page. They also held poker games where they would raffle off prizes to raise even more money, and even arranged motorcades, all those H.O.G. road warriors that knew Larry, to ride for his cause.

Countless people contributed to help us, and I was stunned by the generosity of these charitable individuals. Medicaid also helped. For the first time in our lives, we accepted SNAP benefits (Supplemental Nutrition Assistance Program) for food insecurities. Whether it was permanent or temporary, when support in any form came, we accepted it wholeheartedly. We were honored, showed gratitude, and carried a humble heart. This was not a time to be proud, but a time to allow helping hands to come into our lives, and we received these gifts with dignity and grace. I am forever indebted to these beautiful human beings for their selfless acts of kindness, outpourings of love, support, beneficence, and prayers. It gave me the time to spend with him once he came home and the space we needed just to be able to breathe. It was a privilege to focus on what was really important, and that was time, something that most of us take for granted each day. Larry spent seven months fighting for his life in countless hospitals, nursing homes, and rehab facilities. He was finally deemed fit to come home in January 2022, where he spent the next 17 months surrounded by his family and friends.

Our older son Nick, with personal trainer experience, spent hours with Larry teaching him physical therapy moves, while our younger son, Pete, also helped out. I always felt secure whenever they were with us, as sometimes Larry would unexpectedly fall due to poor balance and paramedics or neighbors would need to be called just to get him off the floor. It was something I was unable to do on my own. One time, Larry was sitting too far towards the edge of our bed while I was helping him to get dressed, and he began to slip. While I tried with all of my strength to pull him back up onto the bed, my back went out, and we both ended up slipping in slow motion onto the floor laughing, although it really wasn't very funny. We sat there staring at each other in disbelief, and I shrugged. We both knew I'd have to call the local paramedics again since our neighbors and our sons were all working. That same day crew would always show up. At that point, we were on a first-name basis with all of them; even Buddy soaked up their attention. He knew they'd never arrive empty-handed, as there was always a treat in their bag of tricks for their best little furry friend, Buddy.

While home, I drove Larry back and forth to outpatient physical and occupational therapies at Helen Hayes hospital, 55 of them to be exact. I pushed him in a transport wheelchair, down multiple, long hallways, with an additional 30 therapies completed at a local rehab establishment. He powered through, but began suffering from knee pain and had to undergo another surgery on his right femur bone from a large infection caused by sepsis that he had contracted nine months prior while in one of the other hospitals. There were so many setbacks during a time when he should have been enjoying every moment he had at home.

Seizures began on February 15, 2023. All of his routine MRI's were coming back clean, so no one could quite understand or explain to us what was happening. The last MRI Larry was given took place in April 2023 and everything looked the same, albeit they detected what they thought was scar tissue from his brain surgery. They didn't know exactly what it was and couldn't confirm whether the tumor was growing back or not. Each seizure (there were many more that followed) left Larry weaker and weaker to the point where he couldn't continue with his physical therapies anymore.

One day, I caught a drastic change in Larry's expression, which shown in his eyes. I was helping him after a shower, and as I was drying his feet, I glanced up to see this immense, overwhelming sadness, and my heart just dropped. I had never seen that look in his eyes in my entire life. At that moment, all the tears I kept from him began to well up. I put my arms around him, and we both cried. It was the unfairness of this struggle; the mental, physical, and emotional pain that a person endures as their body slowly shuts down, and deteriorates beyond their control. No matter how hard one fights, eventually it breaks you. Coping with this disease while your mind is still intact, when you know miracles are now truly unattainable, pushes every boundary of the human spirit. The agonizing sadness, the difficulty in accepting one's fate, destroys you over time. Larry was beginning to give up.

In June 2023, the last seizure was his breaking point. He asked me if he could go back to Helen Hayes for rehab, that maybe they could help him. He was depressed, as he couldn't stand on his own anymore, because he had no more strength left. He said he would go back there for me, that he would do whatever it took to continue to try, so, selfishly I put the wheels into motion.

A Medicare insurance requirement made it mandatory that he first spend one week in a local hospital before he could be transferred to Helen Hayes. There were lots of tests done while he was in Good Samaritan hospital in Suffern, New York. There, it was discovered that the tumor had indeed recurred. From April's last (suspicious) MRI, this tumor had grown a little larger than the first time, and was very different. That's how fast and aggressive this disease is. I immediately contacted his neurosurgeon, Dr. Hanft, as Larry was now bedridden, but there wasn't very much he could do for him at this point, as this tumor had tentacled deeply into his brain. He explained that if he did operate he could very possibly lose Larry on the table. At best, if he survived, his life expectancy would be six more months, as some portions of the tumor were not within surgical reach, and he would remain bedridden, with no quality of life. I explained everything to Larry. He didn't have any more strength left to fight, and he certainly didn't want to live that way, so he bravely made the choice on his own to confront the end. I stood by his decision, as we both knew that he had suffered enough. As much as it was killing me, I tried so hard to find more strength, as I knew I had to get him through this. But, how does one find that fortitude, when inside, you're dying too? I was in agony, falling apart, and felt like my life was disintegrating.

I was grateful for how hospice reached out to help us, but they couldn't provide 24-hour in-home support. Instead, they offered him a room in their private hospice facility where he could be taken care of around the clock. So, in order to get him out of the hospital setting, I felt that this would be a good temporary opportunity, as he was getting antsy and needed a change of environment. I was unable to take care of him at home all by myself, and I needed serious help at that point. So, I began to search for live-in help at home, someone who could stay by my side as we took shifts taking care of him. It was impossible to find anyone willing to live with us, but I kept trying. Either they were not skilled in hospice care, or charged exorbitant fees way beyond our reach, and didn't even have the credentials to justify said fees. Typically these charges are paid out-of-pocket. We didn't have long-term care insurance, and Medicare and Medicaid covered the full cost of the hospice residence, but they wouldn't cover the cost of live-in help at home.

The hospice director offered Larry their last private room. Each room there was named after a tree, and Larry's room was named the

Birch Room. This was particularly ironic, as Larry was raised in an area of Yonkers, New York, that was surrounded by streets that were all named after trees. It was a well-run, beautiful and caring residence with ten private rooms and nurses and attendants continuously staffed. Family, friends, and even pets were encouraged to visit, day and night. They spared no expense. As far as the food menu was concerned, Larry could choose anything from anywhere and they would provide it. They encouraged all of their patients living there that, no matter what ailments they suffered from, now was the time to ask for whatever their hearts' desired.

On his second day there, I sat by his side and explained to him how I was still trying to find someone to help me, so I could finally bring him home. That's when he turned to me and said, "Stop, please, you need to just stop. They're good to me here and I want to stay. I think it would be harder for me to return home and leave this Earth from there, knowing my life would never be the same in my own house. I'm too sick now, I can't do anything for myself anymore, and I don't want to give you memories, places where you'll look and remember where a hospital bed once was, or any remnants of the last stages of sickness that will be left behind. Here, I know I will get the best of care, and you've done everything, more than enough. Now is the time for both of us to relax and just spend whatever time we have left with each other." Larry knew how exhausted I was. He stared at me, and saw right through my facade of strength. He saw how my body was fatigued, weary, how my spirit was dimming, and how my heart was so heavy. This was so typical of him, always putting me before himself. He was the most selfless human being I had ever known. He smiled at me, and I lay down next to him, as he stroked my hair and held me. He spent the next two months there, waiting, and every day I kept asking him if he wanted to come home. At that point, I didn't want anyone else's help. I just wanted him home with me. I was desperate for any kind of normalcy, even though that didn't exist for us anymore. I would have done anything for him, but he just kept telling me "No."

His sister Barbara and her family made countless trips to visit him, and each time, brought delicious Italian food which she had spent hours making just for him. "The gang" would visit often too, and raise their glasses of Jack Daniels to toast their dear friend and rehash funny stories of growing up together. Tony Burgio stopped by countless times to visit, and always brought along the other road warriors. All those Harley Davidson riders; they all loved Larry. The nurses always stopped me before I got to his room, telling me about the roars of laughter, that at times became a little too disturbing, but they let it slide, along with what they "thought" smelled like cigar smoke. "Whatever he wants," they kept telling me. They would close the door to his room so the smoke alarms wouldn't go off. The nurses were amazing, and very kind human beings.

It takes a certain type of person to do a nurse's job. For hospice nurses, it must be incredibly difficult, because they become very attached to the patients and their families, knowing full well it would always be temporary and end the same way. This type of nursing position requires a steady hand, a cool and level head, and an overwhelmingly pure and giving heart. Their focus is on palliative care rather than curative treatments. Each patient staying there is realizing their end-of-life journey.

I would bring our dog Buddy to visit, and sometimes he'd jump up onto Larry's bed to cuddle. Both of our sons were there all the time. Every day visitors came to spend time, to raise his spirits, meander down memory lane, and give reassuring hugs. Larry always knew he was never alone. From the day he arrived, everyone in this residence treated Larry like a king. He was given anything he wanted, day or night, whenever he wanted it. A professional masseuse even visited him on his first day there, and she worked her magic until he fell asleep. He was so sore from being in bed all the time, but I remember being by his side when he woke up from that much-needed rest and asked him if he liked the massage (knowing the woman did a wonderful job). He answered, "No, because they weren't your hands."

I was the handler, in what was an exhausting and ongoing war with insurance companies, hospitals, rehabs, the slow and monotonous snail pace of nursing homes, horrible drug interactions after countless grueling treatments, his meltdowns, and trials that were dangled in front of us offering little to no hope. I never left his side. The only days when my visits were missed, were the few when I was unable to pull myself together. My husband's illness was a true test that I found myself gradually failing. Towards the end, he told me it was time for us to finally have the "talk." He made me solemnly promise to him that I would go on with my life after he was gone. He didn't want me to drift away from the world. He was worried that I would recluse, descend, and over time, evanescently disappear. He knew me well. He then said he wanted me to find the strength to walk my own path on my own two feet, try to find a purpose, a passion which I loved and would be a driving factor in my life. He wanted me to be happy, and especially to try to find love again. He really wanted all of that for me. He also said I didn't deserve to be alone, and maybe I'd find someone just like him, someone who would be capable of loving me just as deeply.

He looked at me and said he was ok with that, and told me he would even try to help in some way, albeit he would be far away, in a place called heaven. Even as he was leaving this world, he still wanted me to feel protected, safe, and loved. He then promised he would always watch over me as he whispered those same words he told me all throughout our life together, "I loved you before I met you, I love you now, and I will always love you." All these words, as he lay there giving up everything; it was a moment in my life which paralyzed me. All I remember was that there seemed to be no air in the room as I lay next to him, frozen. I tried to assure him not to worry, and I promised him that I would honor what he was asking of me, although now he was asking everything from me. Fr. Ravi, a Catholic priest who visited him daily, confided to me that Larry kept telling him "I'm so worried about Greta." Each day it was all he said, even to the nurses. He was worried about *me*. He was the bravest man I have ever known and loved. I am indebted to God that this disease only claimed his body, for it never stole his spirit, he was clear and mindful, and his heart was right there with me until he let go.

At the very end, I remember him lying in bed, very still. Now unconscious from the morphine, he was finally free of pain. Hospice had abided by my instructions to keep him this way, free of the agony which had finally become unbearable. He placed his trust in me not to let him suffer if it got bad. We had both already said our goodbyes while he was still coherent, but seeing him this way now, and knowing he was still physically with me, left me living within my own inertia. I remained robotic, in a strange and dream-like state. The waiting was intolerable. Every day I asked God what was taking so long. Was this state of deferment something I was purposely given for my own reflection?

The first day passed, and the second day then turned into the third. I was at home that third morning. I took our dog, Buddy, into the backyard for his first early-morning walk before I would go and be by Larry's side. While Buddy was running and playing, I sat down on a chair and gazed out over our backyard. I remember feeling so lost, completely empty inside, as I was no longer able to talk with my beloved. There would be no more phone calls, no more conversations, and no more hearing his voice. How much longer would this horrible disease take to claim him?

I sat there and looked up at the sky. It was an eerie shade of orange/brown on that early August morning, overcast, with unusually heavy clouds. The air felt so thick and it was already starting to get hot. I glanced way up towards the top of some very tall trees which lined the backyard, looking left to right. They were so still, no movement, not a breeze. There was just emptiness, no sound, no typical loud buzzing or clicking from the cicadas. Not one bird was flying overhead as they normally would, especially at that time of morning. I feed the birds every day, so it was inordinately out of character not to see or hear even one. Complete silence. You could have heard a pin drop. It was a sign.

That's when I realized I was experiencing what some people refer to as "the calling." As I've already mentioned, from time to time during my life, I have been able to receive signs. I refer to them as "messages" of sorts. I believe they're all around us every single day, and if we are able to see or pick up on them, that is an incredible gift. My mother had it, and her mother had it. Mom called it a blessing, until it began happening to me. For a while there, I called it a curse because most times these so called blessed "signs" seemed to predict or forewarn of some sort of tragedy. As I previously told you, they got better as time went on. My Ajna chakra *gift* (the Third Eye, the sixth of the seven main chakras in our body) was clearly defined for me years ago when I had the reading with Rena. She saw it instantly. I knew at this moment that my beloved's time was finally here, and I bolted out of my chair in a panic, running as quickly as I could. I brought our Buddy back inside, and took off speeding up the Palisades Parkway towards the hospice residence. I was unaware that hospice was calling my home at the exact same time, telling me to come immediately.

I found my beloved very still, asleep in his bed, his eyes half open staring down, only now his skin was a bluish/gray color, and his breaths quick and shallow. He had changed so dramatically in appearance from the evening before; I was shocked. I thought maybe we would have more time. But, no matter how much one might anticipate the experience, it never quite matches the reality, which was beyond incredibly painful for me.

I felt panicky, as the moment was truly here. I stayed with him, spoke to him, and told him everything in my heart over and over and over. I rubbed his arms, his chest, and gently kissed his lips. I thanked him for being the greatest part of my life and for loving me so deeply, passionately, and unconditionally. I told him to remember that he promised he would wait for me. I whispered to him, and reassured him that we would find each other again. Instantly, I had an epiphany and ascertained that this soul was indeed meant to be with me always. That medium Rena was right. This beautiful soul from another lifetime had found me, and I knew in my heart, that it would one day look for me again.

I lay next to him, and after about 30 minutes, my mouth was dry from the unending talking and crying. I told him that I needed a drink of water, I would come right back, and not to worry. The nurses always encouraged all of us to keep talking to him, because they said that even though your loved one is dying and appears to be sleeping, they can still hear you. They would tell us that they witnessed too many instances to make it coincidental where a loved one would depart only when their bereaved would leave the room. They explained it was as if the soul needed to depart on their own. Larry had already asked me to be with him the very moment he passed, and I gave him my word that I would. I would be there to hold him, and that he wouldn't be alone. Yes, I was scared to leave, but something told me to go.

When I returned, I stood in the doorway of his room and realized that in those few seconds when I left him to go get that drink of water, he died. I had missed it. He wasn't breathing anymore. He hadn't moved, and his expression was the same as when I stepped away for mere moments; it was sheer peace. I approached him, knowing that his spirit was somehow still there, kissed his lips again, and told him that I loved him. I lay down close to him and held him. I placed my head upon his chest, where I used to love listening to the beat of his strong heart. I waited, but silence. Crying, I looked up into his soft, brown eyes, which always held my gaze, but now they no longer looked back. I felt a pain that I had never felt before, and hoped I was dying too.

Such a complex interplay of emotions started running through me. Laying next to him feeling the simultaneity of witnessing the intimacy of his beautiful life force departing, then the visceral sense of his loss, was so deeply traumatic. Even a strange sense of relief washed over me, as he had suffered for so very long. There is a profound vulnerability in the realization of mortality. It is a stark reminder of our human fragility, and it is so tangible. With no control, and certainly no alternative, I let him go. Several minutes of quiet solitude passed, as I lay holding him. It was the twilight of our love; the raw, cruel and unfiltered ending, concluding in its intimate finality.

I got up, summoned his nurse who came in, checked his vitals, and called his time of death. I collapsed into her arms and she comforted me. Fr. Ravi came, and we prayed together next to him. Our two sons came and spent their time alone with their father. Next, the representative from the funeral home arrived, and along with our two sons, all helped to lift my beloved's body onto a stretcher. He was finally at peace, and the long battle was over. He was then carried out of his private room, the last place in which he dwelled, and patiently waited until it was his time. The representative exited with my beloved, and along with him, carried a large part of me.

I lost my beautiful husband Larry to brain cancer. It was the middle of August. Still so young, he died late in the morning on August 17, 2023.

> *"I love you without knowing how, or when, or from where,*
> *I love you directly without problems or pride:*
> *I love you like this because I don't know any other way to love,*
> *except in this form in which I am not nor are you,*
> *so close that your hand upon my chest is mine,*
> *so close that your eyes close with my dreams."*
>
> —Neruda, Pablo, Cien sonetos de amor, Editorial Losada, 1959

I made sure all of the arrangements went meticulously, as he so deserved to be honored. So many people came to pay their respects, too many to count. My husband had made friends from all walks of life, but never one enemy. Everyone loved him. Even our favorite Chinese food restaurant owner, Andy, came to his funeral Mass. At one point during the service, Andy walked in and stood directly in front of me, held out his arms, hugged me and told me he loved me.

Andy was broken-hearted, as he just couldn't believe my husband, his friend, had died. Larry would stop into his restaurant, Ichiban in Pearl River, New York, from time to time whenever he was close by, buying his usual Lottery tickets. He would always purchase an extra one as a gift for Andy, and the two of them would sit and talk about the day's events. Larry really wanted Andy to win the lottery so he and his family could relax and enjoy life instead of working such long hours every single day. He wanted life to be easier for all of them, as they were such deserving people. Larry's heart and generosity touched everyone.

I remember our youngest son, Pete (Lawrence Jr.) tenderly tucking his dad's most treasured Harley motorcycle helmet, or as Larry used to call it, "the brain bucket," into his casket, the one decorated with hilarious stickers that would make a truck driver blush. There were so many years of happy memories wrapped around that helmet, filled with so many travels, and endless riding companions.

Our oldest son Nicholas gave a eulogy, with his brother Pete standing by his side during the Mass. It was unexpected, respectful and insightful, as he spoke about all the years he had spent with his father, and how very grateful he was to have been a part of this man's life. His heart was so broken, defeated, yet he found the words and honored his father, his best friend.

I had requested Bobby Mac and Bob Bailey to each perform a reading, and both were proud to speak on behalf of their dearest friend. The entire gang was present in the church that day. As I listened, I was immensely proud of what this beautiful man had left behind, for life as I knew it would indeed change. His coffin was carried out of the church by our two sons, Bobby Mac, Bob Bailey, Tony Burgio, and one other close friend. There were six men in total, all serving as his pallbearers. That moving and poignant song by Casting Crowns called, "Scars in Heaven" was chosen by me and softly played. Our tears fell down, for all of the suffering he had endured, all of the life he so wanted to still live, but we all knew in our hearts that the only scars in heaven were truly on God's hands that held him now. They walked past Bert, who was standing there with his head bowed down, sobbing. His heart was broken into a million pieces. This profound loss shaped a lasting imprint on all of our lives. We would continue on, and his legacy would forever live within our children and those generations yet to come.

"He was my north, my south, my east and west,
my working week, and my Sunday rest
my noon, my midnight, my talk, my song;
I thought that love would last forever, I was wrong.
The stars are not wanted now, put out every one,
pack up the moon, and dismantle the sun.
Pour away the ocean and sweep up the wood,
for nothing now can ever come to any good."

—W.H. AUDEN, "FUNERAL BLUES (STOP ALL THE CLOCKS),"
AUDEN, WYSTAN HUGH, "ANOTHER TIME" RANDOM HOUSE, 1940

CHAPTER 11

FINDING HOPE THROUGH GIFTED SIGNS

SHORTLY AFTER MY BELOVED'S DEATH, I kept handling things, as if I were running on autopilot. I searched out insignificant tasks and prioritized them so they would need to be taken care of; silly things, something, anything, and when I found them, I was grateful. I needed distraction. I promised my husband that I would take good care of myself and keep going. Who was I kidding?

I kept staying strong and being the handler, yet subconsciously avoided grieving at all costs. I was also unable to remember our beautiful life together before this disease made its presence known. I kept reliving those two years of agony, both of us fighting for his life. Mentally, I thought I was going crazy; I isolated myself and the loneliness was beyond overwhelming.

Then, I lost our young dog Buddy to cancer just six months later. It was a totally unexpected battle I found myself fighting, and losing, again. The day I returned to my house after saying goodbye to our sweet little Buddy, whom we both loved so much, I remember closing the front door behind me. I glanced up at all of the stairs ahead of me. I was broken. I realized I was completely alone now. I went upstairs and crawled into bed. I was emotionally and physically enervated, and never got up. Weeks folded into months and I hid from the world. I drew the shades, leaving the house dark and quiet. I wasn't in control of anything anymore. I wasn't a handler. I was deep into a black hole that I couldn't climb out of. Nothing had meaning. My body was so physically sore, and ached constantly. The infrequent showers I forced myself to take, the place where I screamed from anger, those brutal moments of rage, directing my impiety towards God, never alleviated the pain which felt like an abyss. I hardly ever ate; just enough so the nausea would pass, and I could drift back to sleep. I asked family and friends to give me my space and not to contact me. I told them I needed time. They called anyway. Some knocked on my door. I would pretend. Texts were returned, but brief and untimely. I responded to calls, but made excuses. I never answered the door, only for bare necessities, as I had no interest in eating, and zero interest in talking to anyone.

I don't know how it happened, but one day something shifted, and I felt a small spark of energy, a newfound resolve to persevere. I started to feel hope, and to this day, I still don't know where it originated. Perhaps it was some kind of heavenly grace. But, it was in that moment that I truly began to mourn. My screams of anger softened into quiet cries of despair. It had been such a long time now, between the cancer battle, my beloved's death, and precious time lost in endless limbo. But, I finally began the slow journey of facing each and every single layer of this crippling grieving process. Maybe it was instinct, but I felt that I needed to experience it in its entirety. Without going through this, I knew I would never be able to step back into my own skin.

For the next few weeks, I grieved and pined for things to return to the way they were, as there was just no way of making any sense out of trying to understand or accept anything about what had happened. But, I knew I had to relive everything in order to move forward. I would never wish on anyone what I went through during those dark days. I confronted a living hell, and endured an insurmountable trial by fire. I kept to myself, as that is my way. I had never liked to burden people, bring them down, or make them feel like they had to help me. I was always the one who cried alone. But, now I needed to try to let down my guard, I needed to have my cries heard, and I needed to have my tears seen.

But, I also had this revelation: I realized how fortunate I was to have been given a little more time to love such an incredible man, as hard as

144

it was to lose him. I was aware that things could have been drastically different, and I could have lost him in an instant and without warning. But, instead I chose to find whatever triumph I could in that window of time we were so graciously given, and all of those private talks we had during the 17 months while he was home. Those magnificent heart-to-heart's, things most people don't discuss during their healthy, everyday lives. Those conversations that go beyond casual talk, becoming a catalyst for deep introspection and reflection. That's what terminal illnesses create; exchanges of emotional dialogue, intimate tête-à-têtes, discussing hopes, dreams and wishes filled and unfulfilled.

After much reflection, I was eventually able to slowly walk out on the other side with a clearer perspective of what the priorities should be in my life going forward, and I knew in my heart that the first one would be me. I wanted to try so hard; not so much for myself, but for Larry, and the promise I had made to him. A little over nine months after the death of my husband had now passed, and I finally reached out for help, as I knew something was still very wrong with me. Intensely grieving, I couldn't shake my sorrow.

The therapist I chose quickly offered counseling, grief therapy. I was thankful for the opportunity this afforded me, and I used that time to examine this challenging arc in my life. I did the work, but I was still unable to recall all the wonderful, happy times we had together; I kept dwelling on all the negatives that had happened to us, our family, and how everything had fallen apart. Multiple times my therapist tried to shift the sessions around, trying to guide me to explore more positive emotions, or even try relaxation techniques. She encouraged me to bring in photos of my beloved, from all the years we spent together. I did, but still nothing was working, as I would place the photos on the side of the table next to me, and kept circling back to the subject of cancer, as I paced around her office.

I was consumed with those two years of battle. There were so many issues, obstacles I kept reliving in my mind, and I couldn't snap out of it. Seeing that I just couldn't break out of this unhealthy, negative cycle, she expressed how being stuck in this stage of grief was alarming to her, and how at this point, her prior techniques just couldn't break through the barrier I had created in my mind; how I retrogressed all the time into how he had faced such adversity and anguish. I felt like a hamster on a wheel going around and around, never jumping off, never finding sweet relief. So, this became a turning point in our session one day. She interrupted my train of thought one afternoon, it was going nowhere, and advised me to honor the grief of his loss. She said to me, "You're there right now on this deep plane, let's capture it and go with it. Honor the grief." What in the world did that mean? She explained that now was the perfect opportunity to fully absorb all of the pain, take it all in, process it, for one day I wouldn't be able to emotionally touch upon these deep emotions at the level I could right now. "Dig deeper," she said.

She explained that because I had put off grieving for such a long time, she didn't want me to revert to suppression and avoidance, and said that this would be a validating, healing method, and one which she often used, and that now was the time. She wanted me to engage fully with the pain, express it, then I could allow grief to become a part of my life story, rather than allowing it to dominate me. I told her, "I think I've been honoring the grief on a daily basis for months!" I was the epitome of never-ending reflection of honoring the grief, and it was destroying me. But I wondered, "Is she right? Can I do this method with her, step by step, and then finally disentangle myself from this labyrinth?" I didn't want to dwell on this level of pain indefinitely. She said this would be a way to integrate his loss into my life, and it would allow me to move forward. I broke down in front of her. She explained that her office was a safe space for emotional expression, and to keep going; there would be no more interruptions from her.

At the end, she offered more coping mechanisms, and she validated my deep sorrow. What else was she supposed to do? Have me committed? Unbeknownst to me, I actually made a little progress that day, because the humanity she showed me made me try to move forward a tiny bit. But, I also knew that all the regrets and deep sorrows were still sticking around and wondered when the day would ever come where I could recover and move beyond it. I confessed to her how I was actually praying for a miracle. She knew I wasn't a practicing

Catholic and shot me a questionable look. But, her reply was kind, and that faith could very possibly be a positive force in my life. Another avenue for me to explore. But, she interjected that acknowledgment of a profound loss such as this will only happen over time. So, here I was again. I wondered if it were even possible that resilience and strength could emerge from a broken person such as me. My fear was that my misery would never end, and secretly I actually began to accept my fate, and even considered hiding it from her. I felt I was ready to accept the inevitability of my own death. It would be solace and peace from my struggle. I was at the point of wishing for it. She felt I was suffering from broken heart syndrome, especially after I told her about the many physical symptoms I was starting to experience, and she advised me to see my doctor pronto! She also instructed me to not miss any future appointments with her.

At each session thereafter, progress towards goals always seemed to hit a brick wall. It wasn't that I didn't cooperate; I couldn't. The simplest of tasks felt monumental. I did as she instructed, and connected with others, and I appreciated the support of family and real friends who never gave up on me, who listened and encouraged me. Slowly, I tried to find some comfort in my own company. I became self-sufficient again, thank goodness for that, and I was certainly selective about where I invested my energy. I was still somewhat guarded, that's a hard trait to let go of, but I slowly began to get back out into the world and take some chances, so that was a huge step. Whenever I was asked to go somewhere, I was determined to say yes. But, grief felt so lonely, even in a crowd of people. The only person I wanted to talk to was the one I could no longer reach. I sat surrounded by so many voices, yet the silence of being without him, my man, my compass in life, was deafening.

Time went by and I realized how lonely I was. I eventually had a light bulb moment and thought it would be a good idea to rescue another dog, and so I decided to discuss it with my therapist. She thought it was a brilliant concept, as it would improve my mental and emotional well-being. She told me how animals can provide emotional support, reduce stress and anxiety, and foster a sense of purpose because they give unconditional love, which can be particularly beneficial for individuals experiencing depression, anxiety, or loneliness. They can help reduce feelings of isolation and provide a sense of belonging. I agreed with her and expressed how I missed my dog, Buddy. So, without thoroughly thinking it through, I decided to go for it!

I searched and finally found my sweet, and oh so precious, Harry. This poor little forgotten dog came to me and certainly brought structure, optimism, and a glimmer of hope back into my life. He gave me a reason to get out of bed each morning and care for someone other than myself. He satisfied that caretaker instinct I have. His presence brought some laughter back into such an empty house, as he's a funny little guy with so many quirks. He's very affectionate and thinks he weighs two pounds, so when he jumps onto my lap to give me kisses, the crushing reality of all 95 pounds of him hits home pretty fast. He certainly kept me on my toes!

The only dogs I've ever rescued are older ones, the mutts who grew out of being cute little puppies that everyone wants to play with, and when they grow up are discarded, no longer wanted. The love these animals give to you is unwavering, and so pure. They also grow very protective, they see and hear things we cannot, so I always feel safe in my own house. Yet, truth be told, if a stranger were to come to my door, Harry would, without a shadow of a doubt, encourage them to come in and take anything costly or extravagant, which there really isn't much of. But, what does he know? He just wants to please, then get a treat. If only everyone in the world could open their hearts to rescue an animal, then I think this world would finally be well on its way to being perfect. At the time, I thought I was moving forward in a positive direction. Maybe my miracle would be Harry.

The next morning, the day after Harry came to stay with me, I took him out to the backyard for an early walk. It was another beautiful, crystal clear, blue-sky morning, with not a cloud to be seen. I remember walking into the middle of the yard to supervise Harry a little more closely, and I asked Larry two questions out loud: "Was he home in that place called heaven with our little Buddy by his side, and did he mean what he said to me right before he died, that he wanted me to be happy and to find love again?" I called for Harry, who was done with his business, and as I walked over to clean up after him, I got distracted by a large cross right above my head. I thought, "Another cross? Got to be kidding!" This one extended behind me, and when I quickly turned around there was another smaller cross attached to it directly over our house. I wondered, "Two questions asked, two questions answered?" I realized that this was indeed a sign clearly telling me he was home and wanted me to continue with my life, to find happiness and love. His affirmation was deliberately sent, and I knew he wanted me to move on. In the days that followed, I strongly felt him with me, watching as I continued struggling. Unbeknownst to me, an event was yet to come that would coincide with his sign in a significant and consequential way, and it would point me towards a deeper purpose for my life.

I was still grappling and feeling at odds with emotions I couldn't let go of, and two more months drifted by after Larry's sign, but I just wasn't moving forward. The days went quickly, but the nights were particularly challenging; the suffocating emptiness of his absence was so starkly felt. I kept busy most days immersing myself in my work, but I was slipping, slowly deteriorating. Despite therapeutic support, I felt my spirit spiraling downwards, and I couldn't escape it, my pervasive sadness. It had a grip on me beyond my control. It wasn't until two consecutive days in the middle of August 2024, exactly one year after I lost Larry, that an extraordinary event forever changed my life. To this very day, I still think about it often, and question why.

I had been working from my in-house office when I heard a little bell noise, a chime of sorts, coming from another open program (I'm always multitasking). It was news that posted onto my Facebook feed. I glanced at it, and saw that it was a promo for a new rock-n-roll band called, The Effect. I had never heard of them before, but I immediately recognized the last name of their lead guitarist, Trev Lukather. He was the son of Steve Lukather, the legendary American guitarist! Steve, or better known to his friends as Luke, had been named by Gibson Guitar Corporation as one of the Top 10 session guitarists of all time, and in 1977 he joined the famous band Toto.

Underneath this news promo for The Effect was a blip regarding another music artist, a famous singer who provided the background vocals on one of their new hit songs. It read that this singer was 75 years old, and had just signed with a new record label. I thought, "Oh that's so great! Seventy-five years old and he's still rocking it? Wow, he's right behind Mick Jagger! Now, that's one guy that I swear is going to live to 250 years old, at least." There was a link attached, but I hesitated at first. Suddenly, something about this particular singer's name began to evoke a vague recollection. My curiosity got the best of me, and I decided to go ahead and click it. I wondered, "Exactly who was he?" At this point, I was bored with work, as usual, and my mind kept drifting off to dark places. I was feeling restless, agitated, and honestly just wanted to put a face to a name.

I really didn't know a whole lot about the band this singer used to be the frontman for. From time to time, I would hear a couple of their songs, maybe on the radio or MTV, nothing more. I had definitely heard of them, mainly because they had been around since 1973, which was during my heyday. This famous singer made his debut with the band on October 28, 1977 and changed their fusion sound of jazz and rock over to a more commercial sound of arena rock, stadium rock, and concert rock. The crowd we hung out with at that time was more wrapped up in the disco era which started in 1970 and literally exploded onto the scene after the release of John Travolta's hit movie, Saturday Night Fever in 1977.

The circles we traveled in were all listening to either the Bee Gees, KC and the Sunshine Band, or Gloria Gaynor, all of us taking disco dancing lessons with guys wearing Pierre Cardin three-piece suits, Oleg Cassini and Arrow graphic-print polyester shirts. Girls donned spandex, polyester, velvet and satin hot pants, flared jumpsuits, tight, sexy slit wrap dresses, and very high heels. Everyone, guys and girls alike, wore platform shoes. We frequented all the local disco clubs with bright lights, crowded dance floors, large disco balls spinning while hanging from the ceiling, powerful sound systems with heavy bass, and flashing lights synchronized to the music. The focus on creating a vibrant, energetic atmosphere where people could dance their asses off, was literally everywhere, and boy did we ever! People flocked to tiny dance clubs near the Verrazzano-Narrows bridge in Bay Ridge,

Brooklyn, New York just to feel like a part of the scene from John Travolta's movie. Suffice it to say, rock-n-roll was not on my radar back then.

In the 1980's, my husband and I were starting to raise our family. With both of us working all the time, and trying to keep our heads above water raising two kids, we never seemed to have the time to go to any more big concerts, which would explain my ignorance of when this particular singer's career was really taking off. It was his talent that literally propelled this band into the stratosphere. His voice was a perfect match for the band's new style. Like the rest of the world, I had heard some of their hit songs and liked them, although I never followed them or considered myself a fan. I never even knew their frontman also had a solo career.

My workload wasn't heavy that day, so I took a little break. The link brought me to a brand new song by The Effect called, "It Could Have Been You." It was actually a video and under the link was written, "The Rock & Roll Hall of Famer Appears, Background Vocals by . . ." Apparently this song was a remake of one of this famous singer's songs from way back in the day. So, I listened. I didn't remember the song at all. I thought, "Wow, they really are an excellent band," and I mentally wished all of these young guys the very best. I read that their debut album was coming out soon, and I hoped they would do really well because they were all unquestionably talented. Trev's band was more than refreshing, and I believed they were all going to have great careers, whether they stayed together or not. After listening to this fantastic remake, I resumed working and totally forgot to search for the name of that singer. I swear, sometimes I have the attention span of a gnat.

It's important for all of my readers to know that it's not my "M.O." to follow rock bands or search the internet about rock stars' lives, which would then explain the genre of newsfeed that popped up on my personal Facebook feed that day. So, this rock-n-roll news was definitely a first for me. I'm a typical girl and my usual postings and news promos are that of makeup tutorials, hair styling tips (now with hair pieces), interior decorating, interesting recipes, or once in a while, a short, funny Tik Tok video that my good friend Fran likes to pass along to me, along with those nifty little sex toys, but I've already covered that.

My husband was a true lover of hard rock, but I didn't really have any preferences either way in music. I've always appreciated lots of different genres from rock, R&B, gospel, jazz, soul, and pop. I only just recently got Spotify thanks to my younger son, who tutored me and literally forced me to enter the 21st century, but still shakes his head when I tell him all about my expertise in not only surfing the internet, but how I've finally mastered texting abbreviations: **LOL** = laugh out loud, **IDK** = I don't know, **OMG** = oh my goodness, **WTF** = why the face, **BRB** = big round butt, **TTYL** = Talk to you later. He corrected me on *some*. Listen, I'm old school. I'm that English major who prefers to spell everything out, and I get annoyed when people don't take the time to correct their spelling. I wouldn't go so far as to say I'm pedantic, I actually abhor people who are overly concerned with minor details; I don't agree with emphasizing obscure knowledge in a way that comes across as pompous. But, I do have the utmost respect for the English language. I also admire singers with great diction. It drives me crazy when I can't decipher the words someone is singing. And I won't give you my opinion on specific singers, as that would be hurtful. But, I do give a pass when a song's got a good beat, I'll listen to it and overlook all the mumbling throughout it. As long as I can dance to it, who cares?

I also don't use 200 mph thumbs like high-school kids do, so it takes me forever using my one index finger to text. But, being ambidextrous, I will brag about being able to use both index fingers. Just one at a time, after all, one hand has to hold the phone, right? My son watches me as he bangs his head against the wall. "Use the mic, Ma." Still, when my text is complete, I review it before I send it to make sure it's grammatically correct. I'm a perfectionist, and I ignore the built-in spell check feature on my iPhone, because I know it's wrong. But, maybe my son was right when he suggested I should be put on anal psych drugs. The way he looked at me one day pretty much suggested that I'm a living, breathing, nit-picking buffet of bonkers. I guess it's time that I dial it down a notch and just get with the program. TBD. LOL. ☺

Jelly Roll, Eminem, Ed Sheeran, and especially Teddy Swims now start off my playlist where I have found many new artists that I've come to love mixed into all the classic greats, from Aretha Franklin's "Think," Whitney Houston's "I Look To You," Sam Cooke's "Bring it on Home to Me," Cece Winans'"Goodness of God" and "Don't Cry For Me," Bebe Winans' "Seeing For The Very First Time," Nina Simone's "Feeling Good," Johnny Hartman's "For All We Know," Regina Belle's "Dream in Color," Richard Marx's unusual release of "I Can't Help It." But, the one closest to my heart right now is Neil Diamond's "The Story of My Life," for it tells our story here. Heck, I even put my friend Fran's son-in-law's music on there; his words and notes are so thoughtful, romantic and soft. I didn't do it because they're related; I did it because the guy is genuinely talented. He used to be part of a very famous rock band back in the day, and now composes his own music and is very successful in his own right. Which is why I recognized Trev Lukather's last name; Steve (aka, Luke to his friends) Lukather knows Fran's son-in-law. Such a small world.

Funny thing about algorithms though, they track your online footprints (pretty scary). So, ever since I had read about Trev's band, now all the rock news just kept on coming ... tons of posts were popping up, and I couldn't stop 'em. Why did I need to know that somebody called Flea recalled naked snowboarding and a near brawl with Woody Harrelson, or how Metallica's James Hetfield sung on helium from birthday balloons? (Hey, you gotta admit that is hella funny to do).

After I had listened to that song by the band The Effect, the very next day, I was busy back at work when I received another chime noise coming from Facebook. It was another picture with a link about that band, The Effect. It was now late in the afternoon, and I honestly just wanted to call it a day. Here I was exhausted at 3:30 PM, again, after sleeping nine hours the night before. Battling weariness, combined with a slump in spirits, left me most days in a weird melancholic haze. But, then something occurred to me. I realized at that moment, that I had never, ever heard any noises coming from any postings on my Facebook page before. It had happened the day before, and it was happening again now. I thought maybe Facebook had changed things up a little and that it might be a new feature, so I shrugged it off. However, it has never happened since.

Admittedly, I was intrigued, and decided to click the link because I was kind of hoping there might be another song there before I closed out of my work. Music was a sweet musical escapism for me, a temporary shelter from the challenges of depression. But, instead, this link brought me to a message from Trev; he was reaching out to their fan base, asking them where they thought the band should play next. Apparently, they were playing Europe a lot and were looking for ideas. I thought, "If I respond I'm never going to get rid of this stuff." Then I realized, "Too late, you're already in deep shit now girl," so I playfully texted "New York, that is if you're not afraid, and bring *that famous singer* along with you." I had remembered reading about the highlighted background vocals from the day before, and, I was also trying to be a wise guy. Of course, I thought it was funny and also a little silly adding my two cents, but Trev actually gave me a "like" very quickly (could have been reading it at the same time I added my post, it was that fast) so it was all pretty amusing and I started laughing. It felt good to laugh.

When I X'd out, I was going to shut everything down, but now there was another huge news link right there. I couldn't have missed it if had punched me square in the nose, but this time it was only about that famous singer. This jogged my memory from the previous day, when I was wondering who he was. Then, I got a weird feeling, as though my computer had a mind of its own and was toying with me to the point of being pushy. I even remember saying out loud "This is so weird and creepy, what's going on?" So, I gave in, but instead of hitting that news link, I Google imaged this guy's name. If I could view what he looked like, then I would be satisfied.

Right at the top (you couldn't pay me to explain how THAT happened) there was a picture of a YouTube interview he did in 2018 with Dan Rather, a journalist I had come to like over the years. The picture was titled "The Big Interview, The Large Conversation." I thought, "Well, this link is huge and is very strangely positioned front and center. That's really peculiar. I do like Dan Rather, and enough is enough!" So, I hit it. Then I noticed it would take about an hour, but I figured I'd give it a few seconds. I should have my answer quickly, and then I could finally get out of my office and start making dinner for myself and Harry, then look forward to seeking the sweet oblivion of sleep, my gentle haven from the storms of waking hours.

The segment opened with fast clips of a young man from many years ago, with long dark hair, the lead vocalist of the band, Journey. I recognized the great music right away. Well, who wouldn't have? Honestly, back in the day I never paid any close attention to their frontman. All I vaguely remembered was some guy who wasn't very tall, slight build, long dark hair, prominent nose, great voice. But, as the clips quickly continued, the hairs on the back of my neck began to stand up. I suddenly felt flushed, odd. I didn't understand why, so I hit pause. Something told me I needed to pay attention and make the time to listen. I closed out of my work and resumed the interview.

There was Dan Rather, standing in a music studio, and just like that, in walked Steve Perry. He was a man I didn't recognize at all, but who now appeared to be well into his late 60's. He was such a gentleman, sharing about his childhood, his life's dreams, and his career. I kept thinking how graciously he handled himself. For a guy that fronted a rock-n-roll band back in the day, one would think he'd be a little wild and crazy looking, a la Steven Tyler, but this guy was such a class act, not that Steven isn't, however. On the contrary, the Demon of Screamin' is a pretty cool guy with a friendly and accessible charm. One of his famous quotes is, "It's not about how long you sing, but how many souls you touch." He's also overly generous to many charities. He just happens to be known for his flamboyant fashion sense. It was just that Mr. Perry was dressed rather conservatively, and had a lovely, calm and sweet nature about him.

Mr. Rather was very pleased to present this particular interview. Mr. Perry was composed and answered Mr. Rather's questions, even choosing to share complex memories, mixed with sadness, but also so much hope. He spoke of trying times, where there were many roadblocks, and he almost gave up what he felt was his calling, his dream of singing. But, with his unique and great talent, perseverance, hard work, and encouragement from his family, he pushed on. He drew the most strength and inspiration from his mom, who gifted him a (musical) eighth note gold pendant on his 12th birthday for good luck, and ever since that day, he wears it on a chain around his neck, and has never taken it off. So, he forged ahead and it happened for him: Immense success, and, rightfully so.

It sounded to me like he came from pretty great people who had instilled values in him, people who raised him right, understood what he wanted, and really loved him. He spoke of long ago, of his days touring with Journey, and how he knew when he finally felt he had to leave. It took everyone by surprise when he abruptly left at the highest point of the band's fame. People around the world were shocked that someone could leave in their prime, at the pinnacle of their success. But, no one understood what was really going on behind the scenes. Now, it made sense to me why Mr. Rather was so pleased to be the one to present this interview. He wanted to get the answers to everyone's questions: Why, after ten successful years (albeit releasing a solo album in 1985 when tensions were rising within Journey's dynamic) did he officially leave Journey in 1987? Where did he go, and what did he do? When he did finally reunite with the band between 1995 and 1996, he left again in 1998, only to spend the next couple of decades in the shadows.

Personally, I wondered how he lasted all those years initially, constantly traveling around the world, back-to-back concerts, and living in different hotel rooms night after night. I felt that it certainly would have been an adrenaline rush, and probably was a blast because he was young. However, as time went by, ten years from when he started, I think that someone of his particular caliber would have eventually become burnt out, and would have known when to finally say "enough." He said that in the end, everything began to suffer for him. Yes, sex, drugs, and rock-n-roll all did come with those times. But, when a true artist begins to lose their passion for not only the music, but especially their singing (which is their true heart), then starts augmenting their frustrations behind partying behaviors to try to restore the original luster, then that would take its toll. In actuality, it has for some, which he clearly pointed out, and how he didn't want to become another statistic. Smart guy.

He said he was feeling "toasty," and knew that he needed to stop, jump off the mothership, as they say. I'm guessing, that because of the peak of success he achieved, it must have felt very strange not knowing at first where he would go, but he went for it anyway. He ended up back home, to the place where he came from. All he wanted to do was find himself again, and feel grounded. He tried to reconnect with everything and everyone he had left behind. Initially, he stayed away for roughly seven years, and during that entire time, avoided music. Imagine, owning that beautiful voice, and he didn't even sing in the shower! This is definitely a type of post-traumatic stress disorder, to say the least. So many people would have given their eye teeth to have stood in his famous shoes. They would have loved to have had the opportunity to experience that ride of a lifetime, and yet he walked away. The price of fame became too high, but he said he was grateful for all that he had experienced. I have to be honest here in saying that other people said he was crazy, but my heart felt so heavy for him. I knew exactly where he was coming from.

I think that what a lot of people don't understand or realize, is that behind all that glitz and glory, beneath all those hot lights where everything is focused solely on you, pressures from strenuous shows, each demanding a perfect pitch every time, stands a human being giving their best, who's trying to survive, and wants to be loved, just like the rest of us. When the performance ends, it's not always party time; there's also tons of hard work that goes into everything behind the scenes, and sometimes the strain and the pressures can tear strong friendships or a brotherhood apart. Not everything is as glamorous as it appears. Even stars that burn bright and appear to be perfect, slowly exhaust over time, and eventually burn out.

At this point in the interview, I found that I couldn't stop listening, as I was so impressed with the blunt honesty of his answers, and I respected him. He was so gentle and sincere as he told his story, and sometimes, out of the blue, he would unexpectedly break out into little songs here and there. It brought back memories of when Larry would sing to me on the beach in wintertime. We were so young, and madly in love. We would be having a conversation, and out of nowhere, Larry would start singing so sweetly to me, and it touched me, his innocence. So many years have passed, it was a lifetime ago, and yet here I was reminiscing, and smiling as I remembered it. How we would nestle into each other's arms to keep warm, how he would charm me with his cheesy jokes, how he would serenade me with his quiet songs of love, and then his whispers of devotion, as he nibbled on my ear.

I found myself smiling a lot, as all of it was so endearing and unexpected. I felt I could just listen to him all day. He had this sweet, childish nature, a certain innocence about him, just like Larry, and you could tell that he was playful, and loved to laugh. Something was beginning to resonate with me. A familiarity. So much of his personality mirrored Larry's. I never thought anyone in the entire world possessed this kind of genial, gracious, amiable, and sweet nature, other than Larry, who I thought was one of a kind. Of course, I realized they were two different people, but it was as if I also knew Mr. Perry from somewhere before. It kept gnawing at me, but I just couldn't seem to place it, and, I couldn't turn the interview off.

He mentioned that after he left the band he purchased a Harley Davidson motorcycle and rode it without wearing a helmet, which was legal at that time, with his long hair blowing behind him. Funny, because I then remembered how my husband did the exact same thing. He had a Harley Davidson Heritage Softail Classic. Larry loved riding, or "catching the wind" as some would say. Ladies, there's nothing sexier than a man, made of pure testosterone, sitting in the driver's seat while you straddle that hot engine behind him. If you haven't tried it yet, then I highly recommend that you do. I wish I had ridden with him more, but I was always so afraid of hitting big bumps, flying off the backseat of his bike, and ending up as road kill. If only I could turn the clock back. I swear I'd be glued to his back like a patellid limpet, try dislodging that, while leaving my fingernail crescent marks deeply embedded into parts of his kidneys.

As the interview continued, his vulnerability became evident to me. I was so glad Mr. Rather was able to uncover that, because most professionals are always "on." They don't allow the general public to see that side of their true selves. Mr. Rather kept digging, but in a respectful way. The interview uncovered layers of pretty intense pieces of his life. There were moments that reminded me about things that I had tucked deeply away a long time ago. His words began to hit a nerve, at times too close to home, but then I realized how all of us share instances and life events in common with our fellow man. Well, aside from the enormous fame thing, of course. He definitely shared, and I felt it was hard for him to do that. There wasn't a phony bone in this guy's body.

I found myself feeling a strong connection with Mr. Perry very much like the one I had with Larry, but it was an unsettling affinity, because it had struck without warning and caught me off guard while I was just innocently sitting there. He had a lovely way of speaking, which is what made me feel very comfortable, just hearing his voice. I was totally engaged in the topics he was covering, and I remember letting down all of my guards, and embracing a state of relaxed receptiveness; my mind was open to everything. Then these extremely unexpected moments began. A form of extrasensory perception, which is known as thought telepathy, happened. This is thought transference, a psychic phenomenon.

For instance, while discussing success, Mr. Rather made a comparison to it as that of a jealous mistress. He said, "The more time it wants, the less time you have for yourself, and the more distance from your inner self you become, because this jealous mistress is demanding more and more of your time." Mr. Perry listened intently and after a couple of seconds his reaction to that comment was 100% in agreement, and he replied, "Man, you just nailed it!" That caught me off guard, because those words were a common expression Larry used all the time, it was his catchphrase. Mr. Perry also stated that he thought that the price of fame was too high, which is why he chose to walk away. He wasn't willing to pay it anymore. When Mr. Rather quoted that comparison to him, I instantly saw memories of audiences surging through Mr. Perry's head, then visions of traveling, mostly long stretches of miles across the country, then arguments he had. I felt deep regrets; it was as if something major occurred in his life that was out of his control. He was always going and going and going, and there was emotional conflict and hurt. It was as if I was reading his mind. I wondered, where was the happiness, where was the joy? I'm sure there was plenty to go around in the beginning, yet over time they became overshadowed, and tainted by past mistakes and tragedy.

I started to think about Larry, and I remembered all the times he traveled for business, or went away with his friends, leaving me home alone, either sick from pregnancy, or taking care of young children. The ridiculous squabbles we had, how we hurt each other, and just all the regretted collective errors we suffered through. I thought to myself, "How I wish I had the chance to change the past." So Mr. Perry, man, you just nailed it.

Another instance happened when Mr. Perry spoke about how "If you're lucky, there's pain in passion, that means that you're alive, and we're still here, that's the blessing. Life is that, and there's nothing that we can do about it, and if you're not feeling that, then perhaps you're not really living." Larry always used to say that to me, then he would always follow it up with "Tomorrow is promised to no one." Then there was a moment when Mr. Perry was talking about one of his songs, where "The night was calling, and how it was inclusive for everyone, but it wasn't just the night, it was also love that was calling, and how this particular song was a balance." As I listened, I felt his message strongly, and how this song embodied the spirit of all humans, and I could see it written all over his face, too. He said people didn't need to buy the song, he just wanted everyone to hear his music, feel it, and be moved by it, and that is what would make him happy. So, for him it obviously wasn't about record sales. Like Larry, he had a warm heart and a generous spirit, but above all, an extremely caring and benevolent nature.

On every single one of these topics I just mentioned, I wasn't sitting there listening in on a conversation anymore, and waiting for Mr. Perry's answers. It wasn't "if" I identified with what Mr. Perry was saying. I already *knew* what was in his heart, and how he personally felt about things before he even said it. How would I know his feelings, thoughts, or answers to questions? How strange. After a while I began to feel somewhat uneasy, because this was a six-year old video I was watching, not a real person in the actual room with me. "This is ridiculous," I thought.

I couldn't figure out how it was that I already knew what he was going to say, or how I actually felt what was going on within his heart. How can that even be possible? I know absolutely nothing about this guy in real life. Way too much familiarity was happening, and I kept wondering: "Was it the way he spoke, the tone he used, how his lips moved, his smile, body language, or even his mannerisms and facial expressions?" Perhaps it was all of these on the surface, which would somehow allow me to predict what a stranger might say next. But, there was a naturalness, an ease as though I had known him from somewhere before, which would then certainly render the answer for my ability to understand his thought process, and how he felt about things. It's like when you know your partner so well, as if you're both on the same wavelength, so intimately familiar, and can finish each other's sentences. I understood exactly how his mind and his heart worked, because my mind and my heart were synergistically intertwined with his. But, not from an agreement standpoint; it was coming from a sense of actually knowing, and remembering.

He then explained about an "invisibility factor" he felt in his youth. His parents divorced when he was seven years old, and he blamed himself for things he didn't cause, and began to feel invisible. I had experienced this exact, same feeling when I was young, but I wasn't an only child like he was. I was the last born and felt shuffled to the side, a lot. I also carried this invisible feeling well into adulthood, just like he did. I couldn't believe how, when he was younger, he also isolated in his garage in order to own his individuality, the place where he felt safe, yet at the same time, there was something invisible about it. I did that too.

He explained how people don't want to become performers unless they want to be seen. There's this driving factor of "see me, I'm really here" when you feel invisible, which was always what drove me to find outlets where I could have an audience. Well, we certainly shared a lot in common. But, I think feeling that way, the commonality of his points raised, somehow opened my mind a little further, where a bizarre twist suddenly happened.

While he was talking about invisibility to Mr. Rather, images were surfacing in my head quickly, occurring in intervals from another

161

time and place that I was unable to recollect. It was like a film being spliced in an editing room. Another connection with him was starting to happen. Hazy, fuzzy flashes were coming to me suddenly, and then leaving just as quickly. It was definitely a conversation that took place at another time. But, with whom? Fast clips of a beach. I was walking with someone hand-in-hand near an ocean, and we were talking about invisibility. I thought, "My God, why is this even happening? What is going on here? Why are these images, thoughts, feelings, being projected from him?" Then, Mr. Rather stated that one of Mr. Perry's friends once described him as an enigma. Wow, that surely made me think. I never realized that there was an actual word, a root cause for me being the way that I am. Talk about coincidence. This was another thing I had in common with Mr. Perry, but the walk on the beach felt more like a reminiscence. Could it have been Larry's hand I was holding? We had so many heart-to-heart talks as we walked along that long stretch of shoreline enjoying our very own beautiful and desolate wintertime hideaway. But, I couldn't remember.

But, imagine for a moment how it feels to view a stranger for the very first time, and instinctively, instantly, feel an intense physiological reaction that actually changes your heart rate and your breathing response, because something is undoubtedly happening. I'm not talking about typical instant physical attraction to another person, and please, no offense to Mr. Perry, as he certainly is an attractive man, but that wasn't what was happening. This was more of my brain telling me I was actually remembering things. But, who should I be remembering? Could it have been Mr. Perry? I couldn't piece any of it together! My very core was pulling me; it felt as if it were trying to blur the lines between normalcy and insanity. My common sense kicked in and snapped me back into the moment. I told myself that none of it was real, but as that old saying goes, I wish someone would have explained that to my heart, because it was beating out of my chest. I was at a loss for words, but 100% certain that I knew Mr. Perry. But, from where? When? I had never met him. It did occur to me at that moment that some of the similarities between Larry and Mr. Perry were remarkable, actually, they were striking. But, there were also other strange and unsettling dissimilarities.

As it progressed, I guessed that this interview was a vehicle to promote his new album, as it would only make sense because it was released around that same time, 2018. Unfortunately, with promotional interviews also come many personal questions. Mr. Rather is a compassionate interviewer, but journalists always try to wiggle their way into a person's world and uncover what everyone is waiting to hear, most of which is none of their business. During the next part, he confided to Mr. Rather about finally finding a great love in his life, although it was only for a brief amount of time. She was a brilliant psychologist and had been battling cancer for three years. He first saw her in a movie that was being pieced together in an editing room where he was hanging out with his good friend, Patty Jenkins, a director. The movie was an anthology of short films about the multiple physical and emotional ways that breast cancer affects people during different stages of the disease.

He had seen her in a clip and asked his friend Patty who she was. That's when he learned she had been battling breast cancer which was why she was a part of this film. Even though he had been informed about how sick she had been, and she appeared to be ok now, common sense told him it may not be a good idea to pursue anything. But, instead, he listened to his heart and very much wanted to meet her. With his friend's help, they met and quickly fell deeply in love, despite the brevity of their time together. After only a year and a half, she finally lost her battle with cancer. I sincerely felt so very sorry for them both. Mr. Perry spoke about having been with many wonderful women throughout his life, but to have waited so long, only then to have finally found her, the one who he made a connection with on a deeper level, one like he never experienced before . . . well, one would need to be blind if they couldn't see the hurt and longing in the way he spoke of her memory.

It's been a long time now, but to me the one positive aspect that came out of it was to hear how he didn't keep himself isolated because of a promise he had made to her. One thing that I never knew anything about, was how he stepped away and became somewhat reclusive from the music industry for extended periods of time intermittently throughout his career. But then again, how would I? In this particular case with regards to her loss, I can understand, and unfortunately relate to, how incapacitating life can be when one is paralyzed with grief. But, during their brief time together, she pulled him out of isolation both physically and emotionally, and when she died, a couple of years went by, and after he grieved, he rekindled the relationship he had had with music all of his life. It was all because of a promise he made to this beautiful and special woman.

She made him promise that he wouldn't sink into isolation anymore, and to continue to get out there, share his gift, his voice, and his music with the world. Live his life. And so he did, and very well indeed, with the release of his album Traces. I think she must have been so incredibly thoughtful and selfless, to have put him first and foremost in her mind during her own struggle. To me, that is the personification of love. She loved him and was worried about his future, and she certainly knew better than him, and for him. This was exactly what Larry had wanted for me, and it was at that moment when I realized how Larry's love for me was eternal, for I began to feel a strong sense of his spirit present, sitting right there next to me.

Mr. Perry then quoted a phrase, something he told to his beloved, and he shared it with Mr. Rather, "I loved you before I met you, I love you now, and I will always love you." Well, that did it for me! Hearing him use those very specific words towards his lady love, the same words Larry had always spoken to me, stopped me dead in my tracks. Now I was in shock, total disbelief. My stomach felt sick. I pushed the video back a tiny bit and played it again. Then again. And, again. I was dumbfounded, speechless. How in the world can this man be using Larry's words? In the past, I have heard a common quote used by many people, "I loved you then, I love you still, I always have, I always will," but I have never heard anyone else ever say these "distinct" words, for I knew they were only ours. He then told Mr. Rather that his album, Traces, came to fruition approximately six years after he lost her, as most of it was dedicated to her memory.

As the interview was ending, I realized Mr. Perry was intelligent and thoughtful. I did feel he was a little nervous, as it seemed to me that interviews weren't easy for him. I will use the term *guarded* with some of his responses, as he rightfully should have been. Some questions should be left unanswered. Still, he was kindhearted and shared a lot, even offered much more than what had been asked of him. I realized what a pleasure it had been to have taken the time out to listen to this man, to be able to hear his story, view him and find out who he actually was. But, I still couldn't shake how I was feeling. I was tremendously puzzled. My heart felt so broken, yet bittersweet ambiguity, and I didn't understand why.

From my standpoint, looking at someone at this level of accomplishment, one who most would guess doesn't need any kind of reassurance or encouragement, I believed that he was genuinely a very special kind of person. He had this childish innocence about him, which truly is the most important thing one can hold on to. He still had it, even after everything he went through, he remained untainted, and he survived. I briefly paused the interview and thought, "I guess that no matter what happens to us along the way, no matter how many times our worlds are shattered, even if our dreams become unraveled, a lot of us can still carry this light of hope, this beacon that guides us forward, even when our paths are dim." Somewhere inside of me I began to feel the remnants of my spirit's fire starting to come back to life. All of a sudden, although I felt pangs of wistful melancholy, they were tinged with optimism. I picked up from where I left off, and watched the remainder of the interview.

As it came to a close, with Mr. Rather excitedly sitting with Mr. Perry in the Sunset Sound Recorders Studio in Hollywood, California, Mr. Perry schooled him on how a song was assembled in pieces, and all I could see was the immense happiness he found in every aspect of it, and how at home he was in that small, intimate room. Music. It is truly his life, his world, a part of him, not just a job, not a career. It was the miracle he needed that was once brought into his life at a pivotal point, and it saved him. Just like Larry, who at one time, saved me. I also saw what I think is the most beautiful trait that a human being can possess: I found him to be incredibly humble. Larry was humble. The interview ended and I was glad, because if it kept going I would have had no choice but to close out of it of my own accord. The emotions I was experiencing were too intense, and overall, I wasn't feeling well. Hope swiftly began plummeting into confusion. I felt such anguish, nausea, a pulling coming from deep in my chest. What was happening to me?

I immediately found myself concerned about his welfare. In some kind of protective way, I was hoping that this sweet, gentle, tenderhearted and sentimental man, who was trying to act so strong, would be ok. I was actually worried about him. What an absurd way of thinking about someone I didn't know! I wasn't supposed to have any feelings for him, and I certainly have a sensible side to my personality. However, I am also known as a "creative," and that part of me stays in the background most of the time and observes. I catch the subtle signs that most people miss. It was definitely a strange hour for me, an emotional roller coaster. But, I strongly believed there had to be a sound reason for why I felt the way I did. So, I started to dig.

CHAPTER 12

THE REAWAKENING

I IMMEDIATELY BEGAN TO LOOK around to try and find some close-up pictures of him. I didn't recognize the older gentleman I viewed; I just knew I needed to see him at different stages of his life. I couldn't shake the images that were shown quickly before that interview began. I still felt weird and out of sorts. There was this indescribable pulling. The picture I first found showed him standing next to that young musician Trev Lukather, only now sporting gray hair and wearing a green jacket. It looked pretty close to present day, someone who may be near 75 years old. I needed to delve deeper, to see what he looked like when he was touring with Journey way back in the day, so I kept searching. I needed to confirm and validate this gut feeling and unravel the mystery. I had to make sense of it all.

Google images yielded several close-up stills of him when he was young, just starting out with Journey. He looked like the physical twin of my husband Larry when he was that age! He looked exactly what Larry looked like on the first night I met him at that college mixer in 1974. They had the same face, the same hair, jaw line, and soft eyes which carried the exact same gaze and expression. They even had the same prominent nose, same mouth; even the way his lips curled when he smiled. They had the same slight build. Indistinguishable. Amazing! I was stunned and found myself starting to shake. The only thing I didn't find at that moment was his height. My husband Larry was five feet, seven inches tall. It was only later on that I found out that this singer also stands at the exact same height.

How in the world did this unanticipated turn of events occur? Why did it happen at that particular time in my life, in the middle of August, exactly one year after I had lost Larry? I felt my face and realized I had been crying ever since the interview ended. I never realized it, even as I scoured the internet for pictures. For me, the dots were trying so hard to connect; links, which strongly nudged me, two days in a row, to find out who this man was. They steered me directly into that interview, and as it progressed, made me feel inordinately drawn to him. There were stirrings in me from places I couldn't recall. These sentiments felt so real, yet intangible. To see this man, and how he looked when he was older . . . I experienced such conflicting feelings when I watched that interview. This pulling towards him was soul recognition, and I knew it. It was the second time in my life experiencing this feeling, and it floored me, especially seeing what he looked like when he was younger, for that was surreal. Was there any relevance to it? Where was the connection?

Let me see if I can describe what soul recognition is, and how I felt while viewing Mr. Perry. Hopefully, I can do this without sounding like a redundant bumper sticker. Soul recognition is a core feeling tied to emotions which emanate from a sincere and open heart. It's when your soul encounters resonance with another; a genuine recognition between two vital essences, if you will. All of us carry our own unique energies shaped by experiences, life lessons, and our purpose here. When two beings encounter one another, two who are destined for each other, their spirits align where they find their center point, and it brings an immediate, intuitive, and immense sense of connection, familiarity, a sensation of home. This feeling happens in an instant, and it's never generated from your mind, as there is no thinking involved.

People say that things happen for a reason, but at first I didn't know how to interpret what happened to me. This was definitely a sign, a message, but what do I do now that I've opened myself up to it? Why did all of it point towards Mr. Perry, of all the people on Earth, why him? I felt so connected to this perfect stranger, in every emotional way possible, someone I knew absolutely nothing about. He was an older gentleman who I would have simply passed by in my everyday comings and goings. Is this what's called serendipity? Talk about a head-banging moment! I thought, "Where is that medium Rena when I need her?" There were only a few traits about him that were distinct from Larry's, but not many. Yes, physically they looked exactly alike, but only when they were younger. Both came from different worlds, different backgrounds, and different experiences. They were two completely separate people, with one commonality: Me.

The next day after viewing this interview, I searched and found Mr. Perry's album, Traces, on YouTube. It was truly a creative and beautiful compilation of work, something born from the depths of his heart, and you can actually hear it in his voice. One can feel the legacy of the love he lost, how it's reflected in his songs, as they undeniably capture the essence of their bond, and how their special relationship drove him to find an even greater purpose for his life through this personal and artistic expression. What could be more honest or pure than that? One song in particular really grabbed me by the heartstrings; it was called, "In The Rain." This song stood out from all the rest, as if I was guided to it quickly, and purposely; it was the first one that I listened to, out of the entire album; it wasn't even the first track. It was as if I was impelled towards it. It resonated deeply with me, right to my very core. I wept, but one listen was enough for me. It was a short time later that I realized this was the final touch, my aha moment, the conclusion to understanding what something was trying to communicate to me through this poignant song, which Mr. Perry sang so beautifully.

I wondered, "Where was his mind, what was he thinking when he wrote this?" It was so very haunting. I listened, and found myself thrown right back to that crossroad again. That fork in my life, where I knew I needed to find the strength to help Larry fight one more time. Only this battle was different, a never-ending defeat. For a short while in the beginning, we actually talked ourselves into believing we were going to win and it would all finally just go away. Yes, we were living in denial. "Love will conquer all," people kept telling us. "Don't give up, we're praying for you." But, towards the end we were both so forlorn. We had hoped and believed that maybe we could love all the cancer away. I guess a lot of people feel this way when they live beneath the desperate shadows of a terminal illness. One day, I said to Larry, "God's got to be listening and seeing all the effort we're putting in, right?" He held me. In my mind, I would not surrender, or even negotiate the terms of our battle. It would be the enemy who would be forced to capitulate unconditionally! We had come equipped with an arsenal of weapons, our love leading the charge, only to eventually lose the war, which cancer over time, slyly cheated, shredded all hope, and then mendaciously defeated us. It won, and collected my beloved's life as its final trophy.

From the beginning as I watched that interview, my mind had been swirling with jarring contrasts of emotions; the juxtaposition of joyful memories and a tragic outcome, and the bittersweet profundity of a great loss. My sentiments of present-day sorrow were mingled with the happiness from my past, both clashing. I felt rattled, yet my heart was greatly stirred, and I didn't want to negate the beauty of what was trying to come through. Everything had been placed directly in front of me. Like a standard deck of tarot cards on a table. Pick a card, any card, the choice is yours. It was as if something was trying to guide me all along, up until this point, and then make me take a long, hard look. Without knowing it, my heart chose the Ten of Swords; it is the card that symbolizes the end of a cycle, a period of intense struggle, and the need to release the past and embrace new beginnings. Something was urging me to examine closely an ending that should be just that, a denouement, and to certainly not carry any more war-induced psychological wounds.

It was strange how it all pieced together perfectly only on those two consecutive days. Did it happen in order to give me a reason to finally remember everything before the illness happened and my heartache began? Up until that point, I couldn't recall anything. I kept dwelling, day after day, about Larry's battle with cancer, the finality of losing him, the struggles within our family dynamic, and then finally losing our beautiful and loving dog, Buddy. Grief has a way of focusing your attention on the things that break you, but now it was all coming back.

I felt beholden to this sign which allowed my mind to venture back to the years of the beautiful life I had built with Larry. After those two days, thoughts of cancer started to become further and further from my mind, until all I could see were the great memories I had made with my beloved. To unburden oneself can be freeing, but it still gave me great pause. Was this the beginning of healing? Had synchronicity come to guide me towards closure? Should I share any of this with anyone? I opened my journal, and began to write. A sense of ease washed over me and I felt like I could breathe again. Anxieties started to fade as I wrote about this experience.

I'm a pretty logical person, but weeks later I still couldn't shake this feeling. I went out of my way to backtrack my steps thinking I would find something that could explain why it all happened the way it did. It took awhile, but around the end of September, I finally located that first news posting about the band, The Effect, from my Facebook page, containing that very first link. However, this time it didn't bring me to a video song, and a Google image search of Steve Perry's name did not lead me to an interview. Strange.

While writing, a really crazy thought occurred to me: What if I penned a nice letter to Mr. Perry? At the very least, I wanted to express how (unbeknownst to him) he was my miracle. I had a way to get it to him through a mutual friend too, but I stopped. I knew that would be too intrusive, as I've read that he's very private, just as I am. Common sense told me that my initial, knee-jerk reaction was not the best route to take. Besides, with my luck I'd probably end up getting a knock on my front door from the local sheriff, gifting me with a restraining order, c/o of Steve Perry. No, I decided to let it be. For what it's worth, if I ever did meet him, I would prefer to gain his respect, most certainly not his disdain. My intuition tells me he would take the time out of his day to find a little quiet space, and read my story, so I have decided to send it to him through legal, professional channels, in a courteous manner. I will autograph it, and express my deepest and most heartfelt gratitude. I hope he reads it, for had it not been for him, I know that my life would have turned out drastically different.

I can't possibly be the only person who can pick up on signs, especially when they're intentionally placed directly in front of you. Call it whatever you want: A sixth sense, a third eye, foresight, clairvoyance etc. Labels for synchronicity never mattered to me, although that medium Rena told me she saw my Ajna chakra, the third eye. When these strange occurrences happen, they solidify their existence each and every time. But in all honesty, when they're given, you rarely know what to expect, and there's nothing more heartbreaking when you receive a sign that only briefly shows you a glimpse into a past memory, one which connects with you for a mere flash in time, then it's wiped away. It doesn't allow you to draw a concrete conclusion, as it's too quick.

Some days, I wonder if it would be easier remaining ignorant; just living my life blissfully happy and dealing with things as they come. No, I'm afraid not, and I have my mother to thank for that. As I watched that interview, the floodgates opened and brought back my beautiful life with Larry. But, along with it brought visions of something else, something that I once actually held within my own two hands, a piece of matter that was off the charts amazing, but was now something I could no longer touch. That part of it left me feeling heavy-hearted and drained.

I understand how the actress Shirley MacLaine explored the concept of past lives. She wrote about this topic and explained her thoughts on this subject many times during her public appearances. To all of you naysayers, I beg to differ. She has detailed her belief in reincarnation, and the potential impact of past lives on her present life and career. I know the feeling, whether they are merely snippets of memories appearing in dreams, or signs received strong and deliberate, or sometimes only vague. But, all in all, I can tell you firsthand how synchronicity teases you, frustrates you, and sometimes actually leaves you either emotionally or physically sick.

Yes, signs are very real, and this one in particular was surely the greatest one that ever happened to me. It was forcibly willful, and most certainly directed towards me. It helped to finally start the true, and heartbreaking beginning of acceptance, coming to terms with my loss, and at the same time, pointed me in a direction that enabled me to find a renewed passion for my life. I'll never look upon this particular sign in a negative light; on the contrary, it spotlighted the very path I was destined to walk.

Every day now, as I try to move forward, I am still brokenhearted over Larry's death, but I keep that to myself. You see, I am honoring my promise too. I suppose the hardest thing is the reality that I must surrender to this grief, which is impossible to understand until it is yours. I now believe we must try to rebuild our lives so we can start retracing the steps back to a time when there was once joy. From childhood, I was taught to always be strong and not to show weakness. I thought I was bulletproof, but what I have learned out of all of this is, that true strength is weakness. Life's trials should not be avoided. Our tears must fall. We should then continue to move forward as we try and seek out meaningful possibilities that will arise in the aftermath of this tsunami, and while doing this, keep carrying that little beacon of light that still shines within all of us. Let's begin to nurture the flame of hope and the integrity of our truths.

I remain open-hearted, as it has always been my nature to try to find the good in everything and everyone. Whenever I can, I practice what the great Dolly Parton once said, "If you see someone without a smile, give them one of yours." I'm happy-go-lucky, and I love to joke around constantly. I like to keep things light and always try to make others' days a little brighter. I know, I hear it too; I'm starting to sound like a cliché from an online dating site. But the truth is that I do tend to wear my heart, well, everything, on my sleeve, a personal trait that is perhaps my downfall, and something I should have gotten a much better handle on a long time ago. I'm not cut out to wear a thick coat of armor like the rest of the world seems to have mastered. One might think I'm made of steel since I'm from New York, but honestly, I'm not. I've always told it like it is and I don't bullshit around, but I also aim to treat others with compassion and respect, so I take care, so as not to hurt their feelings. I am committed to treating people with kindness, so I would rather focus on a gentle and gracious delivery, choose my words carefully, and try to find the balance between honesty and tact, which I believe is the key to empathetic communication. Can't we all just get along? ☺

CHAPTER 13

WISTFUL NOSTALGIA

I HAVEN'T A CLUE AS to what Mr. Perry is doing with his life nowadays. I did notice on a Facebook posting that he made his third Christmas album. Apparently, Christmas is also his favorite holiday. I have not celebrated Christmas since I lost my Larry, I just can't seem to find it anymore. It was always my very favorite holiday, the one I truly cherished. We both did.

I used to decorate our home like it was the North Pole. You couldn't move without tripping over or bumping into jolly snowmen, Santa Claus figurines, assorted nutcrackers, singing caroler statues, or angels. Everything was illuminated, shining, gleaming, or sparkling, and mistletoe was always hanging and waiting for the next kiss. The air in our home was always scented with cinnamon and apples. So many years of great memories with family, good company, gifts, and great food. I would make a special breakfast for my family on Christmas morning and then we would open fun gifts while listening to the Yule Log which was playing on our TV. Larry was always the designated garbage-bag holder, but I'd quickly snatch those pretty bows to rescue them, to give them a second chance, so that I could reuse them the following year. Nope, not cheap; just thrifty.

I especially loved decorating our tree with brilliant lights, both white and colored, as bright as the ones in Rockefeller Center. Our tree was always real, the scent incredible, very wide and tall enough where it touched the ceiling (there are still small marks, tiny scratches left there that I don't have the heart to paint over). It was always adorned with old and treasured bulbs which had been passed down to us from generations before. I would hang little pictures of family and friends whom we loved and lost, and of course, lots and lots of tinsel. I always believed that a Christmas tree should not only be festive, but should also be a beautiful reflection of what you hold dearest to your heart. The way one decorates it should tell a story of family, dear friends, memories from the old days echoing the past, with future wishes holding pending dreams yet to come.

Christmas for me, has always been solely about giving. In my sneaky way, I try to find out what would make someone really happy, a gift they could open that they'd never buy for themselves. I'm that nutty lady sitting on the side biting my lip in anticipation, waiting as they open the gift I took my time wrapping with care, then seeing their faces light up! I've always been indifferent as to what anyone ever gave to me. Except in the cases of Larry or my children, that is. Larry was so good to me and always knew exactly what would touch my heart. And, most times it shined rather beautifully; he knew I loved jewelry! Those gorgeous trinkets always came from his heart, and they held promises of forever. I always worried that whatever gifts my children would buy for me would be too costly. Kids mean well, but parents hope that they're saving their money, not spending it. Regardless, I would fuss over their gifts, no matter what they were, for I knew it came from their hearts. I would also go out of my way to make sure that anyone who came to our home to visit for Christmas, even if I didn't know them, would never leave empty-handed. To me, it's a time for giving, a day to tell those you love how you feel about them, and a time for remembrance. It's incredible, this joy of giving, and how you absorb it when it's given back to you in surprising ways, but especially how gratitude threads its way into the spirit of it all.

The top of our tree was always adorned by an angel, but much later on it became a star. I would hang lollipops, candy canes, and Hershey's kisses from its branches, so that everyone, whether young or old, could grab one on a whim while passing by. As the years went by, and our children became adults, they would still pitch in and help to decorate the tree in the evening. We had great laughs, sometimes making a little too merry, but my family quickly learned that the tree wouldn't stay that way. They always came to discover the ornaments they previously placed the night before were no longer hanging in the same spot the next morning. Over time, they didn't help out anymore, they gave up. You see, when everyone went to bed, this control-freak mom would rearrange everything so that it was absolutely perfect; otherwise, she couldn't sleep. I placed the smaller bulbs on the top, ascending in size the further down the tree they went. There was stability and symmetry. Tinsel was also removed, then gently placed back, just a fragile couple of strands at a time falling from each branch to resemble real icicles, never thick, clumped up piles of aluminum thrown at the tree by (maybe, not judging) slightly-intoxicated younger humans who had celebrated a bit too much. Everyone would shake their heads, laugh it off, and chalk it all up to their ditzy Libra mom, who was always searching for that perfect balance.

Thanksgiving Day was always the second runner up on my list of favorites. The mornings always began early with my husband rising and prepping the turkey, with our oldest son Nick assisting him. Although our son attended that famous hospitality and culinary arts university, Johnson & Wales, and earned his degree there, he never continued his career in that industry; instead, he opted to go in another direction. Still, he has his dad's love of cooking, which I'm sure his wife now appreciates. Together, they would run the kitchen on Thanksgiving Day. I wasn't ever allowed in (only in the lowest capacity of sous chef, aka, the chopper or the cleaner upper), as both master chefs prepared everything Italian style, using old recipes learned from Larry's mother, who was a phenomenal cook. She was a natural, and measured everything only by eye. She had been schooled by her father, who had learned the art of food when he grew up in Italy. She came from very frugal beginnings, from people who knew how to stretch a dollar, who lived through the depression, yet never went hungry.

I personally learned a lot from her, especially her gravy recipe and how to make her wonderful meatballs. That's right; it's gravy, *NOT* sauce! This noun is now spoken by a Celtic girl, who has been imbued with true Italian passion. Not many recipes came from my side of the family. But, I still do have a couple of my mom's that were handed down, like homemade short bread, Yorkshire pudding, chocolate fudge, not to mention the millions of cuisine ideas I found, all clipped from magazines, that she stored in a bread box. If I view any more little scribblings on how to make Chicken a la King, or green bean casserole with fried crunchy onions straight out of the can . . . I'm going to throw up! Oh dear God! The poor little thing couldn't cook to save her life; good thing she was pretty.

Thanksgiving was always such a happy day in our home, with me tidying up and decorating the table in anticipation of a fun, engaging and delicious dinner, turning on the TV at 9 a.m. to watch March of The Wooden Soldiers, circa 1934, starring Oliver Hardy and Stan Laurel (which yes, I still watch to this very day). Of course, my favorite also starred in it, William Felix Knight, the American tenor with those bedroom eyes. I had such a crush on him. I was so jealous of the actress Charlotte Henry who played the character Bo Peep; Tom Tom Piper certainly wouldn't have had to tie my bonnet to a weather vane to get a kiss, nor use any tricks to corner me so he could reach in for a smooch, as my lips would have been puckered up ready, willing and able! Larry always gave me a pass on that one, most likely due to the fact that Mr. Knight was not considered competition being that he took his final bow on June 18, 1998. Heaven certainly gained a most beautiful star.

Next was always the Macy's Thanksgiving Day parade, live from New York City, with a star-studded cast, especially those legendary Rockettes, ending with the brightest star of them all, Santa Claus himself! It is a fact that there hasn't been one year I've watched Santa riding his sleigh down 34th Street, topping off the parade into Herald Square, where I haven't cried. To this day, I feel a strong pulling in my heart when I see it. It's a magical emotion which comes from watching him, and everyone all around him, singing and celebrating the start of the Christmas season with the holiday now just a few short weeks away. I feel the anticipation, and somewhere inside of me remains that child who still believes.

But, then reality hits me. You see, the holidays are tough for those of us who are left behind. My entire life has been reimagined for me now, and sadly, that now includes Christmas. When the season begins, I don't have the spirit anymore to put up a Christmas tree or decorate my house. To me, my home has turned into a house. It feels empty. I can't find it in my heart now that I am all by myself. If I wasn't all alone, then that most definitely would be a horse of a different color. But, for the time being, as selfish as it sounds, I'm just going to come right out and say it: I feel bereft and discarded in a way, like that sad little song that Faith Hill sings from Dr. Seuss' How The Grinch Stole Christmas soundtrack, "Where Are You Christmas?" It's a feeling akin to being forgotten. In telling you my heart, I do hope that one day Christmas will come back and remember me, because deep down I just want to be guided back to those bygone days of innocence, and experience that nostalgic Christmas spirit I once felt. But, I can't do it alone.

Those dreams I kept in my heart, those days of growing old with Larry, with both of us being referred to as "Gammie and Pops," awaiting the grandkids on Christmas Day, are now forever gone. For me, it's bittersweet, as a part of my husband still lives on through them, and of course, I will always be forever grateful for that. But, I also know that I'm not cut out to be that *grandma* who entertains the family solo. I miss the teamwork I had with my husband around the holidays; we were such a good balance, and everyone always enjoyed the holiday memories made in our home. So, the time has come for me to bid a final adieu to all the beautiful, and cherished decorations Larry and I collected throughout the years. It's only right that I've slowly started giving them to my children; it is now time for them to make their own memories.

Sometimes, around the holidays, those of us who have been widowed feel a bit like we're starring in some kind of sad movie. I know that for me, I'm definitely very dramatic about it: I'm that lonely soul who's standing outside in the deep, cold snow peering through a window with her nose pressed up against the glass, looking in. All I want is to be on the inside, sitting next to that warm fire, being held closely within someone's arms, caressed and loved and accepted for all that I am. Ok, I'll take my Oscar now. All kidding aside, Christmas lately has just made my heart feel so empty. I visit with everyone I love around this holiday, but there's no enthusiasm, no interest on my part, other than enjoying everyone's company. I admire their Christmas trees and their beautiful decorations, but it triggers memories, a sense of loss, and makes me reflect on the past beauty of what was once my very own. I'm trying so hard to embrace this transition, and acknowledge the profound significance of letting it all go. It's time to reframe the picture of what used to be. So, I fake disingenuous laughter, because I don't want to burden them with my sadness, but anyone who really knows me, who loves me, can clearly see it in my eyes, and it's always the same person, my sister-in-law Barbara. She's the whole package; the sweetest, kindest human being, the type of person you can open your soul to, a person so approachable and genuine, a great listener, non-judgmental, and she never expects anything in return. The world is a beautiful place because she lives in it.

Barbara calls me on it every time. She hugs me and tells me everything is going to be ok, as she slips a glass of wine into my hand, hoping to soothe my sadness, yet the grapes fuel my tears instead. For both of us, the wine lifts the veil, revealing our paradox, how we can be broken, yet still find ways to become whole again. We cry together, because her heart is heavy too, as he was her little brother, the baby boy that she begged her mom to bring into the world.

Ever notice how holidays are joyous, yet carry layers of remorse which tug at our hearts, because we miss those dear family members, friends, or lovers who are no longer with us? Why is that? Why can't holidays just bring sheer joy and nothing else? Shouldn't holidays solely be intended to be a time of warmth and togetherness, allow us to express our love through gifts, while also honoring our spiritual beliefs? I guess what that very wise Mr. Perry said is true: "If you're lucky, there's pain in passion, that means that you're alive, and we're still here, that's the blessing." At Christmastime, the blessings are our lives continuing to live well, and also the remembrance of those whom we have loved and lost. So, I'll accept it and take both sides of that holiday coin any day. I'll keep the laughter, along with the tears, and remain forever grateful while keeping the pain from my passion deeply embedded in my heart.

Unfortunately, somewhere along the way, I learned the hard way how presents aren't promises, and smiles donned are not always genuine. I finally faced the defeat of my loss. And so now, and for any time of the year for that matter, I am forward-looking, keeping my head up, eyes straight ahead, and with the grace of a woman, I am ameliorating dire circumstances to build a brighter tomorrow. And I know that somewhere along the way, Christmas will find me again.

I realize now how it wasn't in the cards for us; it's as if our future fell down in mid-flight. When I visit my grandkids, I'm now known humorously as "Glam Ma," that attractive, single gal who pops by from time to time, but is moving ahead with her life. Who would have imagined that? Oh, I'll be around to make sure I cause just a smidge of chaos, unleash a few sprinkles of mayhem, like loading them up on sugar treats before their bedtime when mommy's not looking (she's such a great and attentive mother, so I need to be a little slick with that one), or when they're older, I'll take them to get their belly buttons pierced, just so I can drive their parents nuts. My kids drove me crazy when they were young, so it's only fair that I return the favor. But, I promise I'll do it in a very loving way. Don't forget: Mischievous is my middle name.

When I think back to when we were raising our two sons, I recall us as being good parents. Actually, Larry was a great father. Me? I was a good mother, I did try my best. Having had two sons, and no daughters, meant there were some very challenging moments growing up where their dad had to step in and guide them, man-to-man, since both of our sons had very thick, hard heads. This was while I held down the fort at home, cooking, cleaning, and also working. I took care of them when they were sick, cheered for them at their sports games, volunteered with other parents in raising money for special events, and even tried helping with homework, despite not being able to understand half of the assigned material; it was so confusing, but I gave a good effort.

In all honesty, however, I wouldn't describe myself as the *motherly* type. I deeply loved both of my children with all of my heart, and I was always there for them. But, I think in my case, history repeated itself a little and this apple didn't fall very far from the tree. My mom wasn't overly-affectionate with me, or very present for that matter, and unfortunately, one learns by example. I can say that I pushed myself and did a lot better than the generation that came before me. I also learned a lot from my mother-in-law, who was very warm, doting and devoted, but unlike her, these days you wouldn't catch me baking a tray of lasagna and bringing it to your home every single Sunday, or fussing over grandkids and wiping crumbs away.

It's just that life pulled the rug out from under me rather abruptly, and this wake-up call shaped me into someone I wouldn't have recognized five years ago. I no longer fit into that cookie-cutter role of "Gammie." "Pops," as they would have called Larry, has passed away, so those days of contentedly turning gray and growing old together have about-faced. That starring role has now admirably fallen upon my little grandchildren's other set of grandparents (my son's wife's family) who are nice, Italian people. They do a great job at baking their trays of lasagna, are very happy turning gray alongside each other, and who have earned the title of "Champion Crumb Catchers." Believe me, I'm grateful to them, as I appreciate the constant stability they provide to their family. After the type of loss I endured, which I wouldn't wish upon my own worst enemy, the labels *grandma, gray-haired, and growing old* seem to have gotten rewound in the shuffling of my life. The clock has been kind to me, something I did not expect, especially after this grief journey. It's as if I'm aging backwards in a way, both inside and out. Healing has made me feel young again, lighter, blessed to still be alive, and appreciative of everything I have.

Still, I'm alone now. But you know what? That's ok for the time being. I rather like the new me, and that doesn't make me a bad person. It just makes me someone that life dealt a brand new set of cards to, and this joker no longer hides her Queen of Hearts under her sleeve; it's right out there in the wide open, and I intend on living my life to the fullest. Yes, I may have acquired a little puffiness under my eyes, along with a few fine lines, and lost some hair, but these are the battle scars one earns after having fought through grief. They are the wounds that are a part of our stories.

Still, I repudiate some of the natural processes of aging, such as turning gray. I realize that societal attitudes towards women with natural gray hair are complex and evolving. However, there's a growing trend of women embracing gray hair and even seeing it as a sign of authenticity, some calling themselves "silver sisters," as they celebrate their personal journey and maturity. Yet for men, it's quite contradictory, as they're considered "silver foxes." They're charming, sophisticated, and confident. Remember, that in my case "Elizabeth Taylor" would sit up in her grave and scream **NO** to me if I did! So, I never will. And, quite honestly, I like changing it up, and some days I'm in the mood to be that beachy, fun-loving blonde, other days I'm an alluring and sultry brunette. Maybe I'll even try my hand at being a redhead to match that fire in my soul. You see, my new motto now is, "Girls just want to have fun!" Thank you Cindy Lauper, another New York City girl, whose New York accent mirrors mine!

I raised my family, devoted my life to them, loved them with my whole heart, sacrificed everything for them, and always put them first. But, the universe decided to point me in a new direction, gave me a gentle pat on my behind, and wished me well as I set forth on a different course into my next chapter. A do-over. Both of my sons want the best for me and offer their encouragement to find whatever it is that will make me happy, even if that means moving away. They want me to find more joy in my life, especially after everything I've been through. I won't be cutting the cord by any means; I'll just be giving it a little slack so I can finally find me, the girl I used to be, somewhere in between all the gaps.

My friends have been nudging me to find another love. "Gret (as they call me), come on, it's time." I wondered quite a few times if it would be easier to sail through the rest of my life solo, or perhaps settle for a compatible partner. I know I'm still young, but if I find someone, I know I'm not going to want a mediocre relationship that lacks that spark and passionate energy. I need more. So, I'm going to stay true to who I am and never accept the choice to live in the shadows of how other people think I should live. Those walls I initially built around myself for my own protection served no purpose, and just slowly chipped away at my spirit. Playing it safe by saying that I would never love again, while guarding my heart, and keeping secrets close to my vest, in the end proved to be without solace. It made me feel restless.

I believe that we need to free ourselves from the confinements we build out of our own ignorance, and I proved it when I tore down those walls, released my guard, gained back trust in myself, and began to breathe again. That was when I realized just how strong I really was. So, have courage my friends, get out there, and see what or who is waiting for you. Don't you think that it's time that we, all the lighthearted romantics, the shamelessly sentimentals of the world, deserve to finally find our true and genuine smiles?

CHAPTER 14

REFLECTIONS
ON SYNCHRONICITY

I THINK A LOT OF us carry self-doubt on our backs, although some don't readily admit to it. Time has had its way with all of us, that's for sure. I don't believe that it's safer to simply stay away. I'm still seeking answers to some elements of insecurities that I carry to this day, but I also manage to hide it beautifully from the rest of the world. The actress. No, I refuse to hibernate, because I am now a woman in progress, growing, developing, and evolving. I know in my heart that life still goes on, whether I choose to allow a day to drift by, or I push myself and plan something constructive to effectuate my time. But, during this period of growth, I'm still eager to participate in life's experiences, and willing to show up authentically, exposing all of my flaws and imperfections.

There's something to be said about stepping out of one's comfort zone. Every day I keep trying my best, but one step forward sometimes turns into one step back. I feel like I'm floating some days, which, at first, aggravated me. But, then I reminded myself to slow down, experience this pause in my life, as there must be a reason for it. We shouldn't expect every day to bring progress. I'm feeling happier, yet now I'm thinking deeply about my life and what I wish to do with it, what will bring me contentment, fulfillment. But, is the final goal fulfillment, or simply the journey, the ride, as we try to obtain it? Is it a matter of choosing back what is, and has always already been, ours? Maybe it was something we loved to do at one time, but it got a little lost along the way. If we believe in it again, how do we do it? How does one truly start over and find the road back to joy again? That is the question.

I started by self-reflecting, and decided not to make any huge life-changing decisions at first; to take my time, so that I would know when the opportunity would present itself. So, no rush. I also felt profound gratitude for the freedom to do this, without needing to quickly sell my home, or find a job like many have to do when they're left widowed. The period following the loss of a spouse can be incredibly challenging, and facing the need to quickly sell a home and secure employment adds significant pressure.

Seek professional guidance, and consult with a financial advisor or estate planning attorney to understand the financial implications of selling a home, including potential tax consequences. Work with a real estate agent, someone who has experience in your area and can provide a comparative market analysis (CMA) to help you determine a fair price for your home. While selling quickly might be a priority, explore different housing options to understand what is best for your current and future needs.

Then, seek a career counselor/job agency, especially if you've been out of the workforce for a while. They can help you identify your skills, revamp your resume, and navigate the job search process. Consider skills gained from previous work experience, or even from managing a household that are transferable to potential job opportunities. You can reach out to your network of friends, family, and former colleagues to let them know you're looking for work. Use online job boards like Indeed.com or LinkedIn to search for opportunities and submit applications that way. If you've been out of the workforce for a while, consider taking refresher courses to update your skills and knowledge.

The second thing I did was to prioritize my well being, working first on the inside, which then led to the outside. Everything has been a self-discovery journey of sorts; laying the foundation towards happiness, and I did it one step at a time. As I reviewed in my mind what that sign was trying to tell me, it became a mirror which shifted my perspectives from distortion to balance. I examined everything that was brought back into my life, and considered all the potential benefits against any disadvantages. In conclusion, I reached a decision to make a more informed choice about how I wanted to revel in what remained of the quality of my life. I decided to discover fulfillment along the way, as I pursued contentment and peace, first and foremost.

Yes, from time to time the thought has crossed my mind, and I wonder what Mr. Perry is up to. I don't know anything about him, but I hope he pursues different genres of music other than yuletide noels. Although, I have to admit that one day I listened to two of the songs released from his latest (and third) Christmas album. However, they weren't all Christmas songs. I tried listening to some of those, and he certainly captured the nostalgia of those tunes beautifully, but being that they were only about Christmas, I immediately turned them off; it was too painful for me. So, I started with his rendition of a song called, "What a Wonderful World." I sat alone, played it on full volume, and purposely closed my eyes as I immersed myself into it, and at the end, I found my face wet with tears. That man sure does know a thing or two about expressing emotion in such an intimate manner. Yes, his voice has definitely changed, yet his diction is pure, stable, and he can still sing beautifully. All of us must come to terms with aging. Let's listen to the positive evolution and the unique qualities that his voice has developed. It springboards off of what once was heralded as a strong and healthy voice, and deemed one of the greatest in all of rock history. It is now simply more resonant, and truly showcases the depth and richness he has acquired.

Another song, "Call Me Irresponsible," was also contained within all the other pieces. Not a Christmas song by any standard; it was a duet with his late father, Ray Perry. I'm sure Mr. Perry's intent was to show respect, admiration, and love towards his father, as it was something the two of them always dreamed about doing, and he felt that releasing it on this album was his holiday miracle. But, I've got to say that it downright broke my heart.

Steve Perry used technology to extract his dad's voice off of an old cassette tape that he thought was lost. His dad was singing into a karaoke machine, and I've read that he sent it to his son back in 1993 for the holidays. Steve was able to successfully clean up the vocals on this old cassette tape, and then combined it with his recording, thus building a beautiful track around his father, allowing them to sing together. An unfulfilled dream of singing with his late father became possible, and he said the experience was a deeply emotional one for him. He said that his dad used to sing this particular Bobby Darin song to him at bedtime when he was a child.

There was a video which accompanied this song created by Tolga Tarhan, a visual artist and designer. The video creatively followed his entire relationship with his dad through animation. It begins with a young Steve disappointed that his father is leaving; there was a divorce which occurred when Steve was very young. It tracks him as he discovers a love of music as a teenager, and how he ultimately becomes an international star. Viewers see Ray watching his son Steve on TV, and then when they eventually meet again when Steve is an adult. Later, Steve visits his dad in the hospital, and then again at his grave. The end of the video shows how Steve ultimately discovers the karaoke tape, and Ray and his son then sing the song "Call Me Irresponsible" through connected microphones.

Ray Perry was a great singer in his own right, and it's true how he left Steve and his mother when Steve was only seven years old. This is so heartbreaking from a child's standpoint, because that kind of pain stays with you for the rest of your life. I'm sure that along the way, Steve found forgiveness for his father, hence the birth of this moving and beautiful new song. I suppose it was a sincere and heartfelt sense of closure in a way. Steve Perry's father, Raymond Francis Perry, died of natural causes in 1998 at age 79.

A close friend just pointed out to me that Mr. Perry recently collaborated with Willie Nelson. Through Dark Horse Records, they just released a duet, a new version of the Journey song "Faithfully" to benefit Farm Aid. Mr. Perry stated that singing with Willie Nelson was always something he had wanted to do. 100% of the proceeds from this recording will go to benefit this organization, which was originally founded by Willie Nelson, Neil Young and John Mellencamp. They organized the first Farm Aid concert in 1985 to raise awareness about the loss of family farms and to raise funds to keep farm families on the land. Farm Aid has raised nearly $80 million to promote a strong and resilient family farm system of agriculture, that's their mission, and they are a nonprofit organization. It certainly doesn't surprise me how Mr. Perry's munificence towards those less fortunate has always been important to him, and in this case, being that he comes from a family of farmers himself, it solidifies his love and respect for this particular cause.

But, other than this, I haven't heard any *current* news about his career lately, so no more postings, no more chimes, and no, I don't go out of my way to follow his social media, as I do not consider myself one of his typical fans. In actuality, I haven't earned that merit, as I didn't know a thing about him. But, now I am trying to acquaint myself better with his music. I am finding myself quite infatuated with his voice, in fact; it's beautiful. Maybe he's decided to retire. But then again, he did sign with that new record label, Dark Horse Records, so something tells me he's got more tricks up his sleeve other than Christmas albums and philanthropic songs. But, I'll always wonder if he truly wants to retire, as it has been said that he does have a tendency to step away. If I were his friend, I would talk him out of it. A wealth of talent still remains untapped, undeserving to lay idle. Besides, I feel in my heart that he wants more.

Some people say it's odd, this quiet and private nature, which is something I also identify with, and always push myself to avoid. I've finally learned not to listen to what other people say about me. I know who I am, and I do admit that at times during my life I took avoidance and evasion too far. Escape behaviors don't protect you; they only give immediate relief, because in the long run, habitually responding this way hinders your life, shields you from stimulus, people, and the world around you, which is unhealthy. I never questioned the reasons why I wanted to escape, but sometimes it had a positive outcome, such as temporary relief from tasks/people I was trying to avoid. But, most times it had negative consequences, because the longer I allowed it to go on, Larry would confront me, and give me no alternative but to address the underlying cause of why I was doing it.

It affected my children, who wondered why I couldn't bring myself to leave the house some days. Larry always pulled the truth out of me, and it all stemmed from the same place; insecurities I acquired in my youth, feeling I wasn't worthy, and the fears of others' opinions of me. So, I retreated for my own protection. I am so sorry now for hurting my family with behaviors that I perceived as shielding me from uncomfortable or distressing situations, yet in reality, prevented everyone from engaging in social activities as a family unit. Words written here cannot repair the harm I caused. I take full responsibility, as I make amends, for words are empty if they are not supported by concrete actions, which carry weight, as I now try to restore trust and demonstrate my commitment to change.

Yes, I can be puzzling, not an easy person to entirely figure out, and maybe even a little difficult or abstract at times. I'm inexplicable to a fault, and even I grasp for explanations as I try to justify it to myself. The only person who was ever able to cut through my mystery, and fully decipher what made me tick, was Larry. He always told me I was so critical of myself, and why couldn't I see what he saw? He saw a woman who was so easy to love. Those who know me well will tell you that I am one of the most sincere people they've ever met, and I love deeply to my very core. But, they worry about me because they also know that I'm someone who's my own worst enemy. I still have a tendency to put others before myself, but like most girls do, I also make the time to prioritize my well-being. There's an expression, "You can't teach an old dog new tricks," and I'm fine with that, as it's not in me to go against my nature. Not that I should be referring to myself as an "old dog." I would prefer to use the term "Poised & P.H.A.T. poodle" instead. PHAT is spelled as the abbreviation P.H.A.T., not the word *fat*. I'm not! By the way, it means "**P**retty **H**ot **A**nd **T**empting." Oh man . . . I just "WOWED" myself out loud, and heard it. The award for the most fascinating conversation I've had all day with myself goes to . . . me!

And now, after having watched that interview, I finally have a name which sums up my sometimes trying personality: Enigma. Yeah, right, I'm laughing as I type it. I never thought I'd fit nice and tidy into *that* box, but I think I do. Some of us have a habit of getting in our own way, and that's when I try my hardest to step out of my safe sanctuary, especially after I made that promise to my husband, because he always recognized that trait in me. I do hope that currently, seven years after that interview, that Mr. Perry will remain involved with music, and that there will be more to come. Like I previously stated, I've heard from multiple sources that he is someone who happens to be very generous and kind. He's got such a good reputation.

There are also articles about him, how open and warm-hearted he is when stopping to speak with ordinary people. That's a huge gauge of one's character when they take time out of their day to speak with someone they don't even know, someone they could have just passed by, or walked away from. Larry was the same way. He could walk with kings, and then walk with serfs. Both, to him, were always treated the same, as he never judged, nor saw any distinction.

It's funny, because I even wondered if Mr. Perry missed touring, just a little bit. I'd bet my life that he does. That had to be so crazy, yet exhilarating! I think that I would miss being on the road if that was my occupation. That's the bohemian part of me talking, yet I also crave the stability of a home base. I know firsthand what it's like to be in front of a live audience and interact with them. I guess I passed up one of my many callings. Then again, it wasn't something I did day-after-day for months, or even years at a clip. The idea of touring presents itself as a very romantic and exciting life, but I think that it's certainly not for the faint of heart. It's a challenging one, whereas the artist is given opportunities to express their art in person. They feed off the audience and give them everything they have. Yes, an artist's life is somewhat like a long and winding road filled with struggles with criticism and self-doubt; it is deeply personal, and over time, can become quite taxing, both physically and mentally. But their *home*, their passion in whatever they do, whether it be acting or music, always travels with them in their heart, and is truly the center of their work, so it drives them. What's important is who they surround themselves with, people who always have their backs, their best interests and intentions, so wherever the road takes them, they're still grounded.

I hope that he thinks about all of the possibilities, the different places he can still travel to, and meet new people, younger generations introduced by his fans, the forebears of his past, who want to showcase his talent to them. I'm sure by now he's turned 76, but I believe age is just a number. A lot of people fall prey to the mindset that aging is something we are supposed to dread; but, surely it is better than the alternative, and nothing short of miraculous, awe inspiring, actually. It's a privilege to be alive yet another year, and worth celebrating. I feel 17 inside, and that will never change. Remaining young at heart feels so good. Outside, I'm holding my own very well, but you won't catch me filling up my face with liquid vials of promised youth, or having my mouth blown up to resemble bee-stung lips. I'll never be one to emulate one of those plastic housewives from TV, although I don't judge someone who wishes to make *slight* improvements; but you have to admit that some people do take it too far. The Twilight Zone is just not in my playbook. But, back in the day, yes, it would've been nice to have lifted my breasts back up to where they once stood, as they now most certainly fail the pencil test. Don't know what that is? Ladies, stand with your shoulders back and arms at your sides. Place a pencil horizontally under your breast crease (where the breast meets the chest wall), release the pencil and observe what happens.

Interpretation:

Pencil falls immediately: This indicates minimal or no sagging. Clearly "the girls" need no support, as they stand beautifully and firmly at attention. I have two words for you, but being that I'm a lady . . . I mean, what are you, 15 years old? Yes, I'm being sarcastic, and yes I apologize for almost using profanity, and yes I was only kidding, but the truth of the matter is, I'm jealous.

Pencil remains in place for a couple of seconds: Well, this suggests moderate sagging. Ok, now you're getting close to my level. You've been around the block, tucked a few miles under your belt, but now gravity is settling in. It's getting real, and time to strap on a little support. *Why is this making me happy . . .*

Pencil remains in place and doesn't budge: This indicates severe sagging. Your boobs are probably sitting on the front of your knees. Welcome to my world.

It would have been nice to have had my tummy tightened from those two basketballs who over stretched my once tight and taught belly, but we just didn't have the money back then for me to have a "mommy makeover" (that's a breast lift & a tummy tuck simultaneously, *ouch*), and I'm not about to take the chance to gamble with the clock now that I've reached my sixties. Back then, I should have had the gumption to raise my own funds by advertising my own Boobituary: "It is with great sadness that I announce the departure of my perfectly upstanding knockers, devoted twins shaped by life, who reached the pinnacle of their success trying to nurture children. Donations may be made in their memory, so as to honor and support what has become a cruel and deflated punch line with striae; those bone-chilling roadmaps etched in braille. In the true name of motherhood, may they one day rise again to the occasion. Amen."

Nowadays I rely on firm and steady boulder holders. You've got to look on the bright side of life, and do like I do; remember that when life gives you lemons, you gotta learn to swerve. Now you have an excuse to wear sexy, racy [yet] supportive bras under your t-shirts. I use what God gave me to my advantage, and I happen to like that Erin Brockovich look of intimates peeking out from under my clothes. There's nothing wrong with teasing lacey indiscretions under a low-cut blouse paired with a nice, tight pair of jeans, and it makes me feel good about myself, feminine. I suppose what's even more fascinating is how I round out my ensemble wearing sneakers or casual flats. Stilettos, well, there's just not enough walls to grab onto for balance, so, no dice. The days of finding my spiked heels stuck in the roof of his car are long gone. Well, one would think, but in my case anything is possible. For now, I'll keep those reserved for the boudoir, if I ever get that lucky again, since there's never any walking involved there. Look, I'm just trying to do the best that I can with what's left of me, as my dad used to say. Yeah, I think I've still got it going on. I'm still hot; heads still turn. At least that's what all of my friends tell me. Hey, just because I pay them to say that doesn't mean it's not true!

If Mr. Perry and I were friends, I would encourage him to tour again, just ease up, take it down a notch; strive for a few cities and not travel back-to-back for years on end. After all, he is 76 years old, and I'd hate to hear that fatigue hindered his performance with all those pretty young groupies, or that lack of sleep slackened his cat-like reflexes. One must stay sharp and alert so as to duck quickly in order to avoid those lethal, sexy g-string projectiles headed straight for his head.

I'd share my dry-eye drops with him and tell him to just go fix his hair (yes, he still has some), snap a set of suspenders onto a nice, new pair of jeans, angle that sexy fedora on his head, slap on a little cologne, throw on one of his famous coattails, then grab onto a mic and pop a Motrin. Go for it! They say it's about getting back what you have given. So, I hope he continues to share the joy, and spread the love. If he does, maybe we should take a page from his book because the rewards would certainly be great. It's not how old you are; it's how old you feel, and how you deal with it. If your health is good, your attitude and mindset can significantly impact how you experience life, no matter what your age. Let your mind convince you that love, joy, and excitement can be brought back into your life again. Reaping all of these benefits is the bonus that circles back to us when we are the ones who initiate it.

I admit that one day I viewed a couple of the videos Journey made way back in the day. Some looked like they were from MTV; other segments were from live concerts. I don't believe Journey made many directed videos, as I think they tried to sidestep that component. Back in the day, rock bands were expected to promote their songs with high-budget visuals, but some chose not to. But, I think that Mr. Perry actually loved it. He was a born performer, as well as a musician, and the camera adored him. I found their songs beautifully written, and Mr. Perry's voice phenomenal. Wow, what diction! Coming from a nit-picking perfectionist's standpoint, he's got my vote. But what surprised me the most was how much I just liked watching him move. I learned that he was their greatest and most successful frontman; the one who paved the path for all those who followed in his footsteps and tried to emulate his voice. To me, he just seemed so carefree and happy. Man, they had fun! I'm not talking about the choreographed segments; he certainly was a natural showman and hit his marks professionally. And no, I wasn't *always* focused on his ass. Ok, well, maybe a few times, I'm only human. And, yes, he had a very nice one, and that's all I'm going to say about that.

There was one specific moment when I watched him in a video, when everything blended together, the music, him dancing innocently, totally immersed and feeling every single note, moving playfully all over the place, strumming his air guitar. I'll bet he wasn't even aware of it. I was just relieved that he never fell off the stage, because he just kept spinning, turning, and going and going and going. Maybe he did, but they never showed that on YouTube. It was my favorite part of the video. Most people watch videos for the music, but when he danced I found myself so immersed, as if hypnotized when you stare at a flame; a flame that was solitary, free, flickering, here for just a moment in time, burning bright and warm, forever dancing.

Artists find a way to connect with all of us; they allow their creative process to touch our emotions which we then interpret in our own individual ways. A song lands or it doesn't, and for me a good barometer is usually those unexpected goose bumps. Yes, I liked the band's songs, but what I loved even more was seeing him so lighthearted out there, doing his thing, dancing, and just disappearing into it all. That was what gave me goose bumps. True happiness is an infectious and satisfying deep state of joy, a fulfillment that we should always pursue. It's a gift of value and purpose that enhances our lives, and promotes growth, and is something that I will always wish for him.

I also discovered a few really great songs by Journey that same day that I never heard before: *Still They Ride, Castles Burning, Stay Awhile, Still She Cries,* and *When You Love a Woman.* They're all beautiful, sentimental songs, which I highly recommend everyone listen to, besides the multitude of their other hits. And, from Steve Perry's first solo album named, "Street Talk," I think the song *Running Alone* is my favorite. Then there was another solo album he recorded much later on named, "For The Love of Strange Medicine." This was Mr.

Perry's second solo effort after an eight-year hiatus following Journey's breakup. It contained a lead single called *You Better Wait* which reached the top 10 on the Billboard Mainstream Rock chart. It was absolutely amazing! Another song called *Home at Last* was only a demo track from 1993 and was considered for inclusion, but unfortunately was never used. But, I accidently discovered it on YouTube and adored it, and highly recommend that everyone try to find it and take a listen. Amazing vocals! But, here's another one from that same album that really surprised me: *Can't Stop.*

Wait . . . **WHAT** ⁉⁉
Oh, you have **GOT** to be kidding me!

An extremely hot, steamy, and sexy little song, if I say so myself. But, come on Stevie! That widow's fire thing started happening again. It finished, and I closed out of YouTube. I had to . . . my clothes fell off.

And, on top of everything, you should've seen how he wore his hair when he made that album. It was **WAY** down his back, very long. It was so sexy, bohemian, Native American; he looked like he was evoking the aesthetic of a tribal leader. Well, he succeeded! Perhaps his overall look was aiming more for an ancient, spiritual, or an otherworldly theme. Doesn't matter; the long hair did it for me.

Oh man . . . good thing we didn't cross paths back then. It's lucky for him that I wasn't single at the time too, 'cause the poor guy wouldn't have stood a chance in hell. I can't tell you how fast I would've climbed that tree. But, I am a lady and I do have my standards: First, we would have needed to have met through a mutual friend. Second, there would be no ascending or descending until after at least three consecutive, successful date nights involving a minimum of one entertaining, enjoyable and engaging appetizer. One messy and unpredictable dinner appropriately seasoned with good communication skills, shared values, and expectations would then follow. Third, I would have phoned my emergency contact to make sure they were in the loop (a code word would be involved) much like preparing for a natural disaster. In the end, if it all worked out, there most definitely would have been a happy ending, but I'm not sure if it would have been Mr. Perry's or mine, but without question, one of us would have been felled.

Too bad Crazy Horse (that great Sioux tribal leader) and his gorgeous, cascading mane drove off on a Harley into the sunset many years ago, but there's nothing wrong with keeping that beautiful image of him forever etched somewhere in the back of my imagination, so, if you're reading this, Mr. Perry, yes, I can hear your howls of laughter. We may not actually know each other, yet, but I assure you, and all of my readers, that it feels simpatico. As if our paths were meant to cross, like a key fitting a lock, a connection meant to free something special. It might have led to a meaningful bond, but geographically speaking, many miles lie between us, and this distance is an illusion, a connection existing beyond the reach of hands. Like twin stars in a vast cosmic dance, we orbit each other, yet this relationship is non-existent. I may be a romantic, but I am also a realist. But, if the opportunity were to ever present itself, I would not say no. In fact, it would be my honor to meet him.

Wouldn't it be nice if he could come to New York somewhere along the way? Personally, I love music and watching live shows and concerts. I would go to see him and I'd bring a whole bunch of friends. I'd be the one mixed into the crowd of happy faces cheering on his show and singing right along with him, that once scrappy little tomboy who is tone deaf and couldn't carry a note in a bucket. The one who learned from the deep love of a man how it wasn't her fault, as she realized her worth. The one who recognized how strength is weakness, and whose tears now easily fall and are no longer hidden. The one who doesn't have a steel bone in her body, and who will forever wear her heart on her sleeve.

So, exactly one year after I lost my beloved, parts of this man's life got tangled up into parts of mine, and I now know the universe planned it purposely. Those two days were incredible, and have not left me to this day. They happened at a defining moment in my life, a pivotal point, and it unleashed a torrent of emotions, while eliciting two phenomena to light: First and foremost, a reminder of a precious gift I had once been given; a great love who was waiting just for me, at the right place, at the right time. Destiny. Most of what I experienced from watching that interview rekindled a rush of memories with my beloved Larry, right down to actually hearing those distinct words of love which Larry always said to me. Uncanny. It was as if these two men were mirroring off of each other. I never imagined encountering such a unique, gentle and compassionate spirit, outside of Larry. They both shared so much in common, the same warm heart and generous spirit, and had caring and benevolent natures. It even brought back memories of when Larry would sing to me on the beach in wintertime. They also loved their Harley Davidson motorcycles. Something happened . . . freely and extensively, and it all brought unforeseen and wonderful consequences.

But, this sign also awoke dormant, inaccessible memories. I felt as if a complete 180 happened, when this second phenomena triggered a sudden shift in its trajectory, showing me glimpses of a past that I was, and still am, unable to fully grasp. Maybe my mind was so open, unintended messages meant for someone else crossed paths and ended up mixed into mine. Stranger things have happened. But, I don't think so. There definitely was a soul recognition that I deeply felt, but it was from a skewed perspective, one beheld on a one-way street with a soul that reached out to me, one whom I didn't recognize from my mind, only from my heart. I sensed a strong magnetic pulling that could not be denied; my body had an overwhelming physical reaction. Every cell in my body recognized, and felt, a deep primal connection.

But, if it were to be Mr. Perry's, which I think not (so don't hold your breath), it would take a miracle for me to travel 3,000 miles just to explore that wonderland of fantasy. But, never say never. Maybe someone will find it in their heart to gift me a nice airline window seat (I do appreciate a nice view), and a comfortable hotel room to rest my head. Sans hair piece. I always did long to see the Golden State of California! Perhaps one day, this little feather will drift in that direction. You'll understand what I meant by that comment in just a little bit.

I want you to understand the reasoning behind my baring all of these intimate parts of myself with all of you. It was to give you insight as to where it all finally brought me, and how I used this knowledge in a purposeful way. I decided to put into practice the lessons learned from it, for I no longer felt despair, heaviness, pressure, or stress. As the days passed, the self-inflicted oppression I lived under finally lifted, and I knew it was time to start healing, time to nurture my well being, and time to take baby steps towards a new life. With insights gained from hardship, overcoming adversity leads to new growth, and when you find acceptance, you find peace, you begin your transition, and it's amazing how your mind acclimates and encourages you to then move forward.

I realized that the answer was there all along in plain sight. I couldn't make a connection when obvious stimuli were placed in front of me, as my therapist tried so many times to do. We used tangible objects, even photos, to evoke memories and emotions. When I was purposely lured to that interview, a complete shift of gears happened, when so many triggers opened the latch to my past. I sat there listening to a gentle voice that made me feel comfortable, and safe. Then I heard songs sung exactly the way Larry used to sing to me, right down to Mr. Perry's hand gestures; so lost in the music, that even his gaze was riveted on the songs. Most importantly, I was so taken aback when he expressed private, intimate words that Larry always spoke to me; they were verbatim. I needed a gradual dawning of enlightenment so I could find the portal to my past.

Mr. Perry was the perfect muse who made that happen, the catalyst who provided the pathway to all those treasured mementos I had tucked deeply away into my heart. Another human being so similar to Larry; someone who the universe knew would capture all of the qualities my Larry possessed. The final element was most notably seeing the striking resemblance of the two of them when they were both young, as it brought me back exactly to where I needed to be; our starting point. You see, I had been trying to pick up the pieces of my life beginning at a crossroad; a crucial moment in time, interrupted by cancer, which metastasized its way into our ideal world, and became our greatest disruption. It was the perfect wrecking machine. This crossroad was a core obstruction that impeded my recovery. Efforts to move forward were barricaded by the consequences of cancer, when my focus should have been to rebuild from the ashes, go back to the place where we started, when we were incredibly happy, instead of focusing on the ruins.

In hindsight, I realize that Mr. Perry lives far away on a distant coast, but he was someone to whom I was pointed, a person I never knew anything about; just a name that slightly rang a bell, with links that convinced me within two days to move beyond doubt and without hesitation. Maybe I'll never know why or fully understand what it all meant. Signs can be received and interpreted as direct and intentional. Other times, synchronicities can evoke meaningful coincidences that seem to be guiding you towards a specific direction, but can veer off the path and leave you open ended. This sign was direct, intentional, yet left me with strong, unresolved emotions still remaining on the canvas.

I definitely surmised that it was the intense physical similarities which he and my husband Larry shared, and I was shocked! This sign provoked old and beautiful recollections, and it altered my course by making everything come back alive. For the most part, it made me feel happy, something I hadn't felt in a very long time. Lucky me, for my husband certainly was a good looking man. I guess I never realized it at the time, or put two and two together because my husband normally wore glasses (he had very poor vision), although he did wear contacts too. But, no one ever mentioned to me that he looked like Steve Perry. Perhaps they were oblivious to it at that time also; but, it was all I saw when I found the pictures. Another funny little tidbit here: Larry wore a coattail on our wedding day, along with the matching formal pants, of course. But, he would have worn jeans and sneakers with that jacket if he knew he'd get away with it. Coattails were Steve Perry's signature look, while wearing jeans and sneakers. Maybe if Larry pulled it off that day, perhaps people would have sat up and noticed the similarity.

They both aged differently as well, which was why I didn't recognize Mr. Perry when the interview first began. But, I still don't believe that this was a coincidence, as my heart and intuition both tell me otherwise. Still, my common sense tells me it's not something that was meant for me to ever understand completely. I still shake my head about it, but for now I'll just chalk it all up to opening up the greatest parts of my life, and restoring my joy. I will interpret it as being a kind, compassionate and divine messenger who gave me the encouragement to finally break through that wall, and guide me back onto the right path to find where all of my best memories, all of my best intentions should forever stay so that I can now, simply, and with all of my entire heart, let it be.

I'm starting to understand what that medium Rena meant when she once told me, "A soul interrupted, yet is still here in this same lifetime, and is meant to be with you always." Yes, Larry's life was most certainly interrupted, as was mine at the three-quarter point, so Rena's prediction was correct. I believe now that is why she looked so somber when I walked away from our reading that day. She saw a premonition, a presage of the pain and heartache that I was fated to suffer. One cannot argue about what she predicted, as her esoteric knowledge was so far out of anyone's league, and I witnessed it firsthand. But, my heart encourages me to keep credence in my intuition, and to not waiver in my faith of knowing that this unique soul was indeed meant to be with me always. Maybe a type of soul metempsychosis occurs, a rebirth, where a soul continues existence in another realm until it is steered once again by destiny. I don't know, but I keep the faith, and I'll wait for something much greater than me to intervene, orchestrate, and guide this soul. I believe that the universe will somehow return it to me, whether it will come in this lifetime again, or in an existence still yet to come. I applaud Rena, a perspicacious, mystical, and truly gifted spiritual advisor, who once foresaw a tragedy, a negative shift, which forked into a brand new beginning.

I've given much thought to the concept of "soul," our life force, our energy, which is a deeper, spiritual essence of intuitive knowing latent within all of us. I believe it animates our mind and body and is distinct from our character. I think that our soul is the reality of who we are, like a reservoir of our beautiful qualities, and manifests in our lives by needing to reveal itself somehow. Maybe it does so through our personalities. Our identity, nature, and disposition must be significantly needed by the soul as its vehicle for expression. Perhaps our temperament needs the soul in order for it to be spiritually infused. It only makes sense. I think our personality is the composite mental, emotional, and physical expression of us. Maybe we are like an outer shell, with our soul being our inner-most kernel.

It's pretty clear to me that our personalities are created by social environment, culture, one's existential circumstance by parents, but I don't think that the soul is conditioned by society. Our persona is created by decisions in response to one's environment over the course of growing up, it's true. Our personalities are very much like a strategy for dealing with life, which develops beginning at birth, and then it becomes traits and patterns. Our self-identity, our uniqueness flourishes from situations throughout our life's history. I think it remains unconscious of our true spiritual nature, our soul essence. In other words, our personality's mind is asleep at the wheel to our soul, the true core which remains free of influence. Our temperaments are focused towards being preoccupied with worldly duties, concerns and problems. I don't think our soul has any awareness; I truly believe it's our innermost and purist truth, our authentic self, uncorrupted by external influences.

I'm grateful I found the way back to my life, albeit I know I will never be the same person I once was. I've archived those sad days into a space somewhere in the back of my mind where they belong. The sickness, and all that came with it, stress, anxiety, sadness, poor decisions made on a whim, impulsive actions fueled by desperation, all no longer deserve significance in my life.

We should not linger on the challenges or obstacles we overcome; only on the happy segments of our lives where we can cherish precious moments that deserve our focus front and center. It's best to look ahead and not dwell on the things that have been. Apologies can be made to those who were hurt along the way; we should acknowledge and take responsibility for our actions.

But, there's absolutely no rush, as the timing doesn't really matter, and to be honest with you, no one is expecting it, especially after all that you have endured. When you're ready, I assure you that those fences can be mended, especially if they were strong and solid to begin with. Weed out the weaker ones, those who can't be reinforced, who remain stubborn and divisive. In those cases, consider it a gift as you walk away.

This synchronicity came to me so unexpectedly, as if out of thin air, at the eleventh hour when everything seemed insurmountable; just when I was at my breaking point. It was the miracle I was begging for, and it guided me to finally push through that block; it removed the blinders to my past, and I concomitantly became mindful of the beauty which was already surrounding me. I implore all of you to look beyond the interference that came your way, cross over it, and become intentional as you find your way back. Take a page out of my book, and revisit the start of your journey. Go back to that time where all the happiness and joy you experienced during the beautiful life you shared with your soulmate was radiant. As you reminisce about these keepsakes, these ephemeral, magical, splendid moments in time, you'll come to realize how they were intentionally all meant for you. Let everything that you fought through merely be reminders of just how strong you really are, and keep the weight of sadness tucked away so you can rebuild your life. While we'd never choose to be an ambassador to grief, we can still move forward and embrace it. We can become someone who can help another walk this painful path. Let us find a way to heal together.

Yes, I too had a love story. Larry always told me to write my own narrative, so I finally took heed, and I wanted to share it with the world. My beloved knew how he was always the wish who was written in me, the muse who awakened my artistic spirit, and the catalyst who unlocked my creative potential. I was so blessed to have had him in my life. One of his last requests was that I venture forward. So, as I do this, I will try to empower others around me. I hope that during the process of sharing this memoir, if someone were to try to muster the courage to heal without resolution, to seek the potentiality of strength to move forward without having all the answers, well, then I will have paid it forward, as we are all in this together; surviving and motivating each other. It can become a ripple effect as we gain back our confidence and restore the traction we need to find our footing. Bestowing kindness on the next person walking in your shoes can only bring you positive consequences. Make it contagious; it can be your lasting memorial to your beloved's life, as it has now forever become mine.

CHAPTER 15

FINDING YOUR
NEW LIFE PATH

WE'RE ALL HUMAN, AND WE all have our meltdowns. There will still be times where you'll wish you could just crawl up into a ball and stay in a quiet corner somewhere and be left alone; to a place of peace where there are no feelings, especially no hurt, or sadness. But, if you've committed to starting your life over and staying on the path to wellness, you cannot live this way on a daily basis. Personal growth and self-development are ongoing processes; both have steps involved, and it's gradual. But, in order to make a better, stronger version of oneself, you need to first realize that you not only owe it to yourself, but also to the one who left you behind, the soulmate who loved you.

On those tender, vulnerable days, go ahead and cry. Let it out, scream, break something, fall down and crash as many times as you need to. All of us have countless broken, unrequited dreams, and unrealized hopes and aspirations that will never come to fruition. Mostly, they will be those special milestones we dreamed of achieving with our soulmates, especially those of us who have children; graduations, weddings they will miss, and grandchildren they won't be able to hold, gently kiss, and sing lullabies to. There's too many to count, and we yearn for what we want back. We didn't ask for it, we didn't expect it, and we certainly didn't deserve it. But, I will tell you this: Never hide your grief. It's sacred and truly defines the depth of your heart. It is nothing to ever be ashamed of, as grief is simply love in its most painful form, and it rearranges every single part of you. Yes, this anguish is an insidious thief of peace, yet it is the penalty we pay, and it is an uninvited, yet necessary, sacrifice. It demands proper attention, and needs sufficient time. Your love story was once something amazing, exceptional in fact, and it deeply touched your life. Allow yourself to feel it, remember it, and fully absorb it. When grief hits, heavy and visceral, mourn as you loved: Passionately, unequivocally, heroically, magnificently, and do it with every fiber of your being.

At the end of the day, we must all surrender and relinquish our resistances. We must accept the death of our beloveds as something we cannot, nor will we ever be able to change, or completely let go of. We are not forgetting them. The love you had and shared is eternal. We're simply giving ourselves the precious time we need to heal in order to move forward. It's vitally important to allow yourself to grieve at your own pace. It is different for everyone, no matter what anyone tells you. There is no time factor when it comes to healing. All of us should view grief as a journey, and with each painful step, the load will lessen. Realize that in the midst of recovery there will be many setbacks, because this nonlinear process is beyond our control. It's critical that you treat yourself with an abundance of patience as you allow the actions to unfold. But I do promise you this: Over time, one day you will rise more and sink less. It will happen slowly, but it will continue. When you change your attitude and keep searching for a joyful outlook instead of dwelling on a dreary one, that's when you'll realize how the little things you find each day can bring you tiny pockets of peace.

Start out by allowing yourself to see the wonder in the ordinary by slowing down and being present. It's a shift in perspectives, as you train yourself to notice the beauty and richness in the everyday moments that often go unnoticed. You can rewire your brain and trick yourself into finding happiness in the minutes, and not fearing every waking hour of every new day, and what the future will hold for you. Find quietude and have eyes that see, and ears that hear. As they say, find the flavor in routine. Instead of rushing, savor your daily practices, like when you drink your coffee/tea. Try to let go of worries and negative thoughts that prevent you from enjoying the present. Appreciate the moment and luxuriate in these small pleasures. Remaining in the present with your grief, while experiencing feelings of contentment, can both coexist.

It's an adjustment, a correction of sorts, as we find things that stabilize our mood, and there are techniques used that can regulate and balance one's emotional state, i.e., exercising, engaging in a fun physical activity, or practicing relaxation techniques where you focus on your breath, or body sensations. Or, you can mindfully seek out positive experiences by trying meditation.

When you focus on an optimistic approach to each new day, outlooks start to appear different, brighter, even if you say they're not real. Always try to create a more comfortable environment for yourself, and stay away from stressful situations. You can reappraise a situation in a more positive light, reframing negative thoughts and patterns. Remember, progression will be slow. Baby steps. Exercising your mind in a pragmatic fashion by envisioning positivity, which may seem impossible, actually works. Time is going to pass regardless.

The small things you plan that are good for you will bring you happy moments which will eventually begin to connect, then start to build on each other. Like I said, training your mind to think in this direction reduces anxiety, calms stress, and restores emotional balance. By learning to turn off that critical voice in your head, and begin labeling your thoughts positively, you can choose good intentions. And you know what? You deserve that.

Then, do what I did, and stop staying isolated in your home. Be curious, as you approach the world with an open mind, seek new experiences, and try to see things differently. Go outside and feel the warmth of sunlight on your skin, listen to the sound of the birds singing, and enjoy something as simple as the smell of fresh rain. Connect with nature, immerse yourself in natural environments like parks, gardens, or take even just a short walk to be conscious of the beauty of plants, animals, and the landscape. It has always been amazing to me how nature never fears the change of seasons. It understands the need for rest, renewal, and how it all leads to new growth. It's a rebirth, as we grow through inevitable change.

This transformation, this reinvention of ourselves, will require a lot of discomfort as we evolve and adapt, but what we finally realize is that it's not about the ending; it's about the beginning of something new. Have you ever heard of the expression, "Sometimes those closest to the tree miss the forest?" We are so focused on our problems or situations, in other words, our *trees*, that we become consumed by these minutiae; we get caught up in so many minor, trifling details that prevent us from seeing the bigger picture, and that is the beauty that has been surrounding us the entire time. As we take a step back, the key is to trust this necessary pause in your life, because it will prepare you to become more resilient as you gain a newfound and clearer understanding of the direction you wish to take as you move forward.

It is a fact that we have the incredible ability to survive, despite our crestfallen experiences. So, why do we resist the yearning to understand what we love and what we fear? It is a form of self protection, and certainly past trauma and heartbreak have everything to do with it. It involves risk taking, as self-doubt and insecurity both come into play, where we fear sabotaging old or brand new relationships. The potential pain can be so frightening that we resist loving again, no matter who they are, so we put up shields. It becomes limiting and counterproductive. Ultimately, barriers may be unknowingly created to prevent emotional harm, but it means missing out on the deeper connection that understanding and embracing love can bring. Staying in a constant state of self-protection can prevent us from taking healthy risks, pursuing goals, and developing our full potential.

It's an ongoing effort, yes, but we must force ourselves to use an application of optimistic principles. We can avoid situations which bring us sadness, and certainly specific triggers that make us feel negative about ourselves, or make us angry, or resentful. Our brains can be controlled in our way of thinking, by paying attention to the present, and drawing on concepts like cognitive control so that we can regulate our thoughts and actions, particularly when faced with disagreements, frictions, underlying tensions either with a friend, or within your family dynamic. It's essentially the ability to override automatic responses and choose behaviors that align with our goals. It helps us to maintain focus, filter out distractions when conflicts arise, and suppress inappropriate actions. We can govern our mental processes by directing attention to the here and now, where we can cultivate our self-compassion, and nurture and foster kindness to ourselves, and be thankful for all that we still have.

As you change your mindset, everything all around you will shift too. Sometimes you've got to use tough love on yourself, push that envelope, so you can begin to trust your instincts after processing the variables, and invite those into your world who uplift and inspire you; don't settle for mediocre connections. Instead, look for sincerity, look for truth. It's called self-respect.

Now, you can embrace your new journey as you love yourself enough to walk away from those who don't empower you. You deserve peace, and being surrounded by those who celebrate your uniqueness. You have earned the ability to live a life that feels good. For you. Not for someone else. Find gratitude and make the choice to search for the positives in the very worst of situations, because when you look for the good, you'll find it all around. Just open your heart and let it in. The more love I allowed into my life, the closer it brought me to finding the wonder and joy in everyday moments. Trustworthy, genuine connections began to emerge, and I am thankful for those who supported, advocated, and comforted me. They strengthened my capacity for resilience, even when it seemed impossible, and taught me how life is still beautiful, even in loss.

When we begin to take empathy for ourselves, we can recognize our emotions and respond in a caring, sensitive way towards others, by first owning our self-worth, and then recognizing it in common humanity. We are part of a greater whole, and most importantly, we are not alone. Seek out social interactions that promote joy and connection. Feeling connected to the world can help us to imagine a better future for ourselves as we become more empathetic and understanding to those around us.

One of my daily, positive mind exercises entails a mental picture in which I envision how I remember my soulmate, Larry. I equate him metaphorically to a bright shooting star. I know, it sounds silly, but it works for me. It is during these moments of daydreaming where I see him quickly blazing across the sky, lighting it up, and everyone wants to share in a part of his light. My husband was highly intelligent, funny, gifted, kind, and gentle. All who knew him loved him. My mind wanders back and remembers how this particular star stopped in its tracks and chose me to share his life with. Then I smile, because I remember.

I was the arms that held him, and set aside all else to protect him when his anxiety and panic would set in. When his mind was heavy, I was his safe place, never his stress. I was where he found comfort, the place he called home. I was the one who stood behind him and always put him first, pushed him to be better, held him up, and encouraged him to shine. He was my rock star. I was the woman he counted upon to always stay real with him, the one who was willing, always strong, and yet in the end, whose heart he broke. But, it was all worth it. We had an extraordinary life, loved each other passionately, completely, and protected each other fiercely.

I am still that hopeless romantic who searches the evening sky each and every night hoping to catch just a glimpse of the bright star I once held and always called my own. As soon as I see it, I make my wish. For the short time he was here, he left a deep, indelible mark on all who knew him, but especially upon that young girl he held so closely that night when he danced with her, and turned into the woman he loved, and to whom he gave everything he had.

As Mr. Perry's famous song says, "Don't Stop Believing." I won't, not as long as I still have breath in my body, for I know destiny will lead me into the next chapter in my life, somewhere surprising, somewhere wonderful, and I truly wish the same for all of you. As each new day begins, I keep trying to fit myself into some kind of new and different "normal," one that is right for me, before that day ends and the next one begins. Still, I confess that within my heart lies a secret fear of losing this fire which still burns within me. People have told me it may slowly, and predictably, begin to diminish and fade away as I move forward on this new path alone. I can honestly say that I could not bear to live the rest of my existence here without unearthing another true purpose, finding more passion, and feeling more love. So, yes, I'll make my wish one more time for the stars to align and bring that kind of joy back into my life.

Now, about that little feather: Nowadays, I feel like that soft, white feather floating in the wind from the movie "Forrest Gump." I wonder, "Just how long will it take until I touch down, when someone, somewhere, reaches for me, picks me up, and presses this fragile plume into the pages of his book?" Until they do, I'll keep floating until destiny decides when the season is right for this little quill to be gathered. I'll keep drifting steadfast and strong, and remain shamelessly sentimental, for that is who I am, and that is who I will forever continue to be. Fate would not have it any other way.

As I try to close this volume of my life, I'll never forget all that my husband and I have endured, but I'll always remember to stay grateful for our gift, that amazing and rare kind of love which we were once given, as none of that was in vain. As I look back and reflect on that brief period of time, where I felt as if I were going insane, it is so evident to me how I lost my spark for life, and why my spirit shattered in private. I realize now that bleeding in silence only allowed my wounds to fester, delaying my recovery. It's all behind me now, as I'm trying to forge ahead in a positive direction, and I'll look for what is waiting for me around the corner. My beloved said he wanted me to find another love, and for the longest time I denied myself that way of thinking. But, now my heart is finally open to all of the possibilities that one day may come, and I realize how I deserve all the good things that life has in store for me.

Yes, now is the first time, in a very long time, that I have embraced the satisfaction of knowing that I have truly begun to find a newer, yet genuine me. I stopped living in fear of illusory shadows, optical illusions that tried to jade me, bringing with them damaged memories that offered no hope. I lifted that heavy weight off of my shoulders, and over time, through all of the pain, I found healing. Not because I forgot. It was because I learned how to move forward with both love and loss together.

All of my husband's suffering, as well as mine, is now in the past; he is free, and the benefit brought forth from it was that it did not destroy my faith in something much greater than me. It refined it. I now look upon Larry's life as a marvel, a beautiful entity that was chosen just for me, and now I know there is a plan. I watched as my beloved agonized, bearing such an incredible burden, dying earlier than a lot of people will, but I also witnessed how brave he was as he went into the light. His passing was one chapter of a much bigger story, forever bookmarked, and one that I was meant to tell. All of us are stars, rarities which form this amazing galaxy, which is merely one of millions. We are all miracles with stories, and we must learn to trust what we cannot see. In the end, through all of the shock, anger, loneliness, regret and grief, I found a scared grace, the divine beauty in the light of acceptance, and I finally made my peace with God.

For now, I've been living a quiet life with my dog, Harry. At this point, I am still taking it one day at a time, but I do my best to keep busy and socialize with family and good, close friends. During the day, I am immersed with the passion I've had all of my life, writing. I've begun a children's book series that explores the great adventures of a character named Wee Pip, who was my favorite, and one and only teddy bear when I was a little girl.

Speaking of socializing, I just returned from another cruise with my great friend Fran. Let me explain to you what she's like, as I think most of you have been wondering. Fran is like having the funniest, and most amusing partner in crime one could ever ask for. We've been friends for over 45 years. We've both moved around a lot, and lost touch here and there, but then one would call the other and the conversation would start off as if we had both spoken yesterday.

There were never any pretenses in our friendship. I call her Zsa Zsa (as in Gabor), since she's a platinum blonde bombshell and currently searching for husband number four. Divorced once when she was very young, but it was not her fault; the guy turned into a lunatic immediately after she married him. She was then scooped up by her knight in shining armor, who rescued her, protected her, and whom she promptly married. After his death, she remarried, and had another long, and happy marriage. So, widowed twice. She loved them both deeply, and again, not her fault, as they both died of natural causes and she's got their death certificates to prove it!

Like me, she was also born in New York City, and is very proud of her Puerto Rican heritage. She is sweet, outgoing, has more vivacity than the Energizer Bunny, amazingly ebullient, is so much fun, and so very good for me. I think most people would agree that she's hilariously alacritous, and always ready to go at a moment's notice! I actually lose weight when I try to keep up with her; so she's a good influence for sure. I have no doubt she will be happily married again in less than a year's time, as she has a heart of gold that's never digging for anything other than a good, decent man that she can spoil rotten with her remarkable and impressive Puerto Rican culinary skills. Man, that girl can COOK!

So, while we circled the Caribbean, to our dismay we discovered we definitely chose the wrong ship. Don't get me wrong; it was a lovely cruise line, yet we were both dreaming we'd be sipping exotic drinks, then dancing the nights away with new and exciting people while flying our freak flags. As we disembarked after seven very *L O N G* days, we looked at each other and laughed as we bid farewell to what turned out to be a geriatric cruise on the sea. The entire time we saw nothing but wheelchairs, scooters, and walkers with tennis balls everywhere. Everybody was either too old, paired up, or gay. So, when three quarters of the ship went to sleep at 9 p.m., we got dressed up to the nines, and sat at the chef's table hanging out with the gays from LA. We had a blast, although not very encouraging considering we were two, very attractive widowed gals sailing over an ocean filled with millions of fish in the sea. Oh, the irony.

There really is so much more to life than what we can just see on the surface. Living fully means seeking and appreciating the layers of meaning beyond what is immediately visible. Each day, as we enjoy the remarkable presence of wonder that surrounds us, we must always remember to keep faith in ourselves, and believe in our individuality as we begin to make honest, new choices for a fresh start in our life. We must all strive to go beyond superficial observations, and that requires introspection, where we should begin to explore our hidden depths, and see unseen dimensions where our intrinsic beliefs lie. It's a spiritual journey, where we question our purpose and meaning, but we must remember one thing that was once written by William Shakespeare. He hit the nail right on the head when he wrote this quote from Hamlet sometime between 1599 and 1601, "*This above all: To thine own self be true. And it must follow, as the night the day, Thou canst not then be false to any man.*"

Profound advice.

Shakespeare, William, "Hamlet" - Polonius to his son Laertes in Act I, scene iii Nicholas Ling and John Trundell, and printed by Valentine Simmes, "bad quarto", 1603

Bring meaning into your life by embracing your authentic self, and understanding your principles, ideals, ethics, passions, and desires by living in alignment with them. As you gain a new perspective and understanding of what you want to do with the rest of your life, you'll start to realize that you're now well on your way to finding fulfillment. It's a process, during which we hold onto our integrity, our core values, and our beliefs, as we shift our focus towards solutions, and possibilities for our future growth. It is where liberation and freedom are born. When you speak your truth, as raw and unfinished as it still may be, it communicates your needs to other people, and clearly tells them what's in your heart, giving them the opportunity to understand your emotions, and intent.

Now is the time to break free from societal expectations, and be who you truly are. If people anticipate that you'll follow a certain path, you might want to think about confounding their expectations by taking your own route. People will always bring their own biases, beliefs, and experiences to their evaluation of you. Be tactful, and don't beat yourself up for not fitting in or for making mistakes. It's going to happen, but you can balance authenticity with social connection and be respected for who you are, rather than for trying to be someone else. There's nothing inherently wrong with not wanting to conform to a specific group's norms. But, having a strong self-esteem, a sense of self, can make it easier to navigate social situations without keeping fear of rejection, or a need to constantly prove oneself. Start by focusing on building relationships based on shared values.

I also recommend that you disregard the culturally advised objective of returning to your "normal" life; instead, clean the slate, and look to find a healthier middle ground, one that allows you to rebuild your life parallel with grief, rather than trying to conquer it. Grief is something that will never end, but it most certainly will change, as it shifts its dynamics. It's more like a passage through your heart, not a permanent place for it to stay. Allow the cycle of healing to turn, because it will bring you to a new starting point where you'll develop a realization, a sense of how your wounds have become wisdom, and what once hurt, won't hold power over you anymore. The storm has passed, you've lived through it, learned from it, and better days are now on their way. Keep going, because you'll see a renewed stamina, a pep in your step for the next chapter to begin. You'll have a better insight of understanding your grief, and it will take you to that place where you find acceptance, and peace.

What a lot of people call *closure* may not ever happen in a single point of arrival, as it's a much more fluid concept. I personally don't believe we should put a lid on our grief, in other words, suppress, ignore, or avoid. That's counterproductive. We should gravitate towards the idea of closure by finding ways to absorb our loss in the positive changes that we make, and allow to unfold, and in the special moments that enrich our lives. If we've failed to achieve that word called *closure*, let's not put pressure on ourselves by feeling ineffective. Keep your eyes on the goals you have set for yourself, and integrate your beloved's legacy into how you live the remainder of your life. So many possibilities are waiting for you. Go, find your joy!

As we move ahead, my wish for all of you is that you never settle. You are so very deserving; worthy of so much more that will come to you in this life, no matter how old you become, no matter how much you doubt. You're still here. You were not destined to map out a rich and vibrant terrain, only to end up navigating this life unfulfilled, nor were you designed to live within common boundaries which feel safe, yet can be terribly lonely. From the day we were all born, our parents passed down their unique gifts to us, and our fates were sealed, as it steered us towards the greatness we were intended to achieve. We must all remember that no matter how far the distance, or how great the journey, one day all of us will be guided again towards another destiny. I hope that when you find it, you'll realize how there is no greater venue, no larger stadium, no brighter lights, and no louder music that can ever take the place of *home*, where someone is there waiting for you with their arms wide open. Let it be someone with whom you find your center point, whether it is your family, a brand-new friend, or a new lover. But, it will be that person who will forever fan your beautiful, warm, and bright flame which yearns to feel free, and still needs to dance.

That little light that I spoke about earlier is something that we all carry within ourselves, and it's stronger than we realize. It connects to our memories, where we have stored beautiful passages, which we have already written our chapters. But, now is the time to softly close the door behind us, turn the page, refocus on where we're headed, remain positive, and begin by picking up the pen from last we left off. Our light will take it from there.

At this point, a lot of you have probably been wondering, "Why did she talk so much about Steve Perry in this book? Why did she go into such great detail about things in his life that have absolutely nothing to do with beyond the synchronicity that happened to her? Is she infatuated with him, like some kind of deranged, groupie fan?" No my friends, I'm afraid not. Here is the truth: Because the man saved my life. And, he doesn't even know it.

You see, there came a time when therapy stalled, and not for lack of trying on their part; it was my inability, my lack of will to heal. My heart was irrevocably broken, and I felt as if there was no turning back. I had reached the point of no return. Even my poor little Harry looked towards me for comfort, somebody new in his life that he needed love from, but there was little reciprocation other than caring well for him, and giving him a good home. I rushed in too fast to rescue someone when I couldn't even rescue myself. Of course, in the end it was the best thing I ever did, and I realize that now, as I love Harry very much. But, even after Larry's sign, during those two months that followed, I kept struggling and I no longer had any desire to verbalize; I assiduously gave it my all, and had talked until I was blue in the face. I felt I was out of options, I was tired, and I reached a dead end. A person knows when they know, whether it be rational or not.

When you walk in broken shoes day in and day out, it wears you down. Sometimes there isn't enough therapy, medications, or prayers in the world to cure that hollow ache Jim Carrey once spoke about. If you want pure honesty, then here it is: I'm surprised at how I didn't die from broken heart syndrome. The waves of grief I endured left me with hair loss, severe chest pains, shortness of breath, cold sweats, dizziness, and irregular heartbeats. I wasn't depressed anymore in a medical sense; my soul was defeated, broken. My doctor was highly concerned and immediately referred me to a cardiologist. There really are no words that can articulate the overwhelming depth of pain that I felt. Yes, it is a fact that some of us, thinking logically or not, need a greater reason, a larger nudge, something remarkable and consequential to happen before we give up. I believe, and now know with my whole heart, that the synchronicity of that divine intervention was the light I needed. This phenomenon was sent to me at the exact moment when it knew I reached my second, and very last, tipping point.

It was the gateway into all of the reasons as to why I should keep going. The rationale behind it led to a paradigm shift in understanding. It enlightened me by showing me insights into a beautiful and forgotten history, and I felt comforted and safe. As simple as reading between the lines of an informational interview, I interpreted unspoken truths that made me take into account the intended meaning. It assembled the fragmented, lost parts of my life that were fractured by cancer, and reminded me that my existence with my beloved really did have something worth celebrating, moments that deserved to be cherished and appreciated, especially for all of the lessons I learned. I have gratitude now for the impact my beloved's life had on me, and for this final gift involving Mr. Perry that I have been given, this buried message which I decoded, and allowed to change my entire outlook; it was a wake-up call. In the days that followed, waves of peace washed over me, and I slowly began to look forward to a bright future filled with growth, possibilities, excitement, and more love.

I'm a huge believer in repaying a kindness. So, this is my way of saying a huge thank you to Mr. Perry. He's 76 years old now, but he could be 106 for all I care. He led a remarkable and unique life, and was a rock legend at one time. I don't want him to be forgotten; my goal is to entice my readers to become aware of his accomplishments, his music. He should also be recognized, not only for his abundance of talent, but for his constant generosity towards the underserved and vulnerable, those with limited resources. He founded the Steve Perry Foundation. He's a silent widowed warrior, a magnanimous person who displays high moral qualities and character with his continuous honorable contributions. So, from a person whose life he illuminated, it's my turn to position the spotlight back onto him with the hopes of a spillover effect, that he be remembered all around the world, and encouraged to keep putting his foot forward, spreading his messages of song, reaching even higher, and to keep dancing. He deserves it.

I feel so fortunate to have experienced that synchronicity with him. The universe, in its infinite wisdom, empathized with me, intervened, and was sure as it guided an extraordinary human being to cross my path, to guide me towards cherishing this beautiful gift of life. I came to terms with my loss, acknowledged how beauty can exist alongside suffering, and I embraced it, for I realized how blessed I was to have lived through such a profound journey with my beloved husband. Ours was a voyage where I surprisingly learned how to find inner strength in the face of despair, and how to shift my focus away from mourning. I grew a deeper appreciation of what emerged by accepting my pain. I have now chosen to celebrate a life well-lived, and my true fulfillment has been found as I honor his enduring legacy. I am blessed with good health, a loving family, great friends, and a rekindled passion; my writing. And, I know that one day there will be another person I'll open my heart to, one that I can laugh with, one that I'll love with my entire being, and one who will draw me into his rhythm, as we dance together in what is left of our journey here. What more could anyone ever ask for?

For what it's worth, I truly hope that I have given everyone here a little boost of spirit and brightened up your day. Maybe you needed someone right now to ask you what you've been doing with your life. Maybe it needed to be me; just an ordinary girl from New York. One who believes that we should allow ourselves to feel this human experience which is profound, and so very short. We were designed to live our lives, be brave in the face of uncertainty, and to forge ahead with a fearless heart. Shouldn't we all aspire to have a fun, satisfying, memorable life filled with love and very little regret? Maybe that's what the universe was trying to tell me during those two days. In the middle of August. To remember what was, to never forget how we loved, to be grateful, and to always continue to encourage ourselves and others so that we may all keep our hearts open to each other, to never say never, and embrace the beauty of all the possibilities that lay ahead. What is it they say? The show must go on!

And for now, my friends, so must we.

I will find you again, my greatest love
As certain as the tide reaches for the shore
As surely as the sun starts warming the land
Through the darkness, as the moon lights the way
I will find you

True lovers divided, by life's brief interrupt
Now step between moments, where ashes were scattered
Yielding to love's promise, yet embers still aglow
Passion's desire still beats to the rhythm of love
Stolen flames flicker, stay with me longer, forever dancing

Across the span of countless lifetimes
With the millions of dawns, twilights, and sunsets
You will forever remain my center point
Such brilliance in the storm
Perpetually, safely guiding me home

Heavenly illuminations for all, be aligned
At just that right place, in just that right moment
To capture yearning dreams, and solace lonely hearts
Forever steering us towards
The Destiny of Our Stars

—GRETA McNEILL-MORETTI

Lawrence Peter Moretti Circa 1974

Greta McNeill-Moretti Circa 1974

Author
Greta McNeill-Moretti
(Present Day)

Larry's Mom & Dad
Nicolas and Cecilia Moretti

Greta's Mom and Dad

James Hugh McNeill

Winfred Webly McNeill

Dr. Greta and her trusted holiday assistant
Christmas, 1962

Our Wedding Day
October 20, 1979

Our Sons, Nick and Pete

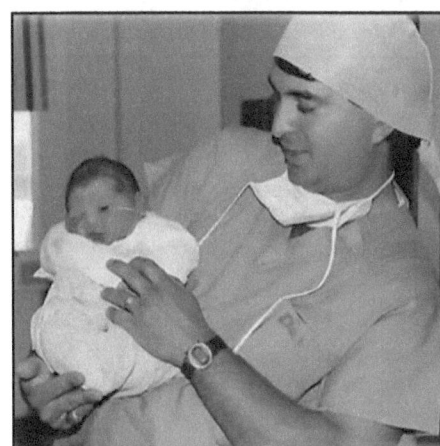
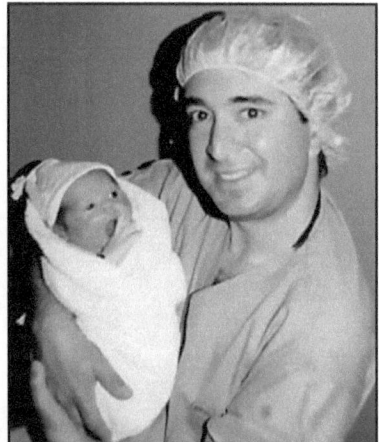

Nicholas Joseph Moretti

Lawrence Peter Moretti, Jr.

My Precious Harry

My Best Pal Lillian
Bronx, New York

Lawrence Peter Berra
(Yogi Berra, One If By Cards)

The Famous "Bertie Boy"

"The Gang"

Bob Bailey, Bobby Mac (Maccariello,) John Donnelly, Mike Losco, Joe DeNardis, and Larry

The "Laronys"
Larry and Tony Burgio

Lawrence Peter Moretti
1956-2023
With All Our Love

ACKNOWLEDGMENTS

My Children

To Nicholas, our first-born son who laughs easily, has many friends, and certainly his father's heart of gold. He works hard, is a peaceful, fun-loving guy and is very happily married to a wonderful, not to mention beautiful, woman, Ariel. They have both given me two of the most precious little granddaughters one could ever hope for: Serafina Rose, who tells everyone "Hello," and loves to dance! And, Lara Grace, who was named in memory of Larry. Nick has a rational way of thinking, and shows kindness and generosity towards everyone. He would give you the shirt off his back if you asked, and you can depend upon him whenever you need him. He's a man of many hidden talents, and even looks a little bit like the actor Jason Statham, only better looking. So yes, he's definitely a charmer, just like his dad! Larry was right-handed, and I am ambidextrous, so between the two us Nick ended up being a lefty. But, it's the loving hand he extended to me which gave me the courage to continue with my passion in life, so that this little feather could finally find its joy, riding the gentle breeze, no matter where it takes it, as she tries to navigate her own way. I love you, Nick.

To Lawrence, Jr., aka Pete, our right-handed, and second-born son, has his father's innocent silly sense of humor, is very outgoing, a magnet around women, another looker just like his dad, and is always overflowing with charisma. He entered the U.S. Marines and served his country proudly. He always wanted to fly, so he embarked upon their air-wing unit and flew in the C-130 Hercules planes, which are tactical airlifter aircrafts used by the United States Air Force and other military forces. His job was Crew Chief/Flight Mechanic, refueling, or tanking, other military aircraft at high altitudes. He performed his services with honor, and found many friends along the way. Some he still has, and some that he lost. He learned teamwork and that no man is ever left behind. Lance Corporal Lawrence P. Moretti. He's always looking for *the one*, but for now is most assuredly enjoying the ride, which sometimes brings him 13,500 feet in altitude, with absolutely no fear of heights, and with a parachute strapped onto his back (well, hopefully), for he never hesitates to jump. I haven't a clue as to where I got this guy from, but I'm sure glad he's mine. He works hard, is a steady part of a union, and a very proud veteran. His constant encouragement led me to believe in myself and find the words I still had left to say. So, with my heartfelt love and thanks to you Petie Boy, Semper Fi. Oorah!

The Gang

First and foremost, I want to thank all five of you collectively

For bringing a brotherhood of loyalty, love, and support to Larry.
You filled his heart with momentous keepsakes,
sharing valuable, unforgettable experiences
bringing richness and joy, as you celebrated the memories
of those early years together.
You're not only friends, but a chosen family.
I love all of you.

To **Bobby Mac,** the best man at our wedding, a person you can always count on, and whose wisdom is far beyond his years. I swear he possesses highly superior autobiographical memories. You're amazing, and I thank you for all of the great ones you brought back to me. All hail the "King of the Electric Slide," for this man possesses rhythm and a true dancer's terpsichorean moves!

To **Bob Bailey,** our sentimental "Deney Terrio." We counted on Bob, our source of kinetic energy, to motivate all of us to get up on our feet, and celebrate the moment, without judgment. Your sweet nature inspired movement and joy in everyone around, encouraged us all to embrace life's rhythms, and to dance, which we did for the rest of our lives.

To **John Donnelly,** whose smile could light up a room, always called me beautiful, and whose heart is bigger than all get out. Who else could blend, half-naked, seamlessly into a Woodstock mural, other than you? You're one in a million!

To Mike Losco, the greatest drummer I've ever known, well, actually the only drummer I've ever known, who never showed up empty-handed (women-wise), has an enormous and sincere heart, always had, and always will have, the greatest head of hair (so sexy and long), and who taught us all how to live our lives, harmoniously and contentedly, to the beat of our own drums.

To Joe DeNardis, our friend whose heart and door was always open on New Year's Eve, where we partied hard, laughed, and kissed in many a New Year. Thank you for your hospitality, kindness, friendship, and allowing us to have a moment at midnight when we all wished upon a dream.

My Editor

To Ms. Lauren Narog, I would like to express my deepest appreciation to Lauren, whose keen eye for detail, insightful editing prowess, and knack for weaving words together have been invaluable. Your passion for storytelling helped to shape this book into the best version of itself. You have been an unwavering guide, and I thank you for your patience, encouragement, and for allowing me to share the story of my life with the world.

To learn more about Ms. Narog, and the editing, proofreading, and writing services she offers:

Email: thefineprinteditingservice@gmail.com

Instagram: @thefineprinteditingservice

My Book Cover Designer / Interior Formatting Artist

To Glen Edelstein, who absorbed every nuance of my ideas and translated the very essence of my story into a compelling and vivid cover; you beautifully and evocatively designed the exterior/interior of my book exactly how I envisioned it. Your attention to detail and professional input were invaluable, and they greatly facilitated the progress of this project. You have the patience of a saint, and it was a joy to work with someone so dedicated and knowledgeable. I sincerely appreciate your meticulous efforts; your work has been instrumental, and I'm deeply grateful for your support and guidance, and for your significant contribution to my book's success. I would highly recommend Mr. Glen Edelstein to any author looking for a talented and collaborative designer.

As a book designer with lifelong experience in the publishing industry, Hudson Valley Book Design's creative director, Glen Edelstein, uses a collaborative approach to the design process. This approach to conceptual book design ensures that your vision for both the interior and exterior of your book becomes a reality. Glen works to ensure that your book is developed as one cohesive package.

To learn more about Mr. Edelstein, book cover designs, book interiors, and typography services he offers:

Website: www.hudsonvalleybookdesign.com

Email: glen@hudsonvalleybookdesign.com

My Website Designer

To Gabriel Edelstein, my sincere thanks for your incredible skill in designing my author website and creating such beautiful functionality that serves as the hub for my work. Your artistic eye and technical expertise built the perfect digital home for my books. You have vision for intuitive navigation and seamless integration, and you created my online presence and made sharing this book so much easier and more engaging for readers. You listened to my ideas and transformed them into a vibrant, user-friendly space that readers now and in the future will love exploring!

To learn more about Mr. Edelstein, website design,

Cave Studios & Productions, LLC

Email: gabrieledelstein4@gmail.com

My Legal Team

To Rothwell Fig, I am deeply grateful to everyone there for their invaluable support, specifically Kevin Brown, Esq. Your legal expertise and insights were instrumental in bringing my story to fruition. Without your help, this book would not have been made possible.

Stephen Ray Perry

My deepest and most heartfelt appreciation, as I give a very special mention here to Steve Perry, as none of this would have transpired without experiencing what the amazing universe so knowingly, divinely, and beautifully brought to me. I will never again question it. Keep spreading your music, laughter, love, and kind beneficence. But above all Steve, may you keep dancing.

WORKS CITED

Auden, W.H., Funeral Blues, Stop All the Clocks, Random House, 1940
  First UK edition, First US Edition, Print, English, Poetry, OCLC 1339262
  LC Class PR6001.U4

Kirkland, John, C., Love Letters of Great Men, (Immortal Beloved), 05/12/2008
Van Beethoven, Ludwig, German composer and pianist
  Publishing House ERSEN and Hainaim, Publishing Co., Ltd.
  United States, Estonia and South Korea, Print (paperback), Pgs. 138
  English Anthology, Poetry, OCLC 259821203, ISBN 1-4382-5724-4

Neruda, Pablo, *One Hundred Love Sonnets* (*Cien Sonetos de Amor*)
  Sonnet XVII (Sonnet 17), I don't love you as if you were a rose), 1959
  First Edition, *Editorial Losada*, Argentina, Print (paperback), Pgs. 124
  Spanish, Latin American Literature and Culture, Poetry

Shakespeare, Gulielmus (William), Hamlet, Polonius to his son Laertes
  (Act I, Scene iii), Nicholas Ling and John Trundell, 1603
  printed by Valentine Simmes, Qquarto edition, the first quarto
  Bad quarto, Early Modern English, Shakespearean tragedy, Denmark

My heartfelt thanks and gratitude to all
who helped breathe life into my story

Remember, the journey forward

Is defined by the life one chooses to create

And it is the outcome which we envision for ourselves

That is all that truly matters

May you all keep wishing upon your special star

So that desires fulfill your heart

And dreams forever become true

THE END

IF YOU ARE IN NEED OF SUPPORT PLEASE REACH OUT TO:

National Suicide & Crisis Lifeline

Call 988   Text 988   or text **TALK** to 741741
https://988lifeline.org

American Foundation For Suicide Prevention

https://afsp.org/

Contact our national office
Toll-Free: 1-888-333-AFSP (2377)
T: (212) 363-3500
F: (212) 408-9684

Hospice Foundation of America

https://hospicefoundation.org/

Knowing the facts about hospice and grief care is critical. If you're in need of guidance about end-of-life options, or grief, we're here to answer your questions at no cost through our Ask an Expert service. Funded by generous donations, staffed by a board-certified nurse practitioner, and the nation's foremost grief experts, your questions will be answered, in most cases, within 24 hours.

(800) 854-3402
(202) 457-5811

1707 L Street NW, Suite 220
Washington, DC, 20036